"*Flip the System UK: A Teachers' Manifesto* is a book with many faces. It is a manifesto, a great overview of current discussions in education – both in the UK and abroad – and a wake up call to both teachers and policy-makers. Still it has [with] a common theme throughout the different chapters: a love for the profession of teaching. A love that is translated in questions about how we can do better as both an individual teacher and as a profession, how we can work together, how we can weigh in on policy, and so on. I appreciate the attempt of the book to rise above the discussions and polarization often found between teachers themselves. The authors do this by pointing out those common goals, this common love. Even if you don't agree with every single contribution in this book, as a teacher you will recognize the common goal."

Pedro de Bruyckere, Educational Scientist,
Artevelde University, Belgium.

"This timely book contains a wealth of detail about education policy, teacher professionalism, and ways to develop agency and collaboration within education. It contains a multitude of thoughts, ideas and opinions from well-known commentators, that will make you think more deeply about where we have come from as a profession, and where we might be going in the future."

"This book is full of detailed analysis, informed opinion, and interesting insights into what has been happening in education over the last couple of decades. It will challenge your thinking and give you a greater depth of understanding about different perspectives on where the profession might helpfully go next. I particularly enjoyed reading the chapters written by Dame Alison Peacock and Dr Debra Kidd."

Sue Cowley, educational author, trainer and presenter, UK.

"There are few books on education you return to time and again...ones you keep handy for reference and renewal. Well here's one - a veritable potpourri of ideas and insights into what to do today, tomorrow, next month and next year to make our schools better. If the educational world's divided into energy creators and energy consumers, here is a treasure trove of ideas to tip the balance in favour of the former at a time when the latter, aided by successive governmental blunders, are in danger of destroying hope itself. And we all know what happens to people when they are without 'hope'. So keep this book by you and return to it time and again."

Sir Tim Brighouse, British educationist and former Schools Commissioner for London, UK.

"This timely book is exactly what is needed for the UK education sector in its current state. It is written by teachers, for teachers, and [the book] speaks up about the need for fundamental change in how the profession is organised, taking it from being managed to being self-managing. Amongst the diversity of voices and essays are practical solutions for how teachers can get involved in the movement, alongside the theoretical background for why their involvement is necessary for the future of teaching. This book presents a powerful articulation of the problem, and a rousing call for a collective solution."

Lucy Crehan, teacher, education explorer and international education consultant, UK.

Flip the System UK

How did we let teacher burn-out happen, and what can we do about it – before it's too late?

This brave and disruptive book accurately defines the problems of low teacher morale and offers systemic, future-proof, and realistic solutions to bringing hope, energy and joy back to the profession. The simple answer is staring us in the face: increase teacher agency. Our rallying cry: our profession needs a return to values of humanity, pride, and professionalism.

From research literacy to a collective voice, better CPD to smarter accountability, contributors to this book demonstrate the huge scope for increased teacher influence at every level of the education sector. Education voices including Sam Twiselton, Alison Peacock, David Weston, and Andy Hargreaves, supported by a broad range of academics and policy-makers, vouch for increased teacher agency and stronger, more powerful networks as a means of improving practice, combatting teacher disillusionment, and radically improving UK education. This text offers an exciting and hopeful perspective on education, urging teachers to work together to 'flip the system' and challenging policy-makers to help … or get out of the way.

Lucy Rycroft-Smith is a maths teacher now working as a writer and researcher and makes regular contributions to the *Guardian* and TES on a variety of educational issues.

JL Dutaut is a teacher of citizenship, media, and government and politics.

Flip the System UK

A Teachers' Manifesto

Edited by Lucy Rycroft-Smith
and JL Dutaut

Routledge
Taylor & Francis Group

LONDON AND NEW YORK

First published 2018
by Routledge
2 Park Square, Milton Park, Abingdon, Oxon OX14 4RN

and by Routledge
711 Third Avenue, New York, NY 10017

Routledge is an imprint of the Taylor & Francis Group, an informa business

British Library Cataloguing in Publication Data
A catalogue record for this book is available from the British Library

Library of Congress Cataloging in Publication Data
A catalog record for this book has been requested.

ISBN: 978-1-138-21479-8 (hbk)
ISBN: 978-1-138-21480-4 (pbk)
ISBN: 978-1-315-44520-5 (ebk)

Typeset in Bembo
by Deanta Global Publishing Services, Chennai, India

MIX
Paper from
responsible sources
FSC™ C013985

Printed in the United Kingdom
by Henry Ling Limited

Contents

Illustrations

Figures

Tables

Foreword

René Kneyber and Jelmer Evers

Education is at a perilous point in history. On the one hand, policy-makers, but also *we* – as in 'everybody' – understand the importance of good education, be it for the strength of the economy, the strength of our democracy, or even the belief that education is its own merit and value. Education must be good, in many senses.

But an education system that boosts the economy and invigorates democracy by assembling perfect citizens doesn't originate miraculously or even organically. For a number of decades, governments across the world have approached this challenge in a similar fashion: proper education requires proper markets, proper targets, and proper accountability, and also plenty of 'proper' testing.

It hasn't worked. Investments have disappeared in the Bermuda triangle of market-based decentralisation; performance-based accountability and incredible stress have pushed many out of the teaching profession. In some countries, strong, countervailing democratic institutions have been broken down, and teacher professionalism has suffered hugely as a result. Now that many countries look, or have started, down a road of falling public expenditure on education, they face the impossible challenge of doing a great deal more with lots less.

Is there really no alternative, as Thatcher used to claim? It seems we are in dire need of one. In 2013, we published a book in Holland, cheekily titled *The Alternative*, on how to build an education system around the notion that good education requires professional teachers. It became a breakthrough success, and a new international version was released in 2015 called *Flip the System: Changing Education from the Ground Up*. A local adaptation came out in Sweden in 2017, and an adaption for the United Kingdom is – obviously – right here in front you.

This book stays true to the series' formula: co-edited by teachers, with contributions by teachers building knowledge with researchers. It is as much about the need of teacher voice on the policy level as it *is* that same voice. It is as much about teacher emancipation as it *is* that emancipation.

Even though many education systems suffer from poor strategy and policy, it is teachers that have made it work and continue to make it work. The crucial question for governments, parliaments, and policy-makers is how they can support and help those teachers to do the best job they possibly can, because in the end teachers will – or kill themselves trying.

Certainly, that requires structural change, long-term plans, and strategic investments. Just as certainly, it is far from impossible for whoever has the heart and spirit.

Dedication

Lucy Rycroft-Smith

Oh, colleagues. I've spent the last year since I left teaching immersing myself in conferences, Twitter, dodgy CPD sessions, teachers-on-tour-drinking, nursery schools, PRUs, universities, forums, and – most tantalisingly – other people's classrooms. I have got to know a great many of you in the last year, and I hope to get to know a great many more. Some of you have made me laugh, some have made me cry. Some of you have consented to play nerdy board games with me. (Others of you have taken the piss, mercilessly). Some of you have taken unflattering photographs of me. Some of you have infuriated me, and some delighted me. Many of you have inspired me. One of you forced me to rant on at you about feminism when we were both clearly too drunk to appreciate it. But we have shared a bond – all of us who have EVER been in a classroom, or a PRU, or even a prison or an oil rig or an online school or anywhere we had the responsibility to educate others where those others were vulnerable or young or disadvantaged. WE KNOW. Some elements of our tiny human lives are common, and that commonality can bring great joy and acceptance and a relief that we don't have to explain and justify ourselves constantly. Teachers NEED other teachers in their lives.

But oh my goodness, how it divides us.

Traditional, progressive, liberal, zero-tolerance, Libertarian, religious, atheist, evidence-based, hippy, lefty. Woolly, old-fashioned, narcissistic, lazy, cynical, naïve, ignorant. We categorise others and elevate ourselves. We form factions and clubs and secret societies. We congratulate ourselves and debunk others. We tout the fashionable opinion and pile contempt on the out-of-date. We blame, we argue, we sneer, we deride.

This book is about THE SYSTEM. If we – anyone who calls themselves a teacher and plenty more besides – are to change THE SYSTEM, we must realise there is a time for this debate, and there is a time to stand together to fight a common enemy. You don't quibble about whose mess-tin is missing when explosives are being hurled at you; you don't care whose grammar is dodgy when someone is shouting for help. You don't argue philosophy in the phalanx. Not yet. The time when we can do this is near, and it will be joyous AND IT WILL BE POLITE. But right now, either you or someone you know in teaching is literally dying because they are at the bottom of THE SYSTEM. Stop calling them a moron for using learning styles and help, please.

So, we want you to know as you read this book that IT IS FOR YOU. Please, please do not think this is a book only for academics or only for researchers; only for teachers or only for support staff in schools; only for headteachers or only for Twitterati. There's a wave of feminism we call intersectional (I'm sorry, Dave, I'm bringing it up again): acknowledging that people's identities intersect, and that the most advantaged (wealthy white women) have often been the significant voice and face of feminism, where the more marginalised have been ignored, excluded, and patronised. If feminism is only for those rich enough and white enough to get it, it's not feminism. So – if system change only happens for those comfortable and healthy and educated enough to seek it (and along their lines of priority), it is not intersectional, and it is not therefore meaningful system change. My system flipping will be intersectional, or it will be bullshit.

So. This book is for you.

It's for the exhausted teachers who neglect their own children. It's for the furious teachers who think they should have personal lives even if they don't have offspring of their own. It's for the teachers who drink, overeat, and take any kind of substance they can to get them through until the end of term. It's for the teachers with tattoos, piercings, extraordinary hair. It's for the suit-wearers who iron their underwear. It's for the trans teachers. It's for the gloriously hirsute teachers. It's for the teachers who pretend they have read things when they haven't, for the teachers with enormous breasts that get sexualised even when they don't want to be, for the teachers who are one precarious lesson ahead of their pupils (and I was that teacher). It's for the teachers who misspell things on the whiteboard and snap at the pupil who points it out. It's for the leggings-and-cardigan wearers, for the single parents, and the polygamous and the asexual teachers, for the bring-your-marking-home-Friday-night-and-bring-it-right-back-again-on-Monday-unmarked teachers. It's for the overweight teachers. It's for the snappy ties and the teacher-jokers. It's for those so short or young-looking they get mistaken for pupils; it's for every teacher that's been asked if they were pregnant when they weren't. It's for the teachers-in-training. It's for the teachers with skin conditions, or BO, or strong accents or who like heavy makeup or who have no hair. It's for the disabled teachers and the BME teachers and anyone who identifies as a woman. It's for the teachers who have to hide their nonconformist personal lives from their pupils or their colleagues. It's for the teachers who painstakingly cycle to work every day. It's for the teaching assistants and the supply staff, the tutors and the mentors. It's for the terrified teachers who shout a bit too loud and grin a bit too wide. I don't care how terrible you are, how crappy your planning or how scruffy you look or how self-important you are or what colour you are or how you smell or how disenfranchised or enthusiastic you are: I AM FOR YOU. THIS BOOK IS FOR YOU.

It is OK to be fallible and it is OK to be different. If we weren't human, and incredibly and richly diverse, our pupils would suffer for it. They will remember fondly your awesome hair and your jokes and your pride in your sexuality; your astigmatism and your BO and your lady-moustache and that time your trousers fell down.

It is also OK to despair, and to feel like you are awful at your job. I have never yet met a teacher who doesn't want to be better − *never* − it's just that often the cost is too high. That cost is set by the exchange rate of the system, and it is bullshit.

I come across two types of responses from teachers, generally, when I tell them about *Flip the System*. There are those who tell me stories of bullying, inspection, depression, exhaustion, results-driven mania, working through the holidays, hideous accountability, and illness. Then there are those who like to tell me their school is different, their headteacher is different, their experience is different. I enjoy and celebrate these stories too. But please be clear − you are not different, not really. You are one career move, one assault, one academisation, one headteacher change, one bullying staff member, or one personal tragedy away from the first type. You are General Melchett. "God, I'd give anything to be out there with them, dodging the bullets instead of sitting here drinking this Chateau Lafite, and eating these filets mignons with sauce béarnaise."

This is privilege (and it is complicated and paradoxical and uncomfortable), and just because the system works for you (right now) doesn't mean it always will, or that you don't need to do anything about it. It means you can − and maybe even should − do more than anyone.

There's another important meaning of the word intersectional here, too: teaching doesn't have to be like joining a convent. We all have other identities: sons and daughters, friends, parents, runners, dancers, activists, writers, philosophers, makers, collectors. It is unreasonable and unworthy to expect any teacher to give up their life for a 'calling', to dedicate their time and energy solely to the wellbeing of the pupils in their care. It is not a choice between having a teaching career and having a life, whatever we may have been sold. You and I are people with rich and short lives to lead, too. Let us live them out of the shadow of Ofsted, in the sunlight of trusted professionalism.

You may read on. (You didn't need my permission anyway, you subversive.)

Acknowledgements

First, this book would not be possible without the support of our families, who picked us up when teaching got the better of us, helped us to believe we were good enough, and supported us throughout the lengthy process of editing this book. So, to our parents, partners, and children, we thank you from the bottom of our hearts. You are as instrumental to flipping the system as you are to our teaching.

We owe a debt of gratitude too to Jelmer Evers and René Kneyber, who handed the reins of this enterprise to us merely at our request, and who have supported us from beginning to end. If their stewardship of *Flip the System* is not a model of collective agency and teacher empowerment, nothing is.

At Routledge, we'd like to thank Alison Foyle, who accepted our quirky proposal and our sheer faith that we could secure contributions from all these wonderful people, and Sarah Tuckwell, Aiyana Curtis and Elsbeth Wright who have overseen the process with patience and sensitivity.

We are also grateful to Jon Severs, Ann Mroz, and Ed Dorrell at TES, who have waved through requests for quotes, and in myriad of small ways have made us feel a little less like the imposters we are prone to feeling like sometimes.

We are obviously indebted to all our contributors, some of whom didn't make the final cut (see above for who to blame!), and some of whom couldn't come through on their initial enthusiasm for a variety of reasons. Your interest was enough. Your efforts were more than we could have expected. Your continued support is an honour.

Finally, our thanks go to colleagues past, present, and future. We've never met one who, even on the most challenging day, even as illness or self-protection took them from the classroom, even as the hammer-blows of punitive accountability rained down, didn't still believe in their heart that education is a noble profession, and that children deserve the best. Those beliefs permeate this book. You permeate this book.

From supply agency to demand agency

Taking back control

JL Dutaut and Lucy Rycroft-Smith

This book is meant as a follow-up to Jelmer Evers' and René Kneyber's incredible volume, *Flip the System*. It was after a presentation by René at a researchED conference that, both looking to recover our professional pride after a bruising few years in Special Measures, we found a new purpose. Those had been years of disempowerment and all-consuming workload, of CPD as cruel and unusual punishment and of health-destroying stress. Now, we would fight back to fitness, not just for ourselves, but for the profession. In the very incubating chamber of neoliberal reform, we would seek out the other voices of dissent, and we would make them heard. We would look beyond their divisions and identify their commonality. We would analyse our findings and we would use them to define teacher professionalism, and to write the teachers' manifesto. We would transform the education system in this country – not with a view to rewriting its curriculum, nor to delimiting its pedagogy, nor still to restructuring it, but to give teachers back the power to effect those very changes. We would show that any education policy that failed to take the profession into account – and that is every education policy since education policy became a thing – was doomed to failure.

We wouldn't stop there. We would show, too, that the system as we know it is nothing more than a heap of those failures. Indeed, every new Secretary of State, at least every one that represents a new Government, makes a point of telling us so. Unfortunately, they do so only rhetorically, to justify their own efforts to sort out the mess. The heap gets nicely decorated for a while, with a new coat of 21st-century progressive sheen or a trendy, matte, traditionalist upcycling. Then the Minister moves on to great office or to the back-benches. As for money, the great Secretary giveth and the great Secretary taketh away. Jobs and talents are lost, or they fail to be developed properly. Then the Government moves to the opposition benches. Rinse. Repeat.

And underneath the heap of those failures – the most recently buried still visible between the cracks, still gasping for air and knocking on a hollow pipe in the hope of rescue – are valiant efforts to educate children, to prepare them for adult life as British citizens, as socially adept individuals, as productive workers.

It is time for a different way of working. It is time to flip the system – to unearth its buried treasures and to recreate it on solid foundations instead of continuing to pile detritus on top of an over-full landfill site.

What we have discovered in our research, what we sensed in our lonely years of classroom isolation, is that where the system promotes networks at all, it only promotes the kind that are predominantly exclusive. Designed to suit the political agenda of the current DfE incumbents, they connect limited numbers of people to limited *ideas*, with limited *knowledge* and limited *collective effectiveness*. The importance of these three features emerges from all the contributions we have received. We have grouped them according to their authors' main priorities, though you will find overlaps and deduce others. Together, they are dedicated to defining professionalism, which we interpret to be the attitudes and behaviours of individuals towards knowledge, towards their colleagues, and towards the ethos of education. More than that, it is clear throughout the book that it isn't enough for teachers to be consumers of knowledge, invitees to collaborations, or receivers of standards. Teachers must also be creators of knowledge, of collaborations, and of purposeful action. In short, they must have agency.

Following these initial sections of the teachers' manifesto, demanding *cognitive agency*, *collective agency*, and *ethical agency*, we look at policy-making itself – of all the networks, the most closed and exclusive by far. Our contributors here show a consistent and disturbing truth: it is this very exclusion of teachers' knowledge, collective capacity, and/or ethical views that results in the system's failure to adequately and sustainably implement policy and reform. This section of the manifesto demands greater *political agency* for teachers.

Finally, we have found, consistent with the original work of *Flip the System*, that the problems we face in the UK are not isolated, and that we need not face them alone. In a world where teachers are set up to compete against each other for coveted places at the top of the tower of PISA, where any learning from each other is mediated by the very same exclusive network of policy-makers, flipping the system means reaching out beyond our national boundaries for a *global agency*. Not only should we never be isolated in our classrooms, but we should not be isolated in our systems. Our agency must be as global as it is national, as national as it is local, and as local as it is individual. The only idea agency excludes is exclusion itself. It is a professional right and a professional duty which can't be given, and can't be taken away. It is the very nature of professionalism.

We offer this book as a manifesto in five parts to define, demand, and devolve professional agency for teachers across the UK. Who are we to do this? We are teachers, and you've made us use our teacher voice.

Part I

The teachers' manifesto

Cognitive agency

JL Dutaut and Lucy Rycroft-Smith

Knowledge input

As teachers, we are called upon to know and make use of a range of information, from student data, through curriculum, to pedagogical knowledge. While an exhaustive list of all the things we need to know in order to function effectively in our education system is beyond the scope of this book, our premise is that all knowledge that is necessary to our performance is equally valuable and valid as professional knowledge, be that the family circumstance of this or that pupil, or the latest research in cognitive psychology. Further, as professionals with agency, it is our contention that it is incumbent upon us, in active collaboration with each other, school and system leaders, to produce new knowledge, and to make decisions about prioritising it. The unchallenged imposition of knowledge *input* (what teachers ought to know) is in fact an act of prioritisation taken out of our hands, and a restriction on our professionalism with devastating consequences for our ability to teach.

In this part, we chart the development of new forms of powerful teacher knowledge through research engagement that is grassroots and, if not totally unmediated, at least more so than has previously been the case. **Tom Bennett** describes the research revolution he and thousands of teachers have lit the fire under. **Peter Ford** tracks the atrocious policy-making that led to the need for this knowledge revolution and reminds us of the importance of universities in developing the research revolution. For too long, he argues, the relationship between schools and universities has itself been mediated by policy-makers. **Jonathan Firth** charts developments in education research that present new powerful knowledge for teachers, and argues that the research itself demands teacher agency in order to be adequately implemented.

Knowledge output

Some forms of knowledge are more valued than others by the education system. Ironically, these most valued datasets are often the least useful in terms of improving outcomes – being, as they are, summative in their nature. From data gathering for half-termly reports that say little to parents about their children's true performance to government-mandated data collection for the purposes of monitoring, league ranking and policy justification, this knowledge, albeit valid and valuable, is given an importance well beyond its true worth. Indeed, it often hampers the development of other forms of knowledge that could have more impact. Our contention is that this form of policy-making is nothing more than the imposition of practices of knowledge *output* (what teachers ought to communicate). It is a further de-professionalisation of our role, with equally destructive effect.

Here, **David Weston** argues that schools should be more than data-rich — swimming in piles of data as Scrooge McDuck does in piles of cash. Schools, David argues, should be data smart — leaner, but investing shrewdly for development and growth by allowing teachers the autonomy, the agency, to prioritise the data that is of use to their practice.

Here, too, **David Williams** describes the Welsh experience of mandated practices that bear little relevance to the job of teaching. As a case in point, David looks at reforms in assessment, and the perverse incentives of policy-making that prioritise political accountability over school and teacher accountability.

David Williams goes further. As a thought experiment, he proposes an entirely new way of conceiving of and carrying out assessment. Our contention, and his, is not that it is necessarily right, or right for everyone. As editors of this book, though, we are entirely convinced that teachers will not only offer different solutions, but different types of solution altogether, to the problems facing education in the UK today.

Julie Smith and **Zeba Clark** offer this section on cognitive agency two concrete examples of teacher-generated, teacher-centred solutions to developing and nurturing professional knowledge. As a senior school leader, Zeba makes the case for internal over external accountability in a forthright, evidence- and experience-based way. Julie, a director of teaching and learning, describes the transformative power of practitioner-led research.

In this way, the following contributions not only demonstrate that the education system undermines the professionalism and status of teachers in the sphere of professional knowledge, but that teachers like Tom, Peter, David, Julie and Zeba exercise that professionalism regardless, often *despite* it. The UK deserves better for its teachers and their students.

Demand cognitive agency

The teachers' manifesto demands that teachers develop and be empowered to develop their professional knowledge, continuously and according to their own priorities, in collaboration with their colleagues. This must include:

- Teacher involvement in academic research as consumers and producers;
- Qualifying and professional standards that require evidence of research engagement;

- Working conditions that make possible the continued attainment of such standards;
- Teacher involvement *at every level* in the design of policy that requires:
    - Any reform of the standards themselves;
    - Any reform that impacts on the knowledge required of teachers to perform their duty, especially with regard to curriculum, pedagogy and monitoring;
    - Any reform that impacts on the knowledge required of teachers to account for the performance of their duty, especially with regard to data collection, assessment and monitoring.
- Accountability measures for all stakeholders and policy-makers that require a commitment to, and the monitoring of performance in, upholding the professionalism of teachers with regard to their cognitive agency as defined above.

Chapter 1

There are no ninjas

Why the research revolution might rescue teaching

Tom Bennett

> "The teacher or school that pursues self-guided, amateur research can easily fall prey to every bias and preconception they are attempting to escape."

In 2013, I started researchED when I was a full-time teacher in a London inner-city school. I was frustrated with the number of pointless tasks teachers were asked to execute that seemed to have little evidence to substantiate them. From Brain Gym to compulsory project work, in the UK at least it seemed that to be a teacher meant having very little say in how and what you taught. To some extent this is understandable – teaching isn't a hobby, nor is it free to provide. The public purse demands and deserves input and oversight.

What appeared obvious as years of teaching passed me was how little regard there was within education for substantiating what it did. Schools and teachers were often asked to evidence impact, but this normally took the form of spurious post-event justification based on instinct or expediency. 'I did this and I think it caused that' is the classic retrospective rationale of every winner and loser that ever was.

More worryingly, I often found that, whenever I asked why we pursued this strategy or that, I would often be told 'the evidence proves it.' I wrote an angry book called *Teacher Proof* that delved into dodgy evidence bases and educational myths that were still common in teaching: multiple intelligences, learning styles, scent-based learning, and so on. If even I – a teacher of philosophy and RS – could discern the problem, it seemed obvious that others could too.

So I started researchED as a conference-based project to bring educators, academics, researchers, policy-makers and everyone else in the ecosystem together: to present the best of what they knew, to challenge, discuss and learn. It proved wildly successful. Eighty percent of our attendees are teachers. Can you imagine that? To suggest teachers would give up their Saturdays in workshops and keynotes on research would have been considered madness five years ago. Since then, researchED has hosted conferences on three continents to over 10,000 people, 80% of them teachers, from Melbourne to Washington DC to Glasgow. Clearly, a chord has been struck.

My frustration then – and frustration still – is that this was necessary. Teachers were not leaving their initial training familiar with the best and latest research in how to teach, the way people learn, remember, focus and behave. Nor were they routinely exposed to the best continual training. Schools didn't consistently refer to substantive research before embarking on long, costly projects and interventions. What an embarrassment we had become as a profession, if we could call ourselves that.

Medicine had its own epiphany centuries ago. It is apposite to remind ourselves that many doctors at first also resisted the advent of empirical science into what they viewed as their territory, believing that 'they knew their patients' needs' far better than any impersonal or remote data. You could hear much the same in classrooms throughout the world. *What does research have to offer me?*, people say to me. I understand it – we grew up in a world where education and research were distant cousins.

Because my own exposure to research had begun so negatively, I suspected there was a con going on (and in some way, there was). But the con was also obscuring the careful, dedicated work of many thousands of ambitious researchers with integrity who wanted to find out the best way to teach rather than be slaves to dogma. researchED developed out of this realisation: that there were dragons to be slain, for sure, but also treasure to be found.

It also made me realise the relevance of something Dominic Cummings mentioned tangentially in a story about his time working with the UK government. Talking about the Cabinet Office, he described a dysfunctional system where, according to him, no one knew what they were doing:

> You might think somewhere there must be a quiet calm centre like in a James Bond movie where you open the door and there is where the ninjas are who actually know what they are doing. There are no ninjas. There is no door.
>
> (Wintour, 2014)

So it is with education. There is no one who will come and rescue teachers from our poorly evidenced plight; where anyone can say anything, research says what you want it to say. My researchED experience has taught me that teachers must become a profession for themselves; that they must work out what works, and when, by themselves, for themselves; that no one will come and do it for them. We have to find out. We have to ask.

There are no ninjas.

Using research to improve practice

There are many ways teachers can access research, but the elephant in the room that must be addressed is workload. Most teachers lack the time or expertise to become proficient in research. While a small percentage may pursue academic studies, most will not. Most have little free time, and research is a specialist activity, not an amateur profession.

The answer lies in seeing the profession holistically. Rather than expecting all teachers to be ninjas, we should aspire collectively to a shared understanding, where some specialise in research and share its fruits with others. We need to acquire a herd immunity to bad science. Here are the key elements of an inoculation programme.

Start a journal club

One practical, sociable way schools and teachers have addressed the problem of assimilating research is to form a journal club. Beth Greville-Giddings is a research lead and teaching assistant in Nottingham, UK, who has become an ambassador for educational research journal clubs. As she describes it on her website:

> Journal Clubs are essentially like book clubs for research. They have been used widely in medical settings since the 19th Century during training and as CPD. Journal Clubs are an informal and social way to discuss research and keep practitioners up to date, whilst providing an opportunity to discuss how research is relevant to practice and developing skills of critical analysis.
>
> There have been an increasing number of schools interested in developing clubs for themselves, particularly since the first researchED national conference in 2013, where Dr Ben Goldacre introduced the suggestion of Journal Clubs as a way for schools to become more research engaged. There are many different ways schools are using Journal Clubs and schools should decide the way that works best for them.
>
> Features of Journal Clubs with high attendance and longevity include mandatory attendance and perceived importance by management.
>
> (Greville-Giddings, 2017)

Create a new role at school: The Research Lead

Rather than have every teacher aspire (impossibly) to focusing on research findings, many schools have found value in creating a new role: the Research Lead – someone whose responsibility it is to find out on behalf of others, to stay abreast of developments and to drive research literacy up in the school (Bennett and McAleavy, 2016).

These leads have come from every strata of the school, from premises staff to head teacher. Sometimes they are paid roles, sometimes not; sometimes they are assigned, and in some schools I have seen, people have simply decided to do it.

The Research Lead can connect the school to the greater world of educational research, while simultaneously acting as a filter. The Lead can convert the school from an island, to an archipelago, to a peninsula, and be a powerful agent of change. In my observations of this emergent role, I have found that several chief variants have emerged.

The Gatekeeper: The lead should be a conduit for research in general, including methodology, current affairs and issues and staying abreast of developments in educational research. This is one of the most common ways that the role has been interpreted.

The Gatekeeper acts on behalf of the school, dedicating a discrete portion of their time to actively pursuing these matters for their colleagues and leadership team. This model draws on the advantages of labour division and specialisation.

The Consigliere: The Research Lead is a special adviser to the head teacher, or senior staff, or governing body, rather than a whole-school resource. While they may still be used as a reference by the larger staff body, their primary role is to assist with change leadership in the school.

The Devil's Advocate: Also known as the critical friend, this Research Lead takes a muscular approach to their responsibilities and assumes an investigative and inspectorate type role. The Lead in this scenario is responsible for challenging staff at all levels (although frequently this was restricted to leadership and management levels) to discuss their strategies in light of relevant research. The aim behind this is not to simply dispute or disagree with the strategy, but to create a dialogue of challenge where individuals are forced to revisit their own motivations and evidence base – experiential, practical or theoretical.

The Auditor: Some Research Leads are tasked with evaluating the whole school's relationship with current research, and then using that baseline evaluation to generate targets and a vision for where the school needs to be. This could mean re-evaluating whole-school teaching and learning policies in the light of, for example, developments in cognitive psychology, or it could be to dispute and dispense with out-of-date practices.

The Project Manager: This Research Lead is given a specific mission to achieve, usually centred around a research-based intervention, either in the exploratory phase of its adoption, or in the investigative phase of forming policy. They might be required to perform a literature review, or visit schools that have previously adopted the strategy in question. Usually the focus of the project will be generated by some perceived need intrinsic to the school, either identified by an external third party, such as Ofsted, or by the leadership team.

Form partnerships with existing research institutions

Some schools and teachers find running their own experiments to be a useful way to examine their practices and prove their educational hypotheses, and I have seen many schools pursue these ends with diligence and honesty. I have even seen staff motivated, re-energised and animated to be part of such a project. But *caveat emptor*: good social science is extraordinarily hard to plan, execute or analyse well. Research requires expertise, experience and care to carry out precisely, and the teacher or school that pursues self-guided, amateur research can easily fall prey to every bias and preconception they are attempting to escape.

One way to avoid this is to form partnerships with institutions and organisations that already carry out research at a professional level, such as universities, educational charities, government bodies and think tanks. These organisations actively seek to recruit schools to take part in their studies. By doing this, schools form partnerships with bodies that can offer advice, training and insight into the object of the research. Just as importantly, the school and its practitioners can offer invaluable insight into the nature and context of the data being collected. In this way, both parties inform and support each other, and wisdom is shared and multiplied. It disrupts the linear hierarchy of 'those who do research' versus 'those who have research done to them' and recreates that relationship in a feedback loop that is at once organic and respectful.

Examples of such institutions are the National Foundation for Educational Research (NFER), the Education Endowment Foundation (EEF), the Centre for the Use of Research Evidence in Education (CUREE), the Wellcome Trust, the University of Durham, Policy Exchange, the Education Development Trust (EDT) and many more.

Reboot initial teacher training and professional development

One reason many teachers are relatively research illiterate is because they are so infrequently exposed to it in the course of their careers. This occurs at two levels:

- They are often not introduced to well-evidenced and substantiated teaching practices in their initial training period; their training is often treated more as gospel or hand-me-down 'truth' than an object of dispute.
- They are often not trained to read a research paper or appreciate the demands, challenges and opportunities that empirical science represents. I can say confidently that most teachers do not know the difference between randomised controlled trials, case studies, literature reviews, qualitative and quantitative research, the file drawer effect, cognitive dissonance and so on (Leat et al., 2014). They should.

Schools and teachers can play a part in their own remedy by rectifying this lack themselves. Of course, it would be absurd to expect every teacher to have the time to do so; teachers are busy to an almost legendary extent. But many teachers will find time for such studies on a part-time or informal basis. Teachers should seek out good quality summaries, original research or even headline data, depending on the time available to them. But where?

Good sources of information about research

Social media – especially Twitter. researchED was started because of Twitter. Its capacity to connect distant parties in disparate circumstances is both levelling and exciting. A trainee teacher can discuss with an eminent academic the exact meaning of their work, and broadcast the result of that conversation to the world. It is a liberating experience to be so connected. For teachers, the opportunity this network represents cannot be over-emphasised. Ideas can be shared instantly, globally, dogma sifted and sieved, circumstances compared and data analysed collectively. Its downfall is that its brevity and conciseness can bring misunderstandings; it is hard to navigate subtleties in this terrain.

Deans for Impact. This relatively new American organisation has produced one of the best summary documents of the best of what cognitive psychology has to teach us in the classroom. *The Science of Learning* (Deans for Impact, 2015) is free to download. It should be compulsory reading for every teacher.

ResearchED conferences (and website). We strive to be knowledge and theory brokers, bringing together everyone working under the education research umbrella. The aim remains to deliver cost-effective days driven by teacher needs, practical support in classrooms and the best voices prepared to speak for free to teachers on a Saturday.

Other organisations are also useful: *Sense about Science*; the *Learning Scientists'* excellent resources website and many others. Now, the humblest educator can access information and ideas that would have previously been impossible to access easily, freely.

What research has proven itself to be useful in the classroom and beyond?

How can research make better teachers? This revolution of access and inclusion is a token gesture if it doesn't make a difference in careers, structures and classrooms. What kind of impact can this research have?

Many teachers have found low-hanging fruit in the study and use of the latest ideas from cognitive psychology. This is a relatively recent phenomenon at the time of writing; most of the research that mistakenly informed classrooms when I trained to be a teacher in the early 2000s was based on over-enthusiastic and misunderstood neuroscience, speculative fictions like NLP and thinly disguised ideological treatises about inclusion and justice that said more about their authors' interests than the working of the student mind. Still today, it can be difficult to distinguish between those trying to sell us something and actual, helpful research. Only increased research literacy across the sector will solve that, but happily, we are already seeing greater use of such theories as working memory, cognitive load theory, spaced practice and a greater understanding of long-term memory. Many of these are explored in detail by Jonathan Firth in this volume, so I won't dwell on them here.

These ideas are open to dispute, of course, but they represent some very robust and well-evidenced techniques to learn and revise. When teachers become familiar with the science as well as the craft of their profession, we start to see something remarkable: the truly professional teacher, with a body of transferrable knowledge, rather than the delivery mechanism we see in many school systems. Knowledge truly is power.

Imagine the scenario when a school leader or policy-maker insists that students learn in a way contrary to all known theories about the human mind. Teachers can push back and press their case – a case that relies on more than simply intuition. Which isn't to say that every educational matter is settled by research and no further discussion is possible; on the contrary, it means discussion becomes possible rather than politically suicidal. Of course, there will forever be resistance against this level of teacher agency or autonomy, but research can, with thought and practice, give teachers a firm backstop against which to plant their feet and push back.

The new world of the liberated teacher

The new era of education research offers a complete short-circuiting of traditional hierarchies in education, where an entrenched, elite priesthood enjoyed sole rights to distribute ideas. When I trained to teach, I believed as my trainers believed; I read the books they suggested; my schema was their schema. It took years of counter-exemplary experience to even begin to chip away at that narrative. I turned first to personal study through a sabbatical at Cambridge University. Then I turned to the great ocean of opinion, fact, data and discourse that comprises social media. Through this process of digital and physical integration, I underwent a complete metamorphosis of ambition, ideology and practice.

Many of the old priesthoods have noticed this paradigm shift and resent it. I've read scornful commentary from some union leaders, university professors, ITT providers, and headteachers about the use of social media to empower and inform teachers. Many territories (for example some provinces of Canada) actively prohibit their teachers from expressing views online that may conflict with the prevailing narrative (or 'bring the profession into disrepute'). Many teachers tell me that they fear to blog, tweet or post because they imagine terrible consequences would ensue. And they might well be right. The terrible consequences are concentrated on the monoliths of tradition, however, and they know it.

I've been complained about twice to my schools for blogs I've written. I've been reported to the Department for Education and the Times Educational Supplement for opinions the complainants found objectionable. Since I started writing a couple of reports on behaviour for the DfE, I've started to receive comments along the lines of 'Should someone in your position be making such statements?' None of this concerns me. I am happy to be inappropriate. If being appropriate means being so anodyne that no offence could possibly be taken, to hell with that. Research and reason have liberated me.

These gatekeepers are standing in the face of a tide that will sweep them away. The capacity for teachers to engage with one another without permission or filter has been unearthed. These worms cannot go back in the can.

References

Bennett, T. and McAleavy, T. (2016). *The School Research Lead*. Reading: Education Development Trust. [online] Available at https://www.educationdevelopmenttrust.com/~/media/EDT/Reports/Research/2016/r-the-school-research-lead-2016.pdf. Retrieved 05/06/2017.

Deans for Impact (2015). *The Science of Learning*. Austin, TX: Deans for Impact. [online] Available at https://deansforimpact.org/wp-content/uploads/2016/12/The_Science_of_Learning.pdf. Retrieved 05/06/2017.

Greville-Giddins, B. (2017). *What Are Educational Journal Clubs?* [online] Available at http://www.edujournalclub.com/journal-clubs/. Retrieved 05/06/2017.

Leat, D., Lofthouse, R. and Reid, A. (2014). *Teachers' Views: Perspectives on Research Engagement*. London: BERA. [online] Available at https://www.bera.ac.uk/wp-content/uploads/2013/12/BERA-Paper-7-Teachers-Views-Perspectives-on-research-engagement.pdf. Retrieved 05/06/2017.

Wintour, P. (2014). *Cabinet Secretary Has David Cameron 'by the balls', Says Former Tory Adviser. Guardian*, 19 November. [online] Available at https://www.theguardian.com/politics/2014/nov/19/cabinet-secretary-david-cameron-balls-dominic-cummings-jeremy-heywood. Retrieved 06/05/2017.

Chapter 2

Beyond the policy VAKuum

An educational journey

Peter Ford

"So how *did* 'neuro-nonsense' end up as educational policy?"

Speaking at the 2015 researchED conference, Minister of State at the Department for Education, Nick Gibb identified examples of classroom practices which were not evidence-based:

> Some classroom practice [...] has been held up to scrutiny and found wanting. I have already mentioned Brain Gym, but alongside it, we can place learning styles, multiple intelligences, discovery learning, and the 21st-century skills movement as hollow shells of their former selves.
>
> (Gibb, 2015)

Acknowledging that such practices still exist, Gibb emphasised that they are now being actively challenged, citing the opportunities afforded to teachers by social media as fundamental to that challenge.

Such is the significance of social media that leading teacher bloggers are increasingly influential in educational discourse. Education secretaries, senior politicians and the sector watchdog (Ofsted) all name-check teacher bloggers:

> It is so encouraging that a growing number of teachers – indeed the most popular teachers on the web, like Andrew Old, whose blog has received more than 600,000 hits; Tom Bennett, with almost eight and a half thousand followers on Twitter, and Joe Kirby, with almost 2,000 – are arguing for a restoration of knowledge and direct instruction; in short, standing up for the importance of teaching.
>
> (*The Mail Online*, 2013)

Gibb (2015) described teacher activism on social media as a remarkable example of a grassroots movement driven not by worthies on high but by teachers on the ground "burning the midnight oil as they tweeted, blogged and shared ideas about how to improve their profession." He noted that the movement had not emerged from universities, accusing academics of being too invested in the status quo. The point of the speech appeared to be that this new movement challenges poor classroom practice in ways that traditional hierarchies did not.

As a specific example, learning styles have become something of a bête noire in educational policy circles. Tom Bennett (2015) teacher blogger, 'behaviour Tsar' and founder of researchED, has felt compelled to write:

> This weekend saw another outbreak of the learning styles zombie virus. [...] Learning styles? Really? Do we have to dig up the coffin and douse it in holy water again? Cut off the head and stuff it with garlic bulbs and consecrated hosts? It seems we do. Van Helsing, to the horses!

Robert Peel, education commentator and author, wrote the following, reflecting the zeitgeist of many educators engaged in social media discourse:

> Progressive ideas were reframed in the modernising language of New Labour. Classroom fads such as personalisation, independent learning, multiple intelligences, learning styles, 21st century skills, and the social and emotional aspects of learning, rained down on teachers.
>
> (Peel, 2014)

Yet, despite years of campaigning, holding the practice aloft as a symbol of all that has gone wrong in education, learning styles endure.

So what are learning styles?

The answer, an ill-defined construct widely used in educational discourse (Sharp, Bowker & Byrne, 2008), is the product of a research field that includes a number of related constructs, such as cognitive styles, thinking styles and, more latterly, simply styles. Peterson, Rayner and Armstrong (2009, p. 11) define them as "an individual's preferred way of responding (cognitively and behaviourally) to learning tasks which change depending on the environment or context and are thus seen as malleable." They are contrasted with cognitive styles, which are "a person's preferred way of processing ... partly fixed, relatively stable and possibly innate preferences" (ibid., p. 519).

In general usage, learning styles are an admixture of these, based on varying criteria, and purport to identify individuals' preferences with the expectation that tailoring teaching to these will result in identifiable improvements in learning outcomes (Coffield et al., 2004; Sharp et al., 2008). The most widely used model refers to visual, auditory and kinaesthetic preferences (VAK), and though there is little evidence that it has any meaningful use in any particular research field (Sharp et al., 2008), it has nonetheless been adopted by business and other fields, including education (Evans & Sadler-Smith, 2006).

Despite its popularity, Sharp, Bowker and Byrne (2008, p. 309) describe the VAK model as having no empirical validity, being little better than "pseudo-science, psychobabble and neuro-nonsense," and further state that it has been "acknowledged, quite naively, by the Department for Education and Skills (DfES)" (ibid., p. 293).

How did learning styles become endemic in education?

So how *did* 'neuro-nonsense' end up as educational policy? Around in various policy guises from the early 1980s, probably the simplest answer is that Minister of State for School Standards David Miliband introduced it in a policy document on personalisation. At the time, personalisation was a developing policy initiative across Whitehall, and learning styles became a vehicle for personalising learning.

Personalisation was a policy concept concerned with the inclusion of service users in the planning of provision, introduced by the publication of *Personalisation through Participation,* written for think tank Demos by Charles Leadbeater (2003), a Demos associate (Demos Staff overview, 2013) and once senior adviser to the Downing Street policy unit (Leadbeater, 2013). According to Campbell, Robinson, Neelands, Hewston and Mazzolli (2007), the concept of personalisation was at first misunderstood as the individualisation of services, though Leadbeater had described it as a far more complex and socially oriented idea. Although personalisation was primarily about the wider public services, Leadbeater himself connected it to education, giving rise to personalised learning, the idea that learners should be engaged in setting their own targets, devising their own learning plans and choosing from a range of ways to learn (Campbell et al., 2007).

The problem with personalisation, as pointed out by Campbell et al. (2007), is that the abilities of an individual to self-actualise, to understand what goals are appropriate and to contextualise aspiration within a complex and fast-changing social environment are considerably affected by factors such as social capital and parental involvement. Despite these issues, personalisation was included in David Miliband's *Personalised Learning: Building a New Relationship with Schools*:

> How do we achieve both excellence and equity?
> The solution is to build on what the most successful teachers do best, to create an education system with personalised learning at its heart. This means a system in which every child matters; careful attention is paid to their individual learning styles, motivations and needs; there is rigorous use of pupil target setting linked to high quality formative assessment and marking; lessons are well paced and enjoyable; and pupils are supported by partnerships with others beyond the classroom.
>
> (Miliband, 2004, p. 2)

Here, David Miliband clearly links personalisation to "individual learning styles," in effect transforming them from what was an unpromising research concept to a lynchpin for turning personalisation into a workable educational practice. What's more, Miliband's use of learning styles only has a passing resemblance to Leadbeater's policy aim of individualised learning.

Clearly grasping at straws to make a policy aim implementable, Miliband had seized upon an ill-defined research construct that appeared to fit the bill. Unfortunately, the problems that Schlesinger (2009) identified with regard to personalisation (social capital, parental involvement and the ability to conceptualise ambition and aspiration beyond immediate circumstances) are not resolved by learning styles. They offer only a superficial policy prescription to meet a much more complex aim.

How has the concept of learning styles survived for so long?

The efficacy or otherwise of VAK aside, the most interesting aspect of learning styles is not what they do or don't achieve, but how they can still be the source of considerable contention ten years after Miliband's policy initiative.

Professor Stephen Ball offers some insight into this longevity:

> schools may pay some attention to a policy and 'fabricate' a response that is incorporated into school documentation for purposes of accountability and audit, rather than to effect pedagogic or organisational change.
>
> (Ball et al., 2012, p. 10)

In effect, learning styles emerged as a convenient pedagogic mechanism to link personalisation to classroom practice. Whilst the intent of the policy may have been to right some social wrong, it eventually became a means to evidence practice in schools and classrooms. It is as likely as not that over time the original intention of learning styles was forgotten, if it was ever properly known. Somewhat chillingly, the act of compliance itself becomes the point of the policy.

Conclusion

The journey of learning styles from policy initiative to pedagogic pariah raises a number of questions for education. First, how does the sector avoid such pedagogic placebos? Secondly, does the extent to which the sector is prepared to embrace these practices perhaps explain why educational practice has, if Nick Gibb is to be believed, fallen out with its own academic body of knowledge?

The answer to the first question is that policy-makers need to accept that policy is not formulated in a vacuum. It must relate to educational practice and, more importantly, be envisaged within a practice context. Without a new approach to policy-making, one that works collaboratively with teachers and school leaders – indeed conceives of them as policy-makers, too – it seems likely that policy and practice will continue to be uncomfortable bedfellows, the one blamed by the other for the ills that befall the system.

The upshot from this, and answer to the second question, is that in this institutionalised blame game, academia is relegated to a third party for either side to deflect onto. While there is a clear need for academics to own their research and combat its misuse, teachers must also be given every chance to access and evaluate research as part of any new policy-making consensus, without reliance on social media or the need to burn the midnight oil.

To arm teachers with critical knowledge and actively engage them in defining and developing education must be core aims of flipping the system – to develop a strong, myth-free and, most importantly, myth-proof profession.

References

Ball, S. J., Maguire, M., & Braun, A. (2012). *How schools do policy: Policy enactments in secondary schools*. Abingdon: Routledge.

Bennett, T. (2015, November 4). *Why does the idea of learning styles keep getting resurrected?* Retrieved from https://www.tes.com/news/blog/why-does-idea-learning-styles-keep-getting-resurrected

Campbell, R. J., Robinson, W., Neelands, J., Hewston, R., & Mazzolli, L. (2007). Personalised learning: ambiguities in theory and practice. *British Journal of Educational Studies*, *55*(2), 135–154.

Coffield, F., Moseley, D., Hall, E., & Ecclestone, K. (2004). *Learning styles and pedagogy in post-16 learning. A systematic and critical review*. London: Learning and Skills Research Centre.

Evans, C., & Sadler-Smith, E. (2006). Learning styles in education and training: Problems, politicisation and potential. *Education and Training*, *48*(2/3), 77–83.

Gibb, N. (2015, 5 September). *Nick Gibb: The importance of the teaching profession*, transcript. Department for Education. Retrieved 30 May 2017 from https://www.gov.uk/government/speeches/nick-gibb-the-importance-of-the-teaching-profession

Gove, Michael. (2013). I refuse to surrender to the Marxist teachers hell-bent on destroying our schools: Education Secretary berates 'the new enemies of promise' for opposing his plans. *Daily Mail* online. Retrieved from http://www.dailymail.co.uk/debate/article-2298146/I-refuse-surrender-Marxist-teachers-hell-bent-destroying-schools-Education-Secretary-berates-new-enemies-promise-opposing-plans.html

Leadbeater, C. (2003). *Personalisation through participation*. London: Demos.

Leadbeater, C. (2013). *About me*. Retrieved 15 March 2013 from http://www.charlesleadbeater.net/about-me/about-me.aspx

Miliband, D. (2004). *Personalised learning: building a new relationship with schools*. London: Dfes.

Peel, R. (2014, July 8). *Gove's unfinished business*. Retrieved from http://quarterly.demos.co.uk/article/issue-3/goves-unfinished-business/

Peterson, E. R., Rayner, S. G., & Armstrong, S. J. (2009). *Herding cats: In search of definitions of cognitive styles and learning style*. ELSIN Newsletter, Winter 2008–2009. Retrieved from http://www.elsinnews.com

Schlesinger, P. (2009). Creativity and the experts: new labour, think tanks, and the policy process. *The International Journal of Press Politics*, *14*(1), 3–20.

Sharp, J. G., Bowker, R., & Byrne, J. (2008). VAK or VAK-uous? Towards the trivialisation of learning and the death of scholarship. *Research Papers in Education*, *23*(3), 293–314.

Chapter 3

Experts in learning

Jonathan Firth

"Our research knowledge must be better than the 'common sense' understanding of an intelligent non-teacher if it is to be considered professional knowledge at all."

Flipping the system means putting teachers back in control of educational practice, and this book is therefore acutely concerned with the locus of judgements made within teaching. The gradual centralisation of education since the late 1980s, with decisions over content and pedagogy increasingly taken by government departments, can be seen as a direct challenge to teacher professionalism. This question seems more urgent than ever: do we want our teachers to be homogeneous 'delivery agents', or to be autonomous and diverse professionals who are experts in learning?

Within this debate, a 'what works' approach to teaching practice – whereby research evidence is used to guide teaching practice – is sometimes seen as a threat to teachers' professional judgement, on the basis that externally set standards (often based on out-of-date or cherry-picked research results) are imposed on teachers from the top down. In this chapter, I argue that research-based knowledge about learning, in particular the intricate and often counter-intuitive functioning of human long-term memory, is actually a key tool for the emancipation of teachers and for flipping the system towards greater teacher agency. Armed with this knowledge and an understanding of their own learning context, teachers will always be in a better position to say what works for their learners than any external authority.

Criticisms of evidence-based practice

It is important, first of all, to set out why evidence-based practice has been seen as a threat. One factor is that it implies an imposition of teaching practices with little or no regard to whether these practices are appropriate to the setting – a criticism of centralisation rather than of the use of evidence per se. However, there is a further concern about the nature of the desired improvements, well expressed here by Biesta (2007, p. 5):

> Evidence-based education seems to favour a technocratic model in which it is assumed that the only relevant research questions are questions about the effectiveness of educational means and techniques, forgetting, among other things, that what counts as 'effective' crucially depends on judgments about what is educationally desirable.

It is certainly true that efficacy in learning and memory is an empirical matter that does not address moral questions of purpose. However, the idea that studying 'what works' is insufficient does not make it any less worthwhile, nor does it impede discussion of values and purposes. In practice, there is already a great deal of discussion about what young people might need to learn for the workplace of the future or to enrich their lives, yet the technical question of how best to impart knowledge and skills tends to be neglected. It is entirely possible to consider how to apply learning science effectively in concert with the already rich and emotive debate over what should be taught.

Research and teacher agency

Most parts of the UK have witnessed an increasing level of interference in teaching practices as well as curriculum content under the general label of raising standards (Alexander, 2014). Such moves tend to be accompanied by heightened accountability measures, reducing teacher agency and prompting teachers to become compliant and unadventurous in their professional practice (Sachs, 2016).

In opposition to this, some voices have called for increased levels of professionalism and autonomy among the teaching profession. A positive example in recent years has been the promotion of teachers engaging with and carrying out their own research; the British Educational Research Association (BERA) stated that "teachers and teacher educators can be equipped to engage with and be discerning consumers of research …[and] may be equipped to conduct their own research, individually and collectively" (2014, p. 5). In his report on 'Teaching Scotland's Future', Donaldson (2011) recommends that narrow interpretations of the teacher's role must be challenged in order to facilitate engagement with research.

This perspective on professional practice has much to recommend it. Professionals who have more control are less stressed (Marmot et al., 1991), while the ability to make meaningful changes is highly motivating and prompts creativity in the workplace (Amabile & Kramer, 2011). Teaching, from this point of view, is better viewed as a disciplined improvisation rather than as the fulfilment of a precisely programmed series of actions, a perspective that is supported by the finding that the level of detail in teachers' lesson planning reduces in line with their years of classroom experience (Sawyer, 2004).

Greater research engagement has the potential to lead to a more responsive form of accountability (Halstead, 1994) whereby practitioners continually analyse and modify their own professional processes. Doing so requires teachers to have control over what they do in the classroom, and so the movement towards teacher research engagement has an intrinsic link to teacher agency.

Knowledge and intuition

Debate about teacher agency is part of a broader discourse around professionalism. Teachers, of course, feel that they should be viewed, treated and remunerated as professionals. However, the quality of the decisions that any professional makes depends on their knowledge and skills.

The role of research evidence in professional practice is to suggest improvements and to modify harmful or ineffective practices – just as if our learners were using poor study strategies, we wouldn't hesitate to correct them (and they probably are – see Hartwig & Dunlosky, 2012). Initial teacher education can be conceptualised as a process where inexperienced teachers are guided in the development of these professional skills, with CPD activities aiming to foster and extend them throughout the teaching career. The term 'skill' should be used with some caution, though. In an era where the politics of pedagogy has come to focus on its practical skills rather than theoretical understanding, the importance of theory and values-based teacher education needs defending (Donaldson, 2011; Brown et al., 2016).

The focus here is on professional practice that is grounded in an understanding of theory; one of the main contentions of this chapter is that it is important to teacher professionalism that we engage with research into human long-term memory. Our research knowledge must be better than the 'common sense' understanding of an intelligent non-teacher if it is to be considered professional knowledge at all. This is especially important given that assumptions about memory tend to encompass a range of inaccurate views, such as the widespread concept of 'permanent memory' – the idea that memory for a single experience, once well learned, does not change (Simons & Chabris, 2011).

Indeed, memory as a field of study has been described as inherently unintuitive (Bjork, 2011). There is good reason therefore to think that without adequate training, a teacher would be working with highly inaccurate notions about how new information is processed, taken in, consolidated and later retrieved. Memory is not the only research area that can affect teaching practice, but it is a particularly fundamental one, given the pedagogical importance of learning and retention. Inaccurate assumptions could impact on a great many teacher decisions, from designing materials to deciding when to finish working on a task.

What about the role of experience? As governments increasingly push for schemes that place untrained graduates directly into teaching roles, it would be useful to know whether a more accurate understanding of memory can develop over time. Here, research into other professions such as lawyers and judges suggests that even years of experience cannot overcome memory biases and misconceptions (Magnussen et al., 2010). Psychological research into cognition and prejudice also suggests that experience alone cannot be relied on to overcome biases in thinking (pupils' flawed revision strategies may be further evidence of this!).

Our intuitive thought processes are rapid, and largely automatic. One example (Kahneman, 2002, p. 451) involves the application of basic arithmetic to a puzzle:

A bat and a ball cost £1.10 in total. The bat costs £1 more than the ball. How much does the ball cost?

This type of thinking may well give us a quick but inaccurate response – 10p. However, we also have a slower and more effortful mode of thinking, which is more sensitive to training (Kahneman, op cit.). When we scrutinise our own answer using this more deliberate system, we realise that the obvious assumption is incorrect – the ball must cost 5p, and the bat £1.05.

As teachers, a key metacognitive function of this more effortful analytical thinking is the ability to check intuitive reasoning, modifying judgements on the basis of our theoretical understanding. It's not the case that intuition is always (or even often) inaccurate; these abilities have evolved through human prehistory for their survival value, and in some areas of interaction intuition serves us well – for example, snap judgements of personality and mood appear to be largely accurate (Ambady & Rosenthal, 1992). However, other domains, such as statistics, seem to inherently run counter to human intuition, with assumptions leading to systematic errors (Tversky & Kahneman, 1974).

For reasons discussed above, there are good reasons to think that the domain of learning and memory is a highly unintuitive area where theoretical knowledge has an important role to play as part of pedagogical expertise. Yan, Bjork and Bjork (2016) have shown that even when effective learning strategies are tried out or their logical benefits explained (in a way analogous to teacher CPD), research participants tend to still stick to their inaccurate hunches. However, if people had both explicit training *and* practical experience of better strategies, they did adjust their behaviour and thinking. This research finding concords with a view of professionalism where neither experience nor factual know-how alone can fully equip a teacher for their role, but a synthesis of theoretical understanding and practical experience can.

Key evidence – learning and memory

What, then, are the main evidence-based principles of memory that can inform our professional practice? Let us consider some relevant facts about human memory.

Memory is easily distorted

Memories of events are not discrete entities. Instead, they are interlinked in networks which psychologists and linguists refer to as schemas (or schemata). Taking in new information is not a neutral process, but is influenced by the state of prior knowledge and beliefs – new information can influence these schemas, but likewise old memories can distort new ones. Memories can also be distorted by later information and questioning, with people often finding it hard to retain with certainty the source of their memories (Schacter, 2001), and even just the process of recalling a memory changes it (Bjork, 2011). As has been recognised for many decades in psychology, taking in new information is a dynamic process of interpretation.

Learning should be distributed over time

Learners often focus on working on a set of tasks until they have 'got it', but immediate performance is an unreliable guide to long-term learning (Soderstrom & Bjork, 2013); the fact that a learner can do something today, tomorrow or even next week does not mean that they will be able to do it in six months' time. Conversely, failure in the short term does not mean that they have not learned.

This dissociation between current performance and long-term learning links to a powerful strategy for learning and review – learning should be distributed over time, with larger rather than smaller gaps between initial learning and review tasks (Rohrer, 2015). More spaced-out learning and practice reduces forgetting and may help learners to mentally connect new information to a broader set of experiences.

Immediate feedback

It might be assumed that immediate corrective feedback is highly valuable to learning. However, a body of research has shown that delaying and minimising feedback can result in better long-term retention (Soderstrom & Bjork, 2013). This may link to the benefits of learners reflecting on problems themselves and overcoming difficulties independently. In addition, Hattie and Timperley (2007) note that corrective feedback is among the least effective options, with feedback based on highlighting the best elements of student work (but not generic praise) having a greater effect.

As with distributed learning, this area of research presents the counterintuitive conclusion that delaying and reducing teacher input can help learning over the long term.

Generation and retrieval

It is increasingly being recognised that repetition and re-reading are ineffective learning strategies (e.g. Dunlosky & Rawson, 2015). So what is preferable?

The 'generation effect' suggests that words produced by a learner, for example when completing a gap fill, will be better recalled than those which are read – a finding that backs up certain forms of active learning.

A similar finding is the 'testing effect' (also called 'retrieval practice') – memory is improved when learners have to recall information, relative to repeated re-reading, even in the absence of any feedback (Roediger & Karpicke, 2006). This suggests that educators would benefit from looking at testing in a fundamentally different way – not as assessment, but as a technique for building new memories (Karpicke, 2016). It is important to clarify that retrieval from memory doesn't need to involve a test – it could include writing or discussion, for example.

These areas represent matters of near-universal agreement in psychology, and although the best way of applying such principles to education is still a matter of ongoing research, they offer considerable potential benefits to the teacher. They are easily applied – techniques such as spacing out topics or delaying feedback needn't involve changes to materials or tasks. What's more, the resulting efficiency gains from these factors represent potential time savings which could ease some of the pressures of teacher workload.

It is worth adding that the discussion of the role of memory in education thus far should not be interpreted in the narrow sense of advocating simple memorisation. A pupil's memory plays a role in every aspect of learning and is used every time they have a conversation or read a text, and it underlies the development of well-integrated conceptual understandings.

Sources of research evidence

Finally, it is important to consider the sources from which teachers get research information. This, too, can represent a form of centralised control, or a means of empowerment of the practitioner. There is a developing grassroots movement among teachers seeking to engage with research-based practice; teacher-led conferences as well as local meet-ups are important means of sharing knowledge, as are social media and practitioner blogs. Publications such as TES are increasingly featuring research evidence based around memory, too.

The role of governments is more problematic. They could in principle give good-quality generic guidance, but recent experience suggests that they often don't; instead, their use of evidence displays considerable distortions based on their ideology and agenda (Alexander, 2014). In a model which features increased teacher agency, the role of governments and other superordinate authorities would see the informed practitioner as the locus of decision making. Their role would be to support rather than dictate to the practitioner, for example by:

- funding teacher access to research journals, as happens for NHS doctors;
- maintaining high standards of initial teacher education;

- supporting teacher research projects with time and funding;
- facilitating and supporting equal-status cooperation between the teaching fraternity and other sectors of academia.

Of course, professional development does not happen in a vacuum but within learning communities, with teachers influencing and supporting one another. Some schools have introduced a 'research lead' position, facilitating dissemination of new educational research evidence among staff. Local school and/or college clusters may be helpful, drawing on a broader pool of knowledge. Pupils and parents, too, can be engaged in the discussion of effective learning, helping to democratise the educational process.

Conclusion

Engaging with research can empower the professional rather than being used to challenge or replace professional judgement. In effect, we must flip the evidence-based learning discourse, allowing the research to take its rightful place as an integral component of our professional expertise. Failure to do so will weaken our professional standing at a time when it is already under threat.

Research evidence can benefit a range of domains, but human memory is one that is especially relevant to education. It is also one in which misconceptions are widespread, and intuition – or even years of classroom experience – cannot substitute for an evidence-based theoretical understanding. This chapter has outlined several areas of research from cognitive psychology that are directly applicable to teaching.

Evidence-based professionalism is more likely to emerge under the ideal conditions of good institutional support, teacher autonomy and access to appropriate resources and role models (Drew et al., 2016). But in the absence of such conditions, individual teachers can boost their expertise in learning as part of a grassroots movement, helping our profession as a whole to say to governments and other authorities, 'we understand research in learning and our work is evidence-based … is yours?'

References

Alexander, R. (2014). Evidence, policy and the reform of primary education: A cautionary tale. *Forum, 56*(3), 349–375.

Amabile, T., & Kramer, S. (2011). *The Progress Principle: Using Small Wins to Ignite Joy, Engagement, and Creativity at Work.* Cambridge, MA: Harvard Business Press.

Ambady, N., & Rosenthal, R. (1992). Thin slices of expressive behavior as predictors of interpersonal consequences: A meta-analysis. *Psychological Bulletin, 111*(2), 256–274. doi:10.1037/0033-2909.111.2.256

BERA (2014). Research and the teaching profession: Building the capacity for a self-improving education system. Final report of the BERA-RSA inquiry into the role of research in teacher education. London: Author.

Biesta, G. (2007). Why "what works" won't work: Evidence-based practice and the democratic deficit in educational research. *Educational Theory*, *57*(1), 1–22. doi:10.1111/j.1741-5446.2006.00241.x

Bjork, R. A. (2011). On the symbiosis of remembering, forgetting, and learning. In A.S. Benjamin (Ed.) *Successful Remembering and Successful Forgetting: A Festschrift in Honor of Robert A. Bjork* (pp. 1–22). New York: Psychology Press.

Brown, T., Rowley, H., & Smith, K. (2016). The beginnings of school led teacher training: New challenges for university teacher education. *School Direct Research Project Final Report.* Accessed 14 January 2017 at http://www.esri.mmu.ac.uk/resgroups/schooldirect.pdf

Donaldson, G. (2011). *Teaching Scotland's Future: Report of a Review of Teacher Education in Scotland.* Edinburgh: Scottish Government.

Drew, V., Priestley, M., & Michael, M. K. (2016). Curriculum development through critical collaborative professional enquiry. *Journal of Professional Capital and Community*, *1*(1), 92–106. doi:10.1108/JPCC-09-2015-0006

Dunlosky, J., & Rawson, K. A. (2015). Practice tests, spaced practice, and successive relearning: Tips for classroom use and for guiding students' learning. *Scholarship of Teaching and Learning in Psychology*, *1*(1), 72–78. doi:10.1037/stl0000024

Halstead, M. (1994). Accountability and values. In D. Scott (Ed.), *Accountability and Control in Educational Settings* (pp. 3–14). London: Castell.

Hartwig, M. K., & Dunlosky, J. (2012). Study strategies of college students: Are self-testing and scheduling related to achievement? *Psychonomic Bulletin & Review*, *19*(1), 126–134. doi:10.3758/s13423-011-0181-y

Hattie, J., & Timperley, H. (2007). The power of feedback. *Review of Educational Research*, *77*(1), 81–112. doi:10.3102/003465430298487

Kahneman, D. (2002). Maps of bounded rationality: A perspective on intuitive judgment and choice. *Nobel Prize Lecture*, *8*, 351–401.

Karpicke, J. D. (2016). A powerful way to improve learning and memory: Practicing retrieval enhances long-term, meaningful learning. *Psychological Science Agenda*. Accessed 24 June 2016 at http://www.apa.org/science/about/psa/2016/06/learning-memory. aspx

Magnussen, S., Melinder, A., Stridbeck, U., & Raja, A. Q. (2010). Beliefs about factors affecting the reliability of eyewitness testimony: A comparison of judges, jurors and the general public. *Applied Cognitive Psychology*, *24*(1), 122–133. doi:10.1002/acp.1550

Marmot, M. G., Stansfeld, S., Patel, C., et al. (1991). Health inequalities among British civil servants: The Whitehall II study. *The Lancet*, *337*(8754), 1387–1393.

Roediger, H. L., & Karpicke, J. D. (2006). Test-enhanced learning taking memory tests improves long-term retention. *Psychological Science*, *17*, 249–255. doi:10.1016/0140-6736(91)93068-K

Rohrer, D. (2015). Student instruction should be distributed over long time periods. *Educational Psychology Review*, *27*, 635–643. doi:10.1007/s10648-015-9332-4

Sachs, J. (2016). Teacher professionalism: Why are we still talking about it? *Teachers and Teaching*, *22*(4), 413–425. doi:10.1080/13540602.2015.1082732

Sawyer, R. K. (2004). Creative teaching: Collaborative discussion as disciplined improvisation. *Educational Researcher*, *33*(2), 12–20. doi:10.3102/0013189X033002012

Schacter, D. L. (2001). *The Seven Sins of Memory*. Boston: Houghton Mifflin.

Simons, D. J., & Chabris, C. F. (2011). What people believe about how memory works: A representative survey of the US population. *PloS One*, *6*(8), e22757. doi:10.1371/journal.pone.0022757

Soderstrom, N. C., & Bjork, R. A. (2013). Learning versus performance. *Oxford Bibliographies Online: Psychology*. New York: Oxford University Press.

Tversky, A., & Kahneman, D. (1974). Judgment under uncertainty: Heuristics and biases. *Science, 185*(4157), 1124–1131. doi:10.1126/science.185.4157.1124

Yan, V. X., Bjork, E. L., & Bjork, R. A. (2016). On the difficulty of mending metacognitive illusions: A priori theories, fluency effects, and misattributions of the interleaving benefit. *Journal of Experimental Psychology: General, 145*(7), 918–933. doi:10.1037/xge0000177

Chapter 4

From data rich to data smart
Empowering teaching, not monitoring teachers

David Weston

> **"At the heart of these scenarios is the eerie sense that everyone has to play the game. Data is king, even if it doesn't really represent a recognisable reality."**

"It's all take, take, take. I can't remember the last time someone asked me what I need," she said, as she burst into tears in front of me. We both looked nervously at the classroom door, wondering if a member of the management team might come in and ask what was happening. She looked at me with a fearful expression that said, "I'm supposed to keep this hidden, I'm supposed to toe the line. This is what being a professional means these days."

I visit schools in England regularly to talk to teachers about how they are learning and growing. The conversation above was not, sadly, a one-off. I speak to so many people in schools who spend their lives looking nervously over their shoulders, wondering if they are about to be 'caught out.' It might be a teacher nervously entering their latest set of test scores into the data management system. It might be, like the colleague who burst into tears, an experienced head of department who has been asked to deliver training sessions on 'Outstanding Teaching.' It might be a headteacher putting on a brave face as she feels the 'school improvement advisor' breathing down her neck.

At the heart of these scenarios is the eerie sense that everyone has to play the game. Data is king, even if it doesn't really represent a recognisable reality. Everyone is monitored and your job is to attempt to exceed your minimum targets at all times. Perform, deliver, be measured. Play your part, prove your worth, don't fall behind.

It doesn't have to be this way. I have visited schools filled with joy. Places of learning where teachers are scholars of research, where intellectual rigour and debate are cherished, where management efforts are focused primarily on growth instead of monitoring. These are schools filled with a sense of collective efficacy, where everyone works together to examine evidence of learning, rather than places of judgement and 'us versus them.' The challenge levels are high and professional accountability is strong; these are not necessarily always relaxing places to work, but they are endlessly stimulating, nourishing and, above all, professional environments.

One such school is Cleveland Road Primary School in East London. It's a large primary school with four classes in each year. I visited the school to discuss the way that staff there engage in professional learning and development. I asked one teacher about his working week.

Him: "Well, every week we meet as a team of teachers to do planning. We have a look at what's coming up in the curriculum and review whether there are any difficult areas for the pupils which have come up in the last week. It's a great way to share ideas and get on the same page with each other. We have our team of Teaching Assistants with us too, and that helps them work across the classes."

Me: "So, it's a professional development session?"

Him: "Oh no, that's not CPD, that's just the way we work."

Everything about this school showed that teachers saw learning as threaded through every activity. They had embedded what Dame Alison Peacock calls the 'holy trinity' of curriculum knowledge, professional dialogue and constantly gathering evidence about pupils' learning (i.e. formative assessment).

This is a teacher-led approach to running a school. School leaders are not engaged in monitoring and telling, but they create an effective and challenging environment where every teacher is stretched to learn and contribute. As Cleveland Road's headteacher, Veena Naidoo, put it: "We know our staff and we know them well. We prioritise excellent conversations and we develop our team leaders to have exceptional subject knowledge and expertise."

Veena, like most of her senior colleagues, has had training in being a coach. She knows that great professional conversations aren't mandated through systems but also don't happen by accident. They work hard to model and develop supportive discussions. These conversations are rooted in the evidence gathered from the classroom and also in the aims embedded in the curriculum. They are empowering, not fear-inducing.

Like Cleveland Road, many of the most effective schools I visit focus on learning and on empowering teachers. While there is a quiet, background process of checking on effectiveness, most of the evidence gathering is targeted, to empower teachers and teaching assistants to make smarter decisions. Data systems are designed to enable teams to explore patterns and issues, to give visibility and clarity to staff about the effectiveness of their practice.

This approach is light years away from what is seen at the other end of the spectrum. Many schools design burdensome data systems with a view to rapidly identifying 'weak performance' and to otherwise allow senior leaders to make decisions about the training that should be given to staff based on test scores or one-off observations. Staff are asked to input data on six or more occasions per year, built on the mistaken underlying assumption that all the numbers are comparable and generalisable across teachers, classes and subjects.

Teachers are monitored through lesson observations and scrutiny of samples of pupil work. This is undertaken by generally untrained observers, despite the evidence showing the unreliability of this approach (Coe et al., 2014). Generic and often highly subjective judgements are made about aspects of practice that need to be improved.

Philippa Cordingley from the Centre for the Use of Research and Evidence in Education (CUREE) led a piece of research into the difference between successful and less successful schools.

She noted that all schools "undertook intense monitoring," but that

> in the absence of steps to ensure that everyone understood the principles/rationale behind the practices that were being monitored, this tended to erode into an unhelpful emphasis on compliance. By contrast, Exceptional Schools placed a great emphasis on building a shared understanding of the school's model of pedagogy and its underpinning rationale. By ensuring that all development focused on identifying and removing barriers to learning and building a shared model of and language for teaching and learning, the extensive monitoring in Exceptional Schools worked to build coherence for learners and develop a commitment to collective efficacy.
>
> (Cordingley, 2016)

Exceptional schools are not just data rich, but data smart. They recognise both the uses and the limits of that data. They ensure that the right information is used at the right levels. They are wary about aggregating entirely different sets of numbers in an attempt to create something superficially comparable. They recognise that data collection and appraisal observations can improve a workload burden which must be minimised. They create cultures where the most important user of information is the person who can act on it most rapidly and who has enough other information to contextualise and interrogate it. Others ask tough questions, provide alternative perspectives and inject expertise.

This surely makes sense. If I collect assessments that suggest that a pupil in my class has underperformed, then the person who can act most helpfully on that is me. I know the backstory of the pupil; I can immediately act to tweak my next lesson, to seek the right support from my colleagues and to have the right informal discussion with the pupil.

By the time that this has been aggregated to a team level, passed up to senior leaders, re-aggregated and discussed, then not only is there a huge time lag from the moment of learning, but the data has lost all of its nuance and context along the way. Anything suggested from class-level analysis will more likely be transformed into a sledge-hammer approach to deal with a complex and nuanced mix of statistical, psychological and pedagogical issues.

Every school can be data rich. That's the easy bit, but if we stop designing systems and cultures that funnel data to the top of the tree and push decisions and training back down, we can flip the system. We can enrich and empower teachers with approaches steeped in autonomy, professionalism and genuine expert accountability. We can make every school data smart.

References

Coe, R., Aloisi, C., Higgins, S., and Major, L. E., (2014) *What Makes Great Teaching? Review of the Underpinning Research*, available at http://www.suttontrust.com/wp-content/uploads/2014/10/What-Makes-Great-Teaching-REPORT.pdf [accessed 17/05/2017].

Cordingley, P., (2016) *Pockets of Excellence: Beacon or Blindspot*, available at http://www.curee.co.uk/node/3289 [accessed 17/05/2017].

Chapter 5

Breaking free of the machine
Lessons from Wales

David Williams

"If there is even a whiff of top–down accountability attached to tests, the numbers will go up, in perfect correlation with their meaninglessness."

In homage to R. S. Thomas.[1]

After the slow poison and treachery of the seasons

For fourteen years, I have seen almost every assessment system used by schools perverted, degraded and ultimately discarded; teachers and pupils treated as cogs in an Orwellian accountability machine with only one goal: to make the numbers go up. Because as long as the numbers keep going up, things are getting better. Right?

If politicians are in power, their vested interest is in numbers going up to prove their reforms successful. If they are not in power, their interest is in suggesting the numbers are in fact nonsense, in order to achieve power. Both of these political stances work against fair and honest assessment. In fact, the effects can be horrific. The machine encourages quick fixes. It encourages and honours head teachers who prioritise short-term success over long-term improvement. It supports the myth of "super teachers" and "super heads", some of whom have imploded under the pressure of this portrayal.

Part of the machine ... nerves metal ... and blood oil

The machine drives teaching to the test, extra revision sessions after school, in the holidays, on INSET days, on weekends and even on exam day. It forces good teachers out of the profession. It damages the reputation and status of schools and teachers. And, unforgivably, it ignores some remarkable accomplishments.

In Wales, when we got rid of SATs and moved to Teacher Assessment, many of us were rather smug. Year 6 and 9 curricula consisted largely of past papers, and TA seemed to offer the freedom to focus on building knowledge rather than exam technique. If you want to see how the machine has perverted and degraded that, just compare the KS2, 3 and 4 outcomes of the same cohorts in Wales and laugh at the ridiculousness of it – we're not so smug now!

At the time, value-added was also all-important. When I took over Literacy Intervention, I met a boy who couldn't read at the end of Year 8. I promised him I would do everything I could for him. He went on to learn to read and write well enough, through hard work and determination, to exceed all of his previous expectations; he got an E. Grit? I didn't know the meaning of the word until I met this boy, who'd felt like a failure for at least five years and still had the guts to persevere right to the end. I couldn't be prouder of him to this day. Results like his were read out and celebrated along with those who had achieved their ten A★s.

Then, the pressure to make the numbers go up intensified. It was perhaps a tinkling mountain spring of pressure at first – a political speech suggesting school results weren't high enough, that Local Authorities should support headteachers to do more. Like the spring, pressure to improve ran downhill from Inspectors to Local Authorities to head teachers to teachers and to pupils. I remember the county paid the local FE college to run revision sessions for borderline pupils during the Easter holidays. Then they paid teachers to do this in school instead. Then they stopped paying and it became expected. All the time, the stream of pressure was becoming a river, and at some point that river fell off a cliff to smash all those in its way against the rocks of "below expected standard". The boy who learned to read and got an E against the odds? A drag on the statistics.

As Cynddylan passes proudly up the lane

What if there is another way, a silk thread of hope to lead us out of this manipulated data labyrinth?

The answer lies simply in who we are accountable to.

We will always be accountable to pupils and their parents, but this alone is not enough. If we are to be accountable in an intelligent manner we must be so to those who know how the system works: fellow professionals, other teachers. We must be accountable to someone who is invested in the fairness of the assessments, rather than their outcomes alone, namely the person who is going to teach the class next. This doesn't mean the Year 2 teacher having a go at their Year 1 colleague, or secondary teachers moaning about feeder primary schools. It means sitting down and designing assessment systems with each other to actually find out what the pupils understand – I mean really understand, not just what you can get them to do in the short term.

But what I am proposing is a subversion of the system – a removal of any incentive other than fairness and transparency. In essence, I am suggesting we deliberately restrict access to the test data we create to anyone with a vested interest in numbers over standards, that we refuse access to this data to anyone except you and the teachers who come before and after you. Change, trust and honesty all require bravery.

What's living but courage?

The reward could be an assessment system which lasts, one that works for the benefit of pupils and teachers, not politicians, and that doesn't require us to redesign everything we've ever done overnight.

The first stage is to sit down with a teacher who is sending you the pupils they have worked with and to decide how, how often and when you are going to assess. I was forced to assess hundreds of pupils receiving reading intervention, or who had just arrived at the school, every September. And whilst, on the whole, this gave us confidence, over three years of testing, that progress was sustained, it also caused problems I am sure you can easily imagine. Firstly, perhaps most obviously, if you stick a hundred Year 7s in the gym and try to get them to fill out those lottery slip response papers, some of them − shock horror! − will perform poorly. Secondly, you don't get to reflect on the data or plan in readiness for the new term, because, well, it *is* the new term and you have to get the help to the right pupils quickly. And there were other issues too − too many to detail here.

Standardised tests have their place, but you may decide not to run them in September, but June, not in the gym, but in the familiar surroundings of their own classroom. What matters is that the person carrying out the test has no incentive in inflating or deflating results, that the test is repeated, and that you and your colleague are prepared to look honestly at the data without any sense of recrimination. This is where they were. This is where they are now according to this test. What is happening? Why? How can we help each other and the pupils to improve in a sustainable way?

We must remember that, whilst testing must inform our judgements about how pupils are progressing, they must not become the judgement. When they do, the ineluctable outcome is that teachers teach to the test.

So the challenge is this: what can you assess and reassess in a meaningful, impartial manner? How many assessments can you reasonably carry out and discuss? What can these assessments really tell you about what the pupils have learned? What assessments were most reliable? What might be better?

The best part about this bottom-up reform is that it is incremental. You choose where you want to start. You decide how you find out if that has been achieved. You don't move on until everyone is satisfied it works.

You start with a little assessment spring of hope, use it to help pupils, keep it genuine and hold your nerve. The more useful this assessment becomes, the more it will grow. If there is one thing everyone can learn from Wales, it's that if there is even a whiff of top-down accountability attached to tests, the numbers will go up, in near-perfect correlation with their meaninglessness. And if you continue to let the assessment system run you, rather than you running it, in the words of every teacher ever: "It's your own time you're wasting!"

What to do? Stay green.
Never mind the machine,

Whose fuel is human souls
Live large, man, and dream small.

Note

1 With thanks to Orion Publishing, all subheadings and the concluding stanza are reproduced with permission from the poems *Lore* and *Cynddylan on a Tractor*. Both poems are available in Thomas, R. S. (2004). *Collected poems*. London: Phoenix.

Chapter 6

Shedding our inhibitions
From external to internal accountability

Zeba Clarke

"Change will remain ad hoc and piecemeal until senior leaders unite to challenge political orthodoxy across the system."

As a teacher and leader, I've spent a good deal of time pondering the nature of good classroom practice. I've been observed and carried out observations. I've read as widely as I can, from blogs to books on pedagogy and leadership. Now that a close family member is making his own journey through the thickets and hurdles of teacher training, I'm regularly being asked what good practice is, and how to achieve it. Particularly contentious is the starter-core-plenary model that is still the basis for much of the lesson planning evidence PGCE candidates must amass. There is considerable divergence between what is officially regarded as good lesson planning and delivery and the actual day-to-day practices of more experienced teachers.

This means that the real nature of excellent classroom practice remains an open question, one that continues to be highly contested on social media as fresh generations of teachers engage with the issues, such as traditional versus progressive pedagogy, knowledge-based learning versus skills-based learning. In the real world of teachers and classrooms, these are reductive dichotomies for a much more complex process. I know that when I am observing colleagues, I look for:

- Secure subject knowledge;
- Focused short- and long-term aims;
- Challenging expectations;
- Tailoring for the group in question;
- Fluidity/flexibility in responding to the needs of the students;
- Satisfaction with the environment and progress being made.

I don't expect to tick every box, every lesson: I've observed colleagues supporting students through redrafting or editing activities, or just beginning to tease out the complexities of an idea or task, and their initial thoughts are, understandably, scattered and chaotic.

In practical terms, Allison and Tharby's pedagogical principles of Challenge, Explanation, Modelling, Questioning and Feedback produce approaches that can be practised, perfected and developed by all teachers and will support the kind of sustained learning that we welcome in our classrooms (Allison & Tharby 2015). These measures are more sophisticated and flexible than the classic four-part lesson plan that so many teacher training institutions favour. The classic *settler–main starter–core–plenary* format effectively straitjackets new teachers into an approach that meets neither teachers' nor learners' needs.

Perhaps more dangerous than their inflexibility is the assumption that these stand-alone lessons can produce sustained learning. As teachers, we know that most valuable work is carried across a week or fortnight, perhaps longer. It is simply not possible to teach students to produce excellent analytical essays, short stories, lab reports, mathematical studies or artworks in a single lesson. Ron Berger's work on developing craftsmanship and pride in one's output is a much-cited exploration of how to instil critique skills, pride and ambition in even very young students; it requires structured time, review and redrafting. However, the culture of what Fullan and others (Fullan et al., 2015) call 'punitive' accountability all too often leads us to step away from the detailed, time-consuming work that ensures students treat their own work with respect and develop their ability to produce outstanding results.

In the UK, external accountability has been embedded over the course of more than two decades. I completed my teacher training in 1992, the year John Major's government introduced league tables as part of the Citizen's Charter and the year Ofsted was formed under the Education (Schools) Act 1992.

In the intervening years, under Labour, Coalition and Conservative governments alike, league tables have dominated educational policy, coupled with a fetishisation of imposing free market principles and monetising aspects of education (Ball, 2003). But, based on the 2015 PISA rankings, the UK continues to struggle with reading and maths skills. Using the English Baccalaureate as a measure of school performance is leading to a decline in the numbers of students taking subjects other than a narrow range of English, Maths, History, Geography, one language and three sciences, particularly in selective schools (Greevy et al., 2012, and Long et al., 2017). This obsession with results, whether PISA or GCSE, limits students and teachers.

First, there is a negative impact on school leaders: instead of encouraging teachers to broaden students' horizons, the imperative is a narrow focus on one set of exam results. Fear of external judgement leads to an over-dependence on data and an obsessive targeting of those students on pass/fail borderlines. This leads to a reductive school culture of micro-management instead of an expansive one where everyone is fully engaged in teaching and learning, surely a betrayal of the very nature of education. Senior leaders and managers need the courage to trust their staff and, more than that, to empower them to focus, not on league tables and incessant data production, but on getting their students to master the knowledge and skills they need to progress through school and beyond. Instead, staff feel exposed, exploited and undermined, while students feel stressed and pressurized to perform. External accountability fosters a factory environment, not an educational one.

Innovation and experiment are set aside for tried-and-tested methods, familiar texts and safe topics across all subject areas. This reliance on 'safe' pedagogy often goes hand in hand with a climate of competition between colleagues and departments and fosters a climate of isolation where teachers only feel at ease when they have closed the classroom door. Collaborative planning, shared materials and a collegiate approach are regarded with suspicion as time-consuming, potentially undermining and uncertain. Yet these are some of the means by which improvement across whole educational systems, such as the Ontario school district (Fullan & Quinn, 2015) and Singapore (Ng, 2016), can be embedded.

The de-professionalisation of teachers has been widely noted by educational researchers from Stephen Ball's description of the 'terrors of performativity' (Ball, 2003) to Gewirtz et al. (2009), but seems to have had little impact on educational policies or political attitudes to the teaching profession. Instead, the critique of punitive accountability fostered by ranking schools has been ignored, and its proponents in educational research portrayed as 'The Blob', defined in the *Spectator* as "the amorphous coalition of a bloated education bureaucracy, teacher unions and education research establishment" (Sewell, 2010). In the intervening years, there has been a hardening of opposing views within 'The Blob' itself, with culture wars between educators favouring traditional approaches and those leaning towards more progressive teaching styles. Divided, we are easily conquered.

This 'us-and-them' attitude of politicians and their functionaries towards educators has also disadvantaged students: their experience of school becomes increasingly disconnected from the world outside. Where technology is making information more accessible and timely than ever, in the UK, the curriculum seems to be narrowing (Greevy et al., 2013), and the focus on data and results sidelines students themselves. We are told that students need personalised development plans, but what this means in practice is finding ways of making students conform. Those students requiring Individual Education Plans often find themselves marginalised.

Despite this hostile environment, some teachers are taking matters into their own hands. In leadership literature, there is an increasing emphasis on protecting colleagues, sheltering them from political demands and enabling them to develop their own cultures of collaboration and shared practice (Buck, 2014; Myatt, 2016). The research conducted by David Frost (2014) into non-positional teacher leadership, based on the HertsCam Teacher-Led Development Work programme, has particular relevance for British teachers. Good leaders are increasingly reminding their colleagues of the core questions at the heart of a good school: what do we want for our students, why do we want this, how do we achieve it?

For those of us who find ourselves teaching without direct support for this kind of initiative, it may be harder, but the wealth of materials on the internet produced by committed teachers offers a pathway to improving one's own practice. We can create collaborative environments and seek out opportunities to share ideas and approaches, at least informally.

As middle managers, department heads and year heads can make more efficient use of meetings within their departments, and take an active role in building a climate of collaboration by encouraging colleagues to work together on specific projects and supporting cross-subject discussion and observations. However, change will remain ad hoc and piecemeal until senior leaders unite to challenge political orthodoxy across the system.

We need to move away from a dialogue of punitive accountability, and the internecine wrangles between traditionalist and progressive educators, while of some value, are false trails in this key undertaking. Punitive accountability is a dead end which has no place in a school. Those of us who continue to regard teaching as a profession and ourselves as embodying professionalism in our classrooms and staffrooms already have strong internal accountability. That internal accountability is implicit in the planning, preparation and relationships we build every day and is one of our strongest motivators. Effective leadership, teaching and learning take place when that internal accountability is harnessed and celebrated.

References

Allison, S., & Tharby, A. (2015). *Making Every Lesson Count*. Carmarthen: Crown.

Ball, Stephen J. (2003). The teacher's soul and the terrors of performativity. *Journal of Education Policy*, 18:2, 215–228, doi:10.1080/0268093022000043065

Buck, A. (2014). *What Makes a Great School: A Practical Formula for Success*. Leadership Matters.

Frost, D. (2014). *Transforming Education through Teacher Leadership*. Cambridge: CUP.

Fullan, M., & Quinn, J. (2015). *Coherence: The Right Drivers in Action for Schools, Districts and Systems*. London: Corwin/Sage.

Fullan, M., Rincon-Gallardo, S., & Hargreaves, A. (2015). Professional capital as accountability. *Education Policy Analysis Archives*, 23(15). doi:10.14507/epaa.v23.1998. This article is part of EPAA/AAPE's Special Series on A New Paradigm for Educational Accountability: Accountability for Professional Practice. Guest Series Edited by Dr Linda Darling-Hammond.

Gewirtz, S., Mahony, P., Hextall, I., & Cribb, A., eds. (2009). *Changing Teacher Professionalism: International Trends, Challenges and Ways Forward*. Oxon: Routledge.

Greevy, H., Knox, A., Nunney, F., & Pye, J. (2012). *The effects of the English Baccalaureate*. Ipsos MORI, DfE Research Report DFE-RB249, Ipsos MORI Report, DFE-RB249, https://www.ipsos.com/sites/default/files/migrations/en-uk/files/Assets/Docs/Publications/sri-education-dfore-effects-of-english-baccalaureate-research-brief.pdf.

Greevy, H. Knox, A. Nunney F., & Pye, J. (2013). *Revised: The Effects of the English Baccalaureate*. Ipsos MORI. DfE Research Report DFE- RR249R. Available at https://www.gov.uk/government/uploads/system/uploads/attachment_data/file/183528/DFE-RR249R-Report_Revised.pdf. Retrieved 06/09/2017.

Long, R., & Bolton, P. (2017). *English Baccalaureate*. [Briefing paper number 06045, 04 September]. House of Commons Library. [Online]. Available at http://researchbriefings.files.parliament.uk/documents/SN06045/SN06045.pdf. Retrieved 06/09/2017.

Myatt, M. (2016). *High Challenge, Low Threat: How the Best Leaders Find the Balance*. Woodbridge: John Catt Educational.

Ng, P. T. (2016). Whole-systems approach: professional capital in Singapore. In J. Evers & R. Kneyber, *Flip the System: Changing Education from the Ground Up*. Oxon: Routledge, pp. 151–158.

Petty, G. (2015). *The Uses and Abuses of Evidence in Education*. Available at http://geoffpetty.com/wp-content/uploads/2015/04/The-uses-and-abuses-of-evidence.pdf.

Roberts, N. (2017). School funding in England. Current system and proposals for 'fairer school funding'. *House of Commons Briefing paper 06702*. Available at researchbriefings.files.parliament.uk/documents/SN06702./SN06702.pdf

Sewell, D. (2010). Michael Gove vs. The Blob, *Spectator magazine*. Available at http://www.spectator.co.uk/2010/01/michael-gove-vs-the-blob/

Vignoles, A. (2009). Educational marginalisation in the UK. *UNESCO background paper for Education for All Global Monitoring Report 2010*. Available at http://unesdoc.unesco.org/images/0018/001865/186591e.pdf

Chapter 7

Practitioner-led research

Towards professional autonomy

Julie Smith

"The structure of lesson study in particular appealed to me as it priori-tises development over surveillance."

My engagement with practitioner-led research is driven by a need to correct an injustice. Back in the days when graded lesson observations were considered 'good practice', I became increasingly aware of their consequences on teacher morale, and frustrated with the sense of doom that permeated the process. Surely lesson observation should be a supportive experience, during which teachers hone their craft and practise their skill? Instead, I saw teachers' confidence destroyed by arbitrary and irrelevant judgements of their ability to teach.

In a climate shaped by trends of performativity, accountability and new managerialism, should teachers find ways of subverting state educational narratives to reclaim their professionalism? O'Leary (2013) refers to the use of lesson study as one possible alternative to graded lesson observation. In use in Japan since the 1870s, lesson study is growing in popularity worldwide as a means of improving teaching and learning, in addition to redressing the imbalance in the agency of the teacher. According to Cheng and Lo (2003), this type of collaborative action research approach aims to improve the effectiveness of student learning by enhancing the professional competence of teachers through joint construction of pedagogical content.

Alternative methods of teacher-centred development have a long history. The origins of teacher research can be traced back to the Schools Council's Humanities Curriculum Project with its emphasis on the re-conceptualisation of curriculum development as curriculum research. Following the project's influence on teaching in British schools, Stenhouse, who directed the HCP, helped to popularise the concept of 'teacher as researcher' in his text, *An Introduction to Curriculum Research and Development* (1975). Additionally, the Collaborative Action Research Network was founded in 1976 with the aim of supporting action research projects, and encouraging contributions to the theory and methodology of action research. Hopkins (2008) suggests that undertaking research is a way that teachers can take increased responsibility for their actions.

Stenhouse similarly describes the ideal role of good teachers as necessarily autonomous in professional judgement. Therefore, for Stenhouse, the issue of power is also paramount; he perceives the link between research and the art of teaching as a method of returning teachers' self-worth. There is evidence to suggest that our profession's interest in evidence-based and practice-based approaches to improving teaching has not abated. The 'Teacher Development Trust', launched in 2012, cites embedding evidence-based approaches as the main aim of their charity; conferences for educators such as researched focus on evidence-based teaching, and high profile scientists such as Dr Ben Goldacre have reignited debate about the purpose and necessity of educational research.

The structure of lesson study in particular appealed to me as it prioritises development over surveillance. The underlying value system of our current education system favours quantitative, measurable data. The element of measuring effectiveness in lesson study may appease managers who require a demonstrable impact on student progress and attainment, while ensuring teachers remain at the centre of the planning, teaching and evaluation process as professional learning is undertaken in classrooms through collaborative enquiry, and learning is seen in sharper, more analytical detail. Dudley (2012) finds that lesson study is a popular, powerful and replicable process for innovating, developing and transferring pedagogic practice. Furthermore, he suggests that lesson study focuses teachers' attention on the effectiveness of the lesson, not on the effectiveness of the teacher. Thus, teachers can abandon what Ball (2003) describes as the vocabulary of performance, and instead focus on learning through collaborative, classroom-based enquiry.

Reflecting on my own experience of lesson study, the triad of teachers I worked within felt a stronger sense of ownership and autonomy over the enquiry than if we had taken part in a lesson observation based on Ofsted criteria. It is a collaborative process that relied on our professionalism; the ownership of the approach, in contrast to one based solely on accountability, leads to respectful challenge and support from peers. The process of lesson study got us closer to exploring ways of improving student learning and genuinely meeting the needs of specific groups than proxies for learning based solely on Ofsted criteria ever did. The triad's close attention to students' post-lesson interviews put students at the forefront of the planning and reflection process, thereby ensuring they had joint ownership of the learning. However, the structure of the lesson study cycle is far more time-consuming as an evaluative process than a 'quality-assurance' model of observation. For the model to become embedded in practice, time needs to be allocated to ensure collaboration is successful.

Findings of our lesson study were shared and discussed within the workplace, and also with a wider teaching community via a pilot website, praxiseducation.com. This recently launched professional development platform for teachers has twin aims: guiding teachers through the process of carrying out small-scale research inquiries into aspects of their practice, and giving teachers access to a database of ideas that have been implemented, evaluated and written by, and for, teachers. Hopkins (2008) explains that this approach empowers individuals and increases feelings of efficacy, which can lead to a genuinely collaborative and critical research community, committed to informed action.

So, despite working within strict accountability frameworks, can schools create a professional culture where discussion, debate and critical analysis are embedded? Bell and Cordingley (2014) have outlined the key features distinguishing 'exceptional' schools from those that are 'very good'. Exceptional schools invest systematically in professional learning. They have an explicit model of pedagogy, and focus on collaborative learning. Continuing professional development (CPD) is underpinned by theory and research, and CPD is effective because it involves teachers exploring evidence at all levels of input. In my experience, for the current interest in evidence-based practice to have system-wide impact, in addition to being given the time, freedom and training to engage with it, teachers need a shared purpose for research. There is a huge volume of small-scale research undertaken, but an evident lack of synthesis.

Teachers occupy a unique position to comment on individuals' learning; feedback given to students is often more nuanced than assessing students' learning based on grade descriptors. As such, teachers are the best agents to provide an objective assessment of student learning. The wide range of data teachers collect should be used to drive a process of enquiry, but developing evidence-informed practice remains a challenge – research findings are often inaccessible and don't necessarily focus on the knowledge teachers need to improve students' outcomes.

The process of conducting action research does raise certain tensions. Research tasks need to be manageable alongside school commitments; the rhythm and demands of the school year, for example, need to be taken into account. The potential audience for sharing the research needs careful consideration, as do the complexities of the classroom, and pragmatism is needed to match the research question with evidence that is practical to collect. Furthermore, action research should not be seen as a linear process; instead, it is likely to produce unexpected findings – problems and new questions emerge out of the process of enquiry.

None of these challenges are impossible to surmount. Engaging with colleagues as co-enquirers has the potential to contribute to a culture of mutual support, but only if the process has formal recognition from the school's leadership team. Ideally, time and support will be given for teachers to conduct research until it becomes a mainstream activity and a community of enquirers is created. The use of the lesson study pro-forma provides a well-researched, well-documented structure as a starting point on the journey to creating an exceptional school in an exceptional school system.

'Quality' education can take a myriad of forms. It can happen at unexpected moments, and can be exemplified by every child and every teacher in every school. The Sutton Trust's (2015, p. 9) *Developing Teachers* report finds that "when we show trust, the vast majority of children and adults learn, develop and grow". It suggests that "the overriding focus in our current school system is on identifying and dealing with weak schools and weak teachers" – a deficit model. As a result, fear is prevalent and risk-taking discouraged. Their policy recommendation is to increase teachers' professional autonomy, and is underpinned by a more intelligent accountability system, a system of measuring success that genuinely reflects the achievements of schools without perverse consequences. Therein lies my hope that the future of teacher development rests on professional learning, teacher collaboration and a trust-driven accountability system. Only then can we work towards building a 'world-class' education system that we can be proud to be a part of.

References

Ball, S. (2003) The Teacher's Soul and the Terrors of Performativity, *Education Policy*, 18(2), pp. 215–228.

Bell, M. and Cordingley, P. (2014) *Characteristics of High Performing Schools*. Available from: www.curee.co.uk.

Cheng, E. C. K. and Lo, M. L. (2003) *The Approach of Learning Study: Its Origin, Operationalisation, and Implications*, OECD Education Working Papers, Issue 94. Paris, OECD Publishing. Available at http://www.oecd-ilibrary.org/docserver/download/5k3wjp0s 959p-en.pdf?expires=1504692652&id=id&accname=guest&checksum=A94C9534AD DEA6F723996EB92FD5DD54. Retrieved 06/09/2017.

Dudley, P. (2012) Lesson Study Development in England: From School Network to National Policy, *International Journal for Lesson and Learning Studies*, 1(1), pp. 85–100.

Hopkins, D. (2008) *A Teacher's Guide to Classroom Research*. Maidenhead: Open University Press.

O'Leary, M. (2013). Surveillance, Performativity and Normalised Practice: The Use and Impact of Graded Lesson Observations in Further Education Colleges, *Journal of Further and Higher Education*, 37(5) pp. 694–714.

Stenhouse, L. (1975) *An Introduction to Curriculum Research and Development*. London: Heinemann.

Sutton Trust. (2015) *Developing Teachers*. Available from: http://www.suttontrust.com/ researcharchive/developing-teachers/. Retrieved 01/05/2017.

Part II

The teachers' manifesto

Collective agency

JL Dutaut and Lucy Rycroft-Smith

Teaching is a social act. We teach because we are entrusted by our society – our communities – with the role, *in loco parentis*, of educating young people. While this may seem like a truism, even the most superficial experience of the education system will show – despite pockets of excellent practice – that the communication and collaboration between schools and their broader communities is not only mediated by the incentives placed upon them by accountability measures, but actually undermined by them too. This pattern is repeated across the education sector in the ways teachers relate to each other within and between schools, to their students, to policy and reform, and indeed, as we will see in Part III, even to themselves.

Normalising relations

Rob Loe shows that the relational element of teaching can be measured. Indeed, he argues that such measurement can be a powerful, transformative policy lever, yet suggests that this genie should be kept in its bottle. In line with many others across the book, Rob perceives the danger of unintended consequences with regard to the over-simplifying force of policy-making, and of measurement for accountability alone. Instead, he challenges us to conceive ways to favour the relational and communal, while forcing policy-makers to abandon their addiction to the notion of immediate system feedback. Speaking to that notion of immediacy and impatience for change, **Jeremy Pattle** takes us through a teacher's life-cycle to show the destructive effect of valuing experiment over experience and revolution over evolution. He entreats us to put relationships with our colleagues at least on a par with our relationships with remote policy-makers and still-developing research. Speaking to the ill effects of over-simplification, **Debra Kidd** urges us to consider that the values of democracy and tolerance aren't simply taught – they are modelled, embedded and enacted in the very way we teach.

Together, Rob, Jeremy and Debra show that education policy is a mediator of relationships, that the act of measurement itself is corrosive to collaboration. While we would not suggest that measurement should be disposed of wholesale, it seems evident to us that the pace of the political cycle, especially in the accelerated phase it seems to be in presently, is fundamentally at odds with the pace of good education reform.

Institutionalising solidarity

Here, **Steve Watson** shows how democracy, scholarship, activism and solidarity are all collective enterprises, undermined by the education system as it exists, and necessary to bring about a new relationship between teachers and their profession. **Ross McGill** goes on to identify a rich seam of opportunity for solidarity rising from the ashes of a broken system of professional development. Further, headteacher **George Gilchrist** shows how even well-intentioned policy fails when it doesn't take into account the collective strength of professional teachers; **Howard Stevenson** proposes a reinvention of teaching unions as mass-participation organisations to facilitate that collective strength; and **Alison Peacock** develops her vision for the Chartered College of Teaching as a new collaboration-led professional body, based on human principles of openness and empathy.

What transpires from these contributions is that only when teachers can work together, in as unmediated an environment as possible, can true change be effected. Indeed, this is not only true with regards to improving the working conditions and professional status of teachers, but also crucially true with regards to the implementation of policy; 'buy-in' from teachers is the sword upon which all education policy, be it school- or national-level, eventually falls. As a result, it is incumbent upon teachers to create and to invest themselves in the institutions that will magnify their voices, and upon policy-makers to empower them to do so. We contend that it is insufficient for the latter simply to listen. They must devolve that power, and allow teachers themselves to lead.

Demand collective agency

Therefore, the teachers' manifesto demands that teachers create and be empowered to create their professional institutions and to nurture their collaborations to lead the education system and its reforms. This must include:

- Teacher representation in policy-making at every level – school, trust, regional, national and international;
- Qualifying and professional standards that require evidence of collaborative practice;
- Working conditions that make possible the continued attainment of such standards;
- The creation, or reform, of institutions that represent, employ or otherwise affect teachers in their professional roles, so that they:
    - Are shaped by practising teachers themselves;
    - Foster collaboration across all aspects of education;

- Are democratically run, open, diverse and fair;
- Are evidence-informed and ethos-led.
- Accountability measures for all stakeholders and policy-makers at all levels that require a commitment to, and the monitoring of performance in, upholding the professionalism of teachers with regard to their collective agency as defined above.

Chapter 8

Measuring what matters

The relational foundations of school systems

Robert Loe

"Upward trajectory is the name of the game and students who threaten the stability of that picture (usually the most vulnerable) are airbrushed out of this hyper-real world."

Perception management

The challenges that come with any period of change, such as education is undergoing today, are always balanced with great opportunities. Perhaps the greatest opportunity is to engage with a debate about what education is for and challenge the very system we are seeking to alter or augment. What appears certain is that "the focus on delivering measurable outcomes has neglected the importance of human relationships" and, moreover, it "risks reducing the complexity and texture of human experience to a simple number, leading to policies and services that do not address the core of a problem" (Muir & Cooke, 2012, p. 7). My hypothesis is simple but challenging. It is that true success, be it in academic mastery, community building, public service, employment or any social metric, depends upon getting relationships right; that leadership, in whatever context and at whatever level it is exercised, depends upon the ability to build and sustain relationships; and that real change starts by seeing the world and the workplace differently.

The issue has been that rather than addressing some of the problems we face, the education system, like so many other government policy levers, has sought to react by painting a much simpler version of the world, thereby reframing the size and scope of the issue. If education can't be the answer, then far better to ask easier questions of the system.

Former Prime Minister Tony Blair believed education was the answer to economic instability and social inequality. He declared in 2005 that education was "the best social policy, helping create a Britain where work and merit, not privilege or class, decide how far you go; and the best economic policy, preparing Britain for the future" (Blair, 2005). This is a tough ask of the education system. Yet the combined might of government had no answer to the acute fiscal crisis of 2007. Central banks dampened the volatility of the symptoms, but structural issues remain. Global debt has accelerated and multiplied by trillions since 2007.

The scale and magnitude of the problem is so terrifying that rather than reveal this, politicians respond by suggesting that the issues are much smaller than presumed or, worse, that they don't even exist; everything is going exactly as planned. One of the key policy responses is to manage our perceptions of the problem, or 'spin' it. The strange thing is most people can sense that the economy is faltering, but they enter into a willing state of denial because no one can envisage an alternative.

Instead, we co-construct a counterfeit version of our reality. Alexei Yurchak (2005) described this as a state of hyper-normalisation; we become so embedded in the system that it becomes challenging to see beyond it. The counterfeit world is hyper-normal. Even those who think they are confronting the system become part of the deception because they too withdraw into the fantasy world, which is why their dissent and resistance is ineffective and the status quo remains.

Our inability to reimagine the education system, or at least to create the space to change it in our imagination; the inauthenticity and futility of even the most positive responses to the system; the very need for a text which argues for a 'flipping' of the system, stems from the technocratic ownership of our education spaces. We are told, therefore, that schools can influence social mobility, social stability, even wealth creation and happiness. It matters little what you tell people, so long as it distracts them from having to contend with the intractable complexities of the world; we accept this version of reality as the simplicity is reassuring.

So it is reassuring to pretend that the current English school system is a great tool to encourage social mobility or gender equality, but unsurprising that the grammar schools of the 1940s were largely populated by males of the wealthier classes. When current Prime Minister Theresa May announced grammar school places were to be expanded, many were surprised that grammar schools still existed. More informed pundits were surprised that anyone still saw grammars as an effective means of improving the system. Few questioned whether the school system could deliver any of the social impacts politicians pretend it can. When it comes to this policy, it seems, evidence is secondary to the reinforcement of the link between education, aspiration, qualification and social mobility.

The reality is that "there is repeated evidence that any appearance of advantage for those attending selective schools is outweighed by the disadvantage for those who do not" (Gorard, 2013). Stephen Gorard (Durham University, 2015) argues that "more children lose out than gain, and the attainment gaps between highest and lowest and between richest and poorest are larger." Even the latest annual report from the inspectorate (Wilshaw, 2016) concludes that "the obsession with grammars ... ignores this problem," or at least distracts us from it. "Pupils eligible for [free school meals] appear to suffer marginally less educational disadvantage if they attend grammar schools" (Coe et al., 2008,

p. 219), but that difference, according to researchers at the Centre for Evaluation and Monitoring, "is equivalent to about one-eighth of a GCSE grade" (ibid.). Of course, even that marginal gain assumes that we measure student outcomes accurately and consistently.

It is reassuring to pretend that the norm-referenced standardisation of tests ensures students are examined fairly and the school system judged accurately. Yet this oversimplification is belied by teachers' angry reactions in February 2016 when examiners were informed that the use of an 'exclamation sentence' must start with either a 'how' or 'what' and must be a full sentence – including a verb. How perplexing! That last sentence would, of course, have been marked as incorrect. It would need the addition of a verb – 'How perplexing it was!' – to get a mark. To say that the latter is correct, and the other an abhorrence, is misleading at best. Even the DfE's own justification of this was bizarre:

> A high-quality education in English – and the ability to communicate effectively – is an important part of the government's commitment to extend opportunity to all.
>
> (Gosden, 2016)

One might think it unlikely that any such attempt to artificially standardise our language, for the purpose of easy marking, could a) encourage greater communicative ability, b) promote social opportunity and c) be a measure of a high-quality education. In fact, this artifice was designed so non-specialist markers could conduct their work at greater speed.

That is because it is reassuring to think that we can measure teacher performance by focusing solely on achievement-test scores. The prevailing theory is that if standardised test scores are high, staff are capable. That too is an oversimplification. Kelly reminds us that the idea that

> we can inspect a school as if it were an entity, within which everybody is treated effectively, [...] is an oversimplification. It doesn't do justice to teaching as a profession [or] to the intelligence of the inspectorate, because they all know this is a lie.
>
> (Education Select Committee, 2010, p. 22)

Kime (2015) adds that "even our best methods are not fit for many of the high-stakes purposes to which we wish to put them." The quantitative methods of teacher effectiveness are at best flawed and the qualitative hardly better.

Because we have failed to agree on an adequately nuanced way to measure the complexities of classroom culture, we have reduced it to a series of visible proxies and devalued the story that is told offstage. What matters to a leadership team, under pressure to demonstrate progress, is that the percentage of 'good' and 'outstanding' teaching is greater than it was the year before, that the numbers of pupils with five 'good' GCSEs is increasing and that students have studied a greater percentage of traditional subjects. Upward trajectory is the name of the game, and students who threaten the stability of that picture (usually the most vulnerable) are airbrushed out of this hyper-real world. One of the key school improvement responses is to manage parental and governmental perceptions of the problem.

In 2015, for example, more than 10,000 children were removed from school rolls in the run up to the examination season. Thousands of young people were permanently excluded, moved to alternative providers or were 'educated at home.' As a result, the school population of England and Wales decreased by a staggering 2% in a matter of weeks (Mansell et al., 2016). Simultaneously, journalists exposed a scheme to enter 'vulnerable' students into a three-day ICT course which could boost examination league table performance. Entries went up by 2000% in the summer of 2015 (Dickens, 2015).

It is impossible to blame school leaders for this. We don't encourage honesty in the mechanisms of accountability, so they, and teachers, are forced to co-construct a counterfeit version of reality – and they have become so much a part of that system, so much part of its gamification, that it becomes impossible to see beyond it. We have lost our sense of education's true purpose and devalued the things that really matter.

Relationships matter

And they matter far more than we like to admit or engage with. In the context of a school system, we should not be surprised that relationships matter, because learning is mutual and deeply social. Relationships lie at the heart of the way children develop, with enormous implications for how we view classroom environments. Schools are, and always will be, places for human beings in community. But the fug that has shrouded the English system has blinded us from the reality that learning and meeting are indivisible, that "we must learn to meet … because we must meet to learn" (Bingham & Sidorkin, 2004, p. 5).

Relationships are the source of our greatest happiness and of our deepest pains; they create value, but destroy it when they go wrong. The most important, and sometimes the most challenging, task of a school leader, is to cultivate – and model – healthy, effective relationships.

Evidence tells us that our relationships have a really powerful impact on our thinking, our wellbeing and our longevity on this earth. It influences how fast tumours grow (not whether you develop them but whether they progress). Studies reveal that survival rates of breast cancer are up to four times greater in those women with closer, larger, personal networks. The lowest rates of dementia are found in those men over 50 with the largest circles of friends. Regular face-to-face interaction impacts our reasoning capacity (particularly memory) and influences our wellbeing/happiness and our physical health (Pinker, 2015).

But let us not mistake the need for greater social capital with the need for larger social networks. Both are usually measured by the numbers of people we are linked to, but 'relational capital', i.e. the collective value of all 'social networks', can only come from those people we really know, not those merely known to us. In times of crisis, it is the people we love who are likely to be by our side, not the people on LinkedIn. Indeed, we know from the field of social neuroscience that those with the capacity and intentionality to invest in meaningful personal relationships are healthier, happier and live longer than those who are solitary or who engage with the world largely online (ibid.).

Yet evidence suggests we are more fragmented than ever. Data from the NSPCC (2016) reveals that British children are unhappier than they have ever been, with family relationships and chronic isolation the underlying causes of much of their angst. The ONS recently published a report (Randall & Corp, 2014) that suggested that compared to anywhere in Europe, we're least likely to know our neighbours, and many of us would be unable to call on friends in a crisis. The Mental Health Foundation (Griffin, 2010) concluded that young adults in particular are more likely to experience loneliness than the elderly in Britain, even though a study by Independent Age (2016) concluded that severe loneliness in England impacts nearly two million people over 50. Yet our society, and education as a key agent system of that society, has valued, prioritised and promoted competition and individualism above all else in the hope that we might be distracted from, and forget, the complexities of the world outside.

If you don't believe me, then just ask a school-aged child. Polling of 3,000 of them and their parents (Herring, 2009) suggests that 12% want to be 'sports stars' (interestingly, not just earn a living from sport), 11% pop stars, 11% film and television stars, 9% want to be astronauts, 4% teachers and just 1% wish to be politicians. Compare that to 25 years ago, when students of the same age aspired most to be teachers (15%) and rarely aspired to any profession where individual fame was a primary goal. We do know that reported aspiration to be famous decreases with age, but children remain strongly hooked on the pursuit of fortune. The majority of children respondents today say they "just want to be rich." And even if competition did make us richer, all the evidence suggests that it is unlikely to make us happier; the gratification that stems from wealth is continuously challenged by the impacts of the competition itself (Boston College Center on Wealth and Philanthropy, forthcoming).

The thing that children rarely do at this moment of reflection is to conceive of anything beyond themselves. We know that very few boys, in particular, see themselves working for a charity or good cause when they reach employment age. We do know, however, that those young people who are more civically engaged in later childhood/adolescence have higher levels of what we might call social/cultural capital (Bennett & Parameshwaran, 2013).

Of course, the importance of relationships can appear self-evident, and this presents the most profound challenge. Perhaps the most difficult aspect of this work is that in an attempt to ensure that we begin to value what is fundamental, it has been necessary to measure that which should be valued. Working relationships are too often a by-product of decisions taken with other priorities in mind. They're neglected, undermined or put under intolerable pressure. My research and experience is that relationships can be influenced effectively and intentionally; that we can create the conditions within which people are more likely to form and conduct effective relationships, and that it is possible to look at relationships in ways that enable constructive discussion and actionable solutions.

Measuring what we value

The research of Relational Schools attempts to provide leaders, policy-makers and change agents with conceptual and practical measurement tools to help them work with, and through, relationships at work, at home or in the community, in organisations or in society. We have spent the last four years working with schools to explore these issues, and have developed a robust database of evidence that clearly shows the vital importance of good relationships between teachers and the children they teach, in the achievement of great student outcomes.

This is, of course, something that all good teachers know instinctively. However, by applying the Relational Proximity Framework[1] to their analysis of classroom interactions, the team at Relational Schools has been able to measure the quality of relationships in schools and thus enable practitioners and leaders to recognise and promote would-be tacit knowledge.

In comparing schools, we found that those we might classify as relatively 'relational' not only helped students achieve better academic outcomes, but also brought a wider range of additional benefits. Critically, in schools with better relational qualities, students' relationships with both their peers and their teachers improved as the young people progressed through the school, with a notable decline in bullying levels. These effects are even greater where a school is intentional about building relationships; levels of wellbeing are higher, absences are lower and physical health is improved. In one case, a school – described as being like a 'family' by students – was considered by social services as one of the best environments in the region for looked-after children.

That's because schools are, in the best examples, communities. They are "positive and personal organisations in which people treat others as ends in themselves" (Stern, 2015, p. 76). I have had the privilege of visiting many schools like this, and it is evident that they are like this despite the competitive, individualistic system within which they operate, not because of it. Many more look like miniature societies, "social forms which are negative and impersonal, in which people primarily treat each other as a means to an end" (ibid.), where children don't know each other and even staff struggle to remember each other's names.

We know that public policy, organisational or system-wide change, can either increase relational distance or overcome it. Yet, in the context of our current education system, it has taken the development of our empirical metric to foreground behaviours and practices that are beneficial or destructive. Relationships *can* be assessed and the impacts can now be modelled. Good relational practice can be incentivized and more supportive environments for relationships created.

There's just one problem ...

In 1902, at the height of French colonial rule in Hanoi, Vietnam, deaths from bubonic plague, in the majority-white quarter, forced the authorities to take rat infestation more seriously. Previously, whilst considered vermin, rats were a charming, idiosyncratic part of the landscape. Far from eradicating them, one learned to live with them. Pay was determined per tail of dead rat, and the numbers caught each day, whilst peaking at 20,114 on 12 June, was never less than 4,000. The incentive had worked and the catchers were rewarded handsomely. That is, until surveys revealed that rodent numbers remained stable. Evidence emerged of catchers removing the tails, then releasing them back into the wild, and of others breeding them for the income. The new system had made the situation worse.

It is concomitant with Goodheart's law: the minute a government attempts to measure any element of school experience or, worse, benchmark that data, they become unreliable indicators. The natural response is to anticipate the effect of the measurement and seek to benefit from it.

In attempting to foreground relationships, I have suggested there is a need to enhance its value and status through a robust and verified empirical measure. The great danger is that as we begin to afford greater status to issues such as relationships in schools, student and staff wellbeing or happiness, so their heightened prominence will come at a cost. We risk knowing everything and valuing nothing. Yet it is not, necessarily, the fault of the measure itself but the stories we tell with data. It is not merely a question of *what* we measure but *who* measures, and *when*.

A new measure of school success

The story data tells depends on the person interrogating it, and where they are positioned will influence the way they interact with it. When we measure student outcomes, we rarely engage with the question: what is education for? So, we tell children that superior outcomes are a doorway to university, itself a gateway to white-collar employment, wealth and happiness. And in Beth Green's words, "while we would not deny the goodness of such things, seeing [them] as the 'telos' or 'purpose' of education is dangerous for students, communities, and the institutions of education" (Green, 2016, p. 11).

Our belief is that the development of any society comes through the maturing process of its members, influencing how resources like people, land

and capital are deployed in the future. Redefining the goals of education in relational terms relies on a shared appreciation that the quality of relationships – issues of identity, self-esteem and interdependence – are not just key to personal wellbeing and happiness, but also key to organisational and business effectiveness and social harmony. As a result, education needs to re-articulate its objectives, re-examine assessment outcomes and embed student success within a relational narrative of education:

> It is about building up loving relationships between ourselves and others with whom we share a common life. Therefore, graduates who exhibit attitudes of empathy and trust as well as habits of volunteering and giving, even if they are not earning as much, are still being well served by their schools.
>
> (ibid.)

Accepting that relationships played out at school are likely to influence those seen outside of it, developing and nurturing the relational capability of our children from an early age will help them build and repair the communities and societies in which they will live, work and recreate. Yet, measurement of longer-term, holistic school outcomes are neither straightforward nor popular. It should be of no surprise that with the marketisation of education, schools, like businesses, seek to maximize short-term gains, at the expense of making prudent decisions to guarantee the future stability of the organisation.

One possible solution to the destructive short-term culture in schools would be to set performance targets that encourage schools to consider the long-term development of students. We propose a new measure of school success: 'Destination Seven' (D7). Its aim: to track, and capture, student outcomes seven years after they have left compulsory schooling, so providing a fuller picture of the impact of education on young people and communities. D7 would be designed to foreground outcomes that might point to a flourishing life: socioeconomic status, health and wellbeing, prosocial capability and conduct such as volunteering or civic/political engagement as well as academic performance (celebrating the development of a culture of lifelong learning).

Such a measure would encourage schools to build, sustain and measure outcomes which were far less instrumental, and to treat young people as an end in themselves. It would provide space and permission for teachers to develop qualities within their students that would truly benefit them in later life. More than that, it would force education policy-makers to think and act beyond purely politically expedient, centralised actions. It would, profoundly, flip the system by ensuring the state had very little control of student outcomes in the moment, and enabling teachers to craft education that was valuable for the future.

Note

1 Developed over the past 20 years, the Relationships Foundation, and more recently Relational Research, Relational Proximity is defined as a measure of the distance in the relationship between two people or organisations which determines how well each engages with the thinking, emotions and behaviour of the other.

References

Bennett, M. & Parameshwaran, M. (2013). What factors predict volunteering among youths in the UK? *Briefing Paper 102*, The Third Sector Research Centre. [online] Available at http://www.birmingham.ac.uk/generic/tsrc/documents/tsrc/working-papers/briefing-paper-102.pdf. Retrieved 03/06/2017.

Bingham, C. & Sidorkin, A. (Eds.) (2004). *No Education without Relation*. Oxford: Peter Lang.

Blair, T. (2005). *Speech to local Labour members in Sedgefield on education*. (Transcript). [online] Available at http://news.bbc.co.uk/1/hi/uk_politics/vote_2005/frontpage/4430511.stm. Retrieved 03/06/2017.

Boston College Center on Wealth and Philanthropy (forthcoming). *The Joys and Dilemmas of Wealth*.

Coe, R., Jones, K., Searle, J., Koktsaki, D., Kosnins, A. M., & Skinner, P. (2008). *Evidence on the effects of selective educational systems*. [online] Available at https://www.suttontrust.com/wp-content/uploads/2008/10/SuttonTrustFullReportFinal11.pdf#page=234. Retrieved 02/06/2017.

Dickens, J. (2015). *Uptake of three-day ICT 'GCSE' soars 2,000 per cent*. [online] Available at http://schoolsweek.co.uk/uptake-of-three-day-ict-gcse-soars-2000-per-cent/. Retrieved 03/06/2017.

Durham University (2015). *Grammar schools don't help social mobility*. (15 October). [Online]. Available at https://www.dur.ac.uk/research/news/thoughtleadership/?itemno=25866. Retrieved 03/10/2017.

Education Select Committee (2010). *The role and performance of Ofsted*. 10 November. HL 570 II, p. 22.

Gorard, S. (2013). *Overcoming disadvantage in education*. London: Routledge

Gosden, E. (2016). *Nonsense! Backlash over new school rules on exclamation marks*. [online] Available at http://www.telegraph.co.uk/education/12185164/Nonsense-Backlash-over-new-school-rules-on-exclamation-marks.html. Retrieved 03/06/2017.

Green, B. (2016). *Educating to Love Your Neighbour*. Ontario: Cardus Education Survey. [online] Available at http://cace.org/wp-content/uploads/dlm_uploads/2016/10/Cardus-Cardus_Education_Survey_2016_Educating_To_Love_Your_Neighbour.pdf. Retrieved 03/06/2017.

Griffin, J. (2010). The Lonely Society, Mental Health Foundation. [online]. Available at https://www.mentalhealth.org.uk/sites/default/files/the_lonely_society_report.pdf. Retrieved 03/06/2017.

Herring, T. (2009). *When I grow up I want to be...* [online] Available at http://www.taylorherring.com/blog/index.php/tag/tarrant-lets-the-kids-loose/. Retrieved 05/06/2017.

Kime, S. (2015). *The problem with measuring teaching quality is that there is no agreement over a definition of good teaching*. [online] Available at https://www.tes.com/news/school-news/breaking-views/%E2%80%98-problem-measuring-teaching-quality-there-no-agreement-over-a. Retrieved 03/06/2017.

Mansell, W., Adams, R., & Edwards, P. (2016). *England schools: 10,000 pupils sidelined due to league-table pressures.* [online] Available at https://www.theguardian.com/education/2016/jan/21/england-schools-10000-pupils-sidelined-due-to-league-table-pressures. Retrieved 03/06/2017.

Muir, R. & Cooke, G. ed. (2012). The relational state: How recognising the importance of human relationships could revolutionise the role of the state. Institute for Public Policy Research.

NSPCC (2016). *Childline: 30 years of listening to children.* London: NSPCC.

Pinker, S. (2015). *The Village Effect.* London: Atlantic Books.

Randall, C. & Corp, A. (2014). *Measuring National Well-being: European Comparisons*, Office for National Statistics. [online] Available at http://webarchive.nationalarchives.gov.uk/20160105160709/http://www.ons.gov.uk/ons/dcp171766_363811.pdf. Retrieved 03/06/2017.

Stern, J. (2015). The personal world of schooling: John Macmurray and schools as households. In Fielding, M. (Ed.) (2015). *Learning to be Human. The Educational Legacy of John Macmurray.* Abingdon: Routeldge. p. 76.

Wilshaw, M. (2016). *The power of education.* (Transcript). [online] Available at https://www.gov.uk/government/speeches/the-power-of-education. Retrieved 03/06/2017.

Yurchak, Alexei (2005). *Everything Was Forever, Until It Was No More: The Last Soviet Generation.* (In-Formation). Princeton University Press.

Chapter 9

Walking with dinosaurs

Jeremy Pattle

"At a time when your experience should see you at the peak of your powers, you are most prone to attack from impact enthusiasts."

Old vs new

Many years ago, I attended a CPD day designed to tackle the challenges of the new GCSE examinations. Most of the day fell into the familiar pattern of these events: moments of excitement at new possibilities, followed quickly by realisation of the inevitability of greater workload and limited resources. One moment, however, stood out.

A young teacher, clearly destined for greater things and armed with flipchart and overhead projector, delivered a confident talk to an audience of over a hundred teachers. I can remember neither topic nor content, but there was one exchange I've never forgotten. Well prepared, fluent and at times quite strident, she ruffled more than a few feathers. This came to a head when she suggested a course of action clearly too radical for at least one person in the room.

"I've been teaching for over thirty years, and I resent someone with a lot less experience telling me how to do my job".

The room went silent. The response was calm but brutal.

"While it may be true that you have at least twenty-five years more experience than me, I would like to respectfully suggest that you might have a lot more experience of doing things badly".

He walked out. She returned to her notes.

At the time, I was an idealistic, inexperienced teacher who had met opposition to some of my methods, and was dismissive of those of some others. My character type had been identified as 'enthusiast' at a previous professional development session, and I readily (enthusiastically?) identified with her position and admired her ability to rebuff opposition. I liked the fact that a dinosaur had been put in its place.

The dinosaur was a symptom of a problem with the system. His ideas were entrenched and presumably experience-based. Mine were based on recent theory and a willingness to experiment. I didn't consider that previous teaching generations had had the same approach when they were at the same stage in their careers. In the intervening thirty years, my position has moderated to the point that I recognise my old self as part of the problem.

Revolution vs evolution

The teaching profession is subject to a state of permanent revolution. Teachers, managers and secretaries of state constantly try to make an impact. It is a key part of establishing a career, or, as politicians might have it, 'creating a legacy'. To do that, it is often expedient to undermine existing practice and present alternatives as obvious improvements. This inevitably creates alienation among those whose methods are challenged without fair hearing, leading to resentment and cynicism – and disillusioned enthusiasts make resolute cynics.

Teachers are encouraged to develop a teaching identity, but this is at odds with a system in a state of constant change. We have created a culture where the longer you have been in the profession, the more likely it is that your methods and beliefs will become marginalised and that you will lose willingness to engage with change. Dynamic, innovative staff are an obvious strength in a school and should not be the exclusive preserve of the young. Indeed, at a time when your experience should see you at the peak of your powers, you are most prone to attack from impact enthusiasts.

There is, therefore, a need to rethink professional development. If we want a cohesive education system with professional agency, the system needs a workforce that is motivated and engaged with pedagogy throughout its career, one that includes all teachers, not just those looking for CV-enhancing accolades. Change is inevitable and, looking at the current state of education, desirable, but for it to be effected, it needs to carry hearts as well as minds. All teachers should be invested in their development, and all should recognise the potential of *all* their colleagues (in precisely the way that I, as a young teacher, didn't).

Inadequate systems create cynics. The inevitable question is how a new system might evolve that supports more enthusiasts.

Teachers pressured into achieving targets and delivering narrowly defined 'outstanding' lessons have little scope to explore and develop their own educational philosophy. They have too much to lose by not following the latest strictures. Teachers are compromising their ideals, or failing to develop them altogether. This makes us vulnerable to fads and evidence-free policy. CPD should include greater emphasis on intellectual approaches to the profession.

None of us likes being wrong. Accepting new ideas only to be told *they* were wrong undermines future innovation. For all the success of the scientific method, applying it to teaching often ignores the efficacy of existing practice and the subtleties of a dynamic environment. Teachers are aware of this, and politicians need to acknowledge that expertise within the profession is a resource. Involving teachers more prominently in policy-making would guard against false panaceas.

Just as a positive educational experience is not evidence enough for wholesale system change, so too the effectiveness of an educational system is insufficient grounds for wholesale replication, much less replication of selected parts. This lack of cultural awareness and specificity presents dangers of pupil stress, teacher burnout and lack of future capacity, and bears all the hallmarks of political expediency over rational decision making. Once more, involving teachers in policy-making offers a solution by taking a longer-term view of change.

What if?

We encourage children to be critical, yet our own critical faculties are often taken as obstructive. 'What if?' is a question that should be at the heart of our profession and one we should be encouraged to ask. Rather than negate change, it is a question that embraces it. By establishing a culture of willing and inclusive change, we allow teachers to adapt throughout their careers without feeling threatened. Teachers need to question, contribute and be given a chance to properly assimilate ideas and reconcile them with their own practice.

What if we were to build a new system from the bottom up? This repentant dinosaur thinks that with the energy of our enthusiasm for change, we could rest a lasting edifice upon the foundations of our knowledge and practice – as long as we show due regard for the fossils we unearth as we dig them.

Chapter 10

Complex needn't be complicated

Debra Kidd

"We need a different system: one based on humanity, compassion and wisdom, and tolerant of uncertainty and complexity."

Let's, for a moment, think of a map. What comes to mind? A web of roads, or the undulating contours of topography showing the heights and depths of our landscapes? Do you see straight lines cutting from A to B, or a layered 3D world? Our ways of seeing and our willingness to accept complexity very much impact on our values and what we can tolerate in terms of uncertainty in education.

Learning, like mapping, is not a linear process, no matter how much we would wish it to be. And our ways of evidencing learning are superficial – something like a map – showing an approximation of surfaces, while only ever being able to hint at what lies beneath. This hidden aspect to learning and indeed to all human experience can be frustrating, especially for those who need to show that what they do has 'impact', but it also offers us a wonderful opportunity to recognise and value that which can't easily be measured and to try to ensure that in holding ourselves accountable, we don't create undesirable outcomes in the process.

When we hold a map in our hands, we can have a multitude of responses. We can look methodically in order to see where we need to go next. We can look with curiosity, to see where might be interesting to go in the future. We can look with nostalgia to remember where we have been. We can also look with wonder and simply appreciate the art of the map. As Robinson and Petchenik write in *The Nature of Maps* (1976, 37–38):

> A map does not converse in sentences. Its language is a half-hearted rumour, fractured, fitful, non-discursive, non-linear ... It is many-tongued, a chorus reciting centuries of accumulated knowledge in echoed chants ... A map provides no answers, it only suggests where to look.

I can find no better analogy for a classroom than this. It is a place where we attempt to get from A to B, a place where we work out together where to go next, and a place where we look back and review where we came from. And it can also be a place, if the conditions are right, where we see learning as an object of beauty, and the process of being educated as a form of becoming other – emerging, growing, changing – a mode of what Biesta calls subjectification (2013). I'd argue that this final mode of learning is the holy grail of education, and its enemy is the deadening desire for certainty that drives us through content at pace, without time to wander and discover all that lies off the beaten path.

Andreas Schleicher, speaking about English mathematics education, said that our curriculum is a mile wide and an inch deep – that in our haste to cover as many facts as possible, we discover little, and show scant regard for deep conceptual understanding Yet we see a view promoted from some sections of the education system – and certainly from government – that knowledge is all, that getting children through exams is the end point. Teachers who subscribe to this enticingly simple, linear view tend to dismiss wider concerns about rising numbers of exclusions, or incidences of mental health problems. *That's not our problem*, they say. *What happens beyond the test is not our responsibility*. But it is. It is if you consider the purpose of education to be to prepare children, not only for the world as it is, but for the world as it might be. I'm not referring to some vague notion of an economy consisting of jobs that have not been invented yet, but rather the world as they might create it, not simply experience it. To provide an education that can achieve that goal, we need a different system: one based on humanity, compassion and wisdom, and tolerant of uncertainty and complexity.

To do so, we need to robustly challenge the limited perspective of finding out 'what works' in education. I believe movements to place research at the heart of learning in the UK have been misrepresented to teachers as being grassroots and in the interests of the profession. researchED, the brainchild of Sam Freedman (then advisor to Education Secretary Michael Gove) and high-profile doctor/journalist Ben Goldacre (then advisor to the government on research in education), was handed to a high profile teacher in order to give it credibility (see Tom Bennett's chapter), yet in my opinion its purpose serves the government's agenda very well. I believe it reinforces the single-minded obsession with proving what works without really engaging with the obvious extension – to what end? The focus is simply on getting children through tests – a very basic common denominator in education. Test results should be a by-product – not an end product – of great education.

Elsewhere, other self-proclaimed 'grassroots' organisations such as Parents and Teachers for Excellence emerge consisting of government donors and supporters, advisors and peers, calling themselves the voice of parents and teachers, of whom there appear to be few. They advocate the role of academies in promoting a knowledge-led curriculum that pays little attention to the well-being of children and their wider life experience. Both movements are classic examples of Deleuze's modulations of a control society (1992), in which the dominant institutions and establishments will morph and modify their messages in order to seem radical and of the people, while in reality they simplify and control, reinforcing a central message of compliance.

Classrooms are complex places – systems of emergence in which what we want to happen cannot be easily controlled. There is always the distraction, the unexpected outcome, the wasp in the room, the fart, the snow outside the window. And there is the internal world of distraction – young love, hunger, neglect … We must manage distraction, of course, and how we do so reveals as much about our attitude to complexity as it does about our expectations. The linear, simplistic, lowest-common-denominator option is to take the route of repetition and reinforcement: to make learning memorable by assuming it's not interesting in the first place and knocking it into the head with a hammer. This requires a high level of compliance and is usually accompanied by a zero-tolerance behaviour policy. The complex route, by contrast, seeks out connections, looks to outliers and finds both common cause and unfamiliar pivots, and challenges by posing hard questions about human nature, the state of the world, lessons learned from history and possibilities for the future.

Let me give you two examples from the subject of history. In one school, the teacher talks. He has knowledge. He talks a lot and even writes blogs about how important his talk is. The children listen, then they write down what he says, using a taught method of highly controlled note taking. They are then tested on what has been said, exam style. They are drilled. They pass their tests. But they are not historians. That's okay – there are only a limited number of jobs for historians, and they now have a qualification. But they are not thinkers, either. How will they cope with the autonomy required of them in Higher Education or in the workplace or in life outside of both? In this ideology, it is not the teacher's job to be concerned about this. His duty has been done.

In another school, a history teacher works with the art department to develop a unit of work using project-based learning. Their topic is the Cold War. Every lesson – each an hour and a half long – students spend twenty minutes in a teacher-led lecture. They are then split into two groups and they alternate, one in seminar-style discussion work while the other researches independently. Periodically, there are exam-style questions. The children are under no illusions about how learning happens in universities. But there is more. They are asked in art to create sculptures of the key figures of the Cold War. They learn to sculpt and all the final pieces are recognizable – Thatcher, Reagan, Gorbachev and other key figures. The work is strong, but stronger still is the task to decide where to position them on a chessboard in order to show their influence. This is learning that takes a child way beyond the acquisition of knowledge into a realm of conceptual understanding of power, interdependence and globalisation. It is complex but not complicated. It is an ordnance survey, not a sat nav.

I am clearly not arguing here against knowledge or the acquisition of facts. Indeed, I believe knowledge is necessary to developing critical, creative thinking processes leading to useful, interesting outcomes. But it's what we do with what we learn that affects outcomes for all. Placing students in unfamiliar and uncertain learning contexts in which they learn, in the words of the IB, that "other people, with their differences, can also be right", is vital to a democratic education (International Baccalaureate, 2017).

We have a choice. We always have a choice. We can be reductive and seek the simple in order to maintain an appearance that we are doing that which needs to be done. Or we can embrace complexity and recognise that, in the words of McLuhan, *the medium is the message* – the manner in which we teach communicates values beyond what is being taught. Being professionals means knowing what works, but it also means engaging with the moral context of making it work. And that's not complicated at all.

References

Biesta, G. (2013). *The Beautiful Risk of Education*. Boulder, CO: Paradigm.

Deleuze, G. (1992). Postscript on the Societies of Control. *October*, 59(Winter): 3–7. Available at https://cidadeinseguranca.files.wordpress.com/2012/02/deleuze_control.pdf.

International Baccalaureate. (2017). *Mission*. [online] Available at http://www.ibo.org/about-the-ib/mission/. Retrieved 03/06/17.

Robinson, A. H. and Bartz-Petchenik, B. (1976). *The Nature of Maps*. Chicago: Chicago University Press.

Chapter 11

A manifesto for control

Democracy, scholarship, activism and solidarity

Steven Watson

"As workload has increased and the demands of the job have intensified, never before has there been such a need for an expansion of teacher activism."

Introduction

In this chapter, I want to reflect on the process of reclamation, that is, teachers taking (back) control of education. Evers and Kneyber (2016) symbolize this process as the inversion of a hierarchy, as depicted by a triangle, with government at the apex of the triangle, districts or local authorities at the next level, then school leaders and teachers at the bottom. The 'flipped' system is simply this triangle inverted, so that teachers are at the top. The question is, how can that be achieved? And what would that process involve?

I propose four principles as the basis for change. While I refer to the English context, the principles could be usefully applied anywhere. I refer to these collectively as a manifesto for control and they are: democracy, scholarship, activism and solidarity. While they do not provide a blueprint for the change process, they provide some design principles to help in the development of teacher-led campaigns and initiatives. I have developed these principles from a variety of literatures and experiences in and out of education; they capture the essential features of an approach that could enable and sustain a 'flipped' system.

Democracy

In England, few teachers have influence over strategic-level decisions that impact their work and, in particular, the approach they take to teaching. The culture of leadership and management in schools is increasingly hierarchical and managerial (O'Reilly & Reed, 2010). Many decisions are influenced by centralised accountability and responses focused on narrow measures, such as examination results and progress measures. For decades, successive governments have introduced policies that have greatly undermined workplace democracy.

I am not going to examine the origins or rationale for such policy here (for a description of the historical development of policy, see Walford, 2014); what I will do is argue the importance of democracy and its place in future policy-making if teachers are to regain professional autonomy. Workplace democracy employs democratic principles within organisations; that is, decisions are based on the views and perspectives of those that work in it. This is essential if teachers are to have greater control over their work and over the education they provide. Democratic principles are often classified as representative or direct. Representative democracy involves the election of individuals who deliberate, debate and decide on the electorate's behalf. Direct democracy involves everyone in the decision making process, through voting and collective deliberation. Democratic organisations can feature both these democratic principles (Pausch, 2014). A common argument against organisational democracy is that it slows decision making, and executives should respond to situations without lengthy staff consultations. However, in a school and for the purpose of teacher empowerment, the quality of deliberation and decision making should be prioritised (for the arguments, see Woods & Gronn, 2009).

Research shows that workplace democracy has a number of benefits; it is related to better quality work environments and improved worker well-being (Knudsen, Busck & Lind, 2011). There is evidence of causal effects with greater worker empowerment, improved performance and job satisfaction (Fernandez & Moldogaziev, 2013).

Democracy in schools offers a powerful principle to underpin a flipped system, but it requires participants to be assertive and informed, to deliberate proposals and evidence and to reach joint decisions or vote on alternatives. Democracy alone is therefore insufficient; we require evidence and scholarship, and we require motivation, confidence and action to make things happen, i.e. activism. Given the incessant drive to centralise decision making (Creese & Isaacs, 2016), we need solidarity to oppose these forces and defend local organisational democracy.

Scholarship

Boyer (1990, p. 2) explained that the term scholarship is often used interchangeably with the term research: "to be a scholar is to be a researcher". I, like Boyer, use an expanded notion of 'scholarship' to describe a broad range of research approaches used in the development of theory and evidence to inform educational practice. Scholarship goes beyond research. It involves making connections across disciplines, the application of research to real-world problems and communicating the implications of research.

Yet, recent policy in England has taken a narrower view of scholarship. Teaching is seen as a technical craft rather than as an agential profession and should be guided by evidence from experimental studies based on scientific principles (Department for Education, 2010). Goldacre (see, for example,

Haynes, Service, Goldacre & Torgerson, 2012) influentially expounded the need for 'scientific' evidence in educational research similar to the way it is currently used in medicine. The scientific or experimental approach (frequently referred to as a randomised control trial or RCT) involves randomly assigning an intervention to pupils, in experimental and control groups. A measurement is taken before and after the intervention and, if there is a difference after the intervention, it can be reasonably assumed that the differences are in some way attributable to the intervention. Since the evidence is overwhelming, it is then difficult to argue with the outcome; teachers are encouraged to implement the approach faithfully, and improvements are likely to be observed on the measures that were used in the trial.

However, the exclusive use of RCTs is not consistent with the broader view of scholarship. The experiment reveals a positive/negative result and whether we should/should not adopt whatever intervention was tested. This does not tell us how the trialled intervention worked; there is limited theoretical development. The problem with experimental studies is that interventions have to be implemented in complex contexts: classrooms and schools. To what extent, then, can we faithfully replicate the intervention? There is likely to be at least some variance. Practitioners have to make decisions based on the context within which they work. No matter how compelling a result from an experimental study, cultural practices, as established routines, tend to dominate (see Watson, Major & Kimber, forthcoming). Changing what teachers do is not a trivial task. This is not to reject the need for experimental studies in education, but the idea that RCTs are synonymous with scholarship. Results of scientific procedures and experimental evaluations of interventions have to be treated critically, not as absolute facts. Importantly, because of the complexity of context, teachers need to be seen as agentic professionals with the capacity to lead and participate in scholarship.

While the experimental approach is attractive because of the appeal to statistical certainty, scholarship needs to offer explanations: it needs to generate theory. This theory should be able to explain observations but also help teachers make predictions in their practice. Theory is developed through qualitative approaches which involve observing, interviewing and analysis. The problem with qualitative research is validity. Indeed, it is a vexing problem more generally: what can we know for certain and what can be used to inform practice?

The answer is that it is unlikely we can know anything for certain, and all evidence that teachers are presented with requires judgement. Ultimately, teachers have to weigh up and decide what and how they do things in their classrooms. Although there are many aspects of practice that follow cultural patterns, and some that are prescribed by institutions or guided by policy, it is only the teacher who is in a position to consider context and evidence in an informed way in their particular context.

The difficulty of 'truth' was addressed in a novel way by psychologists and philosophers in the late nineteenth and early twentieth centuries. Charles

Sanders Peirce, William James and John Dewey, among others, proposed pragmatism. William James saw philosophical questions of truth and validity as irresolvable. People can take opposing positions based on robust evidence, each determined from particular contexts. Opposing views argued with evidence and justification are unlikely to be resolved, even if one position may have 'more' scientific or experimental evidence as justification. The issue is over application: how do we make use of that knowledge?

The essence of pragmatism is the validation of knowledge in practical situations, and with consideration of what we are trying to achieve. For example, improving an aspect of classroom practice would involve adapting, developing or innovating existing practice – and this would be based on the identification of an issue by the teacher. A scholarly approach in this situation would involve an analysis of the situation as it is, a consideration of related research and evidence, and the intentional design of a new or adapted approach, as well as some form of evaluation. The two most common methods for teacher–researchers to do this are action research and design-based research. By contrast, the scientific paradigm would lead to the use of an RCT for this purpose. More often than not, however, we want to know how the intervention worked. Additionally, teachers who undertake this kind of research are not in a position to marshal the sample size necessary for a rigorous experimental evaluation.

That is scholarship in the context of classroom practice; but I want to take this further and link scholarship, pragmatism and deliberative democracy. As part of organisational democracy, collaborative decision making requires members of the organisation to deliberate on issues and to reach joint decisions on a course of action. What can be time consuming is if the deliberation focuses on the 'rightness' and 'wrongness' of opposing, often intractable, abstracted positions. Pragmatism offers a way out of polarisation by concentrating on the issue at hand and deciding on a collective course of action. Deliberation for the purpose of democracy is intrinsically linked to scholarship (Habermas, 1984).

The capacity to undertake scholarship is an important aspect of teacher empowerment and flipping the system. Teachers need to be able to undertake scholarship as part of their democratic involvement in an autonomous profession and as an integral part of their own professional learning and development.

Activism

Activism means individuals and groups of teachers arguing and campaigning for improving democracy and the right to participate in scholarship. It is the profession acting to improve and defend itself. It requires the profession and its stakeholders to speak out to improve the quality of education. For teachers, it is easy to become passive as a result of working in an intense and demanding environment. It is reasonable to expect not to have to campaign for working conditions, pay or policy that permits teachers to act as professionals. However, as workload has increased and the demands of the job have intensified, never before has there been such a need for an expansion of teacher activism. Judyth Sachs characterises teacher activism as follows:

> An activist teaching profession is an educated and politically astute one. [...] Teachers in individual schools can work at the school level, regionally, or [...] at the national level to achieve socially responsible goals. Teacher educators, bureaucrats, unionists and others interested in education also need to join together in order to make public and to celebrate the achievements of teachers. They also need strategies to inform those in positions of power and influence of the importance and necessity of a strong teaching profession. It is this kind of profession that can educate our children to be socially active and responsible citizens.
>
> (Sachs, 2003, p. 154)

Certainly, there is evidence of teacher activism developing. No one can deny the success of movements like researchED,[1] for example. Established in 2013 with an inaugural conference involving 500 teachers, it has continued with popular and frequent conferences. It positions itself as a grassroots movement promoting teacher engagement with research, although it is not clear how this group is funded and the nature of its associations with other organisations, think tanks and government. While it claims to be a grassroots movement, there appears to be no democratic structure, and its constitution, if it has one, is not in the public domain. If it were to address these issues, then it has potential in supporting greater teacher empowerment because of its activism and concern for scholarship.

Social media, in particular Twitter, has an active group of teachers, headteachers and education academics who network, debate, discuss and promote the teaching profession. Although it is excellent in facilitating networks and interaction, it is limited in its capacity to make decisions democratically and build consensus. Research on teacher activism and social media would be helpful in assessing its capabilities. There are no current estimates of the extent of activism on social media; however, on Twitter the most followed teacher (Ross McGill, or @teachertoolkit) has 146,000[2] followers internationally. What proportion of this following could be described as activist is unclear. There are 456,900[3] full-time equivalent teachers in England as of November 2016. If building consensus and establishing a sense of solidarity is necessary in promoting greater teacher control, how might social media activism contribute to this cause?

Solidarity

Strength through mass unity has historically been the source of power in struggles against authority. Solidarity is a cornerstone of this manifesto for control. Change can come when people act together. Yet, there is an obvious difficulty:

teachers have different views about various aspects of their work; they are likely to have different experiences and are frequently from different backgrounds. This heterogeneity can result in fragmented groups and internal tensions and even conflict; all this works against developing solidarity. It is important, therefore, to take heed of the words of another key pragmatist thinker:

> It is to be achieved not by inquiry but by imagination, the imaginative ability to see strange people as fellow sufferers. Solidarity is not discovered by reflection but created.
>
> (Rorty, 1989, p. xvi)

In 2004, I was working in a school which was placed in special measures.[4] The headteacher resigned and an interim replacement was appointed. The interim head immediately implemented a regime which meant teachers had to produce considerable amounts of paperwork for each lesson they taught. Teachers were asked to present this paperwork without notice and would face disciplinary proceedings if they did not comply. There was widespread dissatisfaction amongst the teaching staff. A union meeting was organised and was well attended. After many individual accounts of difficulties and increased stress the meeting turned to what could be done by the union. It was clear that the assembled group wanted action. The union representative suggested an indicative vote over action short of a strike. Surprisingly, although there was such strength of feeling, only a small number supported action. No one wanted to stick their necks out; no one wanted to be seen to oppose the measures being put in place. My colleagues had little faith in the power of solidarity. This was not surprising, since unions had been attacked, maligned and undermined under the Thatcher government (1979–1990), and a culture of corporatism and individualism fostered in schools through the 1990s. Divisions and promotion of the individual meant teachers had not developed, or had unlearned, a cohesive and united voice on areas of policy as well as on pay and conditions.

Things change. Recently public-sector workers – who have long been branded a cost to society – are now beginning to realise their importance. Junior doctors have demonstrated solidarity in resisting government attacks on the National Health Service and teachers have been largely united in their opposition to the reintroduction of selective schools. We are about to relearn the importance of solidarity in the teaching profession.

Conclusion

Democracy involves shared decision making and building a joint vision through direct, deliberative and representative democracy. Of course, there will be a wide range of views and some significant disagreements, but a deliberative process offers the means through which compromise and synthesis can be achieved. Scholarship provides a means by which – practically and through drawing on evidence and theory – professional communities can meaningfully co-construct a vision. Activism involves building networks and communicating more widely the needs of the profession and the nature of education. Solidarity requires us to imagine our disparate sufferings as a common obstacle to overcome. Ultimately, to flip the system we need to construct our actions with respect to all four.

Notes

1 http://www.workingoutwhatworks.com/en-GB/About/History
2 https://twitter.com/TeacherToolkit
3 https://www.gov.uk/government/uploads/system/uploads/attachment_data/file/533618/SFR21_2016_MainText.pdf
4 Special Measures is a status conferred on state schools in England when their performance, as judged by the Office for Standards in Education (Ofsted), is considered inadequate.

References

Boyer, E. L. (1990). *Scholarship reconsidered: priorities of the professoriate*. New York: The Carnegie Foundation for the Advancement of Teaching.

Creese, B., & Isaacs, T. (2016). International instructional systems: how England measures up. *The Curriculum Journal*, 27(1), 151–165. https://doi.org/10.1080/09585176.2015.1131171

Department for Education. (2010). *The importance of teaching: schools white paper*. London: HMSO.

Evers, J., & Kneyber, R. (2016). Introduction. In J. Evers & R. Kneyber (Eds.), *Flip the system: changing education from the ground up* (pp. 1–8). London: Routledge.

Fernandez, S., & Moldogaziev, T. (2013). Employee empowerment, employee attitudes, and performance: testing a causal model. *Public Administration Review*, 73(3), 490–506.

Habermas, J. (1984). *The theory of communicative action, volume 1: reason and the rationalization of society*. (Thomas McCarthy, Trans.) Cambridge: Polity.

Haynes, L., Service, O., Goldacre, B., & Torgerson, D. (2012). *Test, learn, adapt: developing public policy with randomised control trials*. London: Cabinet Office Behavioural Insights Team.

Knudsen, H., Busck, O., & Lind, J. (2011). Work environment quality: the role of workplace participation and democracy. *Work, Employment & Society*, 25(3), 379–396. https://doi.org/10.1177/0950017011407966

O'Reilly, D., & Reed, M. (2010). 'Leaderism': an evolution of managerialism in UK public service reform. *Public Administration*, 88(4), 960.

Pausch, M. (2014). Workplace democracy: from a democratic ideal to a managerial tool and back. *Innovation Journal*, 19(1), 1–19.

Rorty, R. (1989). *Contingency, irony, and solidarity*. Cambridge: Cambridge University Press.

Sachs, J. (2003). *Activist teaching profession*. Buckingham: Open University Press.

Walford, G. (2014). From city technology colleges to free schools: sponsoring new schools in England. *Research Papers in Education*, 29(3), 315–329. https://doi.org/10.1080/02671522.2014.885731

Watson, S., Major, L., & Kimber, E. (forthcoming). *Cultural practices, habitus and routines in the post-16 mathematics classroom in England.*

Woods, P. A., & Gronn, P. (2009). Nurturing democracy: the contribution of distributed leadership to a democratic organizational landscape. *Educational Management Administration & Leadership, 37*(4), 430–451. https://doi.org/10.1177/1741143209334597

Chapter 12

CPD

Education's Achilles heel

Ross Morrison McGill

"Cost is not the only consideration. It's time we treated our teachers in a way that allows them to develop professional pride."

I've always wanted to improve my classroom practice. I know I can be even better at teaching. I want to learn. In fact, I love learning, and as a teacher, it is vital I continue to develop to keep up with reform, subject developments and to remain one step ahead of my students. Yet, like many teachers, I have often believed training lacked purpose and learning rarely came from it.

As a result of poor Continued Professional Development (CPD), teachers stagnate at work and become frustrated – forced to take learning into their own hands and succumb to the priorities of others. Despite this pervasive failure to invest in the profession, thousands of teachers still manage to develop and evolve. Each academic year, we shed skin and reincarnate ourselves. Sometimes it's every term, and, in rare cases, every other week when new initiatives are launched as by-products of external governance.

When professional development is in the hands of teachers, designed or chosen predominantly for the greater good of students, training on the job can be targeted, energising and meaningful. Even then, there is little or no breathing space to consolidate prior learning to maintain the desired knowledge and skills our schools depend upon. For a profession so focused on pastoral care, after initial qualification, very little time is invested in teaching staff. Under the new national funding formula, in 2018/19 "more than 9,000 schools in England will lose funding" (Weale, 2016). With shrinking budgets and ongoing pay constraints (DfE, 2016) that have spanned almost a decade, our teachers have every right to feel undervalued and over-stretched.

For the past 20 years, the English system has made effective CPD its weak spot. Schools and their training programmes have crumbled under increasing external accountability. The result? We have created an Achilles heel – our system is insufficiently evidence-based – and poor CPD is at its root, restricting teachers by taking away what they need most: time out of their classrooms to reflect and improve.

A recent report of international research by the Teacher Development Trust found that training is "too inconsistent in quality" and "lags behind [that] experienced by colleagues elsewhere internationally" (Teacher Development Trust, 2015). To flip this narrative, we need CPD placed back in the hands of those who know and understand what works. What could teachers achieve with the time and stability to work with a longer-term, deeper and more meaningful focus?

Teacher empowerment

An achievable change which institutions can genuinely facilitate is to start celebrating the talent we have. For many, thankfully, the type of one-day training course teachers were 'sent on' to return as outstanding practitioners in 'questioning' or 'behaviour management' are already a distant memory. Contextually appropriate, in-house talent is replacing external providers. Not only are the outcomes of CPD potentially improved by this, but it also brings about much needed belief that improvement *can* happen. However, the strategy isn't without risk.

The main danger, in my experience, is allowing a few to dominate that process. Opportunities to develop and lead CPD need to be shared equitably. Another is lack of challenge. Through social media, the teaching profession has shone the limelight on itself. We vociferously share and challenge ideas, and get a better sense of what is working in our school and all over the world. While this is excellent news for CPD – indeed, teachers are increasingly better connected with colleagues online than they are with those in their schools – what about those who do not use social media? Less than 10% of the thousands of teachers I have worked with over the past eight years use social media for professional gain. I suspect this ratio is replicated across the half a million teachers in England. Professional knowledge needs to be networked, and institutions who bring CPD in-house need to ensure they provide opportunities for staff to seek out and respond to challenge.

Although the one-size-fits-all model of CPD is on the back foot – restricted to essential government, inspectorate or school policy updates in many places – we are not yet free of directives justified by that dreaded phrase: 'what Ofsted wants'. No, we are not yet the autonomous, highly educated profession we wish to be. Peter Sellen (2016, p. 7) reports that: "Of the 36 jurisdictions in the dataset, England ranked 30th in terms of the average number of days spent in a year on certain types of professional development". In Finland, a master's degree is the minimum expected of teachers.

The paltry five INSET (In Service Training) days first established in 1988 by Education Secretary Kenneth Baker in England, Wales and Northern Ireland still stands in stark contrast to international evidence; according to former Schools Commissioner for London, Sir Tim Brighouse, to have a real impact on pupil achievement "teachers need to be able to participate in at least 50 hours of development work over not more than two terms" (Brighouse and Moon, 2013).

But time isn't everything. Fifty hours every two terms of sitting in the hall listening to the headteacher talk is unlikely to solve anything. At a Spectator 'Schools Revolution' conference, Dylan Wiliam (2010) summed up the problem:

> The standard model of teacher professional development is based on the idea that teachers lack important knowledge. For the last 20 years, most professional development has therefore been designed to address those deficits. The result has been teachers who are more knowledgeable, but no more effective in practice.

Professional pride

It's no wonder INSET days have a shocking reputation. They're usually enough to make any teacher beg to return to their piles of marking! Though I suggested above that whole-school INSETs are often restricted to announcements and responses to changes from the DfE, Ofsted and Ofqual, it is impossible to overestimate the number of these changes and their impact on workload and morale. Nothing (other than increased funding, of course) would facilitate better CPD (and by it whole-school improvement) more than a hiatus in the political interference that has been, ironically, the only constant in education for at least two decades. Time would be better spent re-learning how best to train and develop staff, in line with research recommendations (Teacher Development Trust, 2015).

But if time is one of the critical factors, and schools spend 80% of their budgets or thereabouts on human resources, there is little scope to invest in CPD once utilities and school building maintenance are also calculated. Therefore, schools must be inventive. I have worked with many to address CPD needs by reducing teaching timetables by one period per week. There is a cost, of course, but those schools who commit to this model can create meaningful, impactful, tailored and sustained professional development. Cost is not the only consideration. It's time we treated our teachers in a way that allows them to develop professional pride, and offering a 'weekly slot' provides the required time for teachers to reflect and consolidate.

Raising morale

Training should not just be for those joining the profession, or those on a course or leadership pathway. Regular, sustained, high-quality staff training should be part of every teacher's daily experience – and is never complete! We always have something new to learn. After all, we are teachers – learning is the very nature of our profession. Dissemination and reflection are our daily bread.

For the past decade, I have worked with schools to slowly modify their professional development cultures. We are not there yet, but many schools are now on their way to developing a marketplace of CPD, available to and led by all teaching and support staff at various levels and at various stages of their careers. This model, in my experience, is very well suited to sustained development, and highly preferable to the top-down, knee-jerk process so familiar to so many teachers. Not only is it more cost-efficient and more effective, the feeling of ownership it brings really raises morale.

The marketplace model allows schools to outline CPD for the year ahead and enables them to:

- adapt and protect important areas for reflection (e.g. marking, planning, teaching);
- showcase to staff a breadth of professional development;
- encourage a range of staff to share ideas with their peers;
- communicate that CPD is planned over time and not a knee-jerk process;
- encourage all teachers to lead and strengthen the culture of action research;
- develop strategy for implementing evidence-based ideas;
- link professional development to appraisal so that objectives are developmental and enquiry-based.

Professional networks

Beyond in-house CPD, teachers should have access to the best available professional networks. Here are a few ways to engage with others for improved CPD:

- The Teacher Effectiveness Enhancement Programme (TEEP): set up in 2002 by the Gatsby Charity Foundation to develop a model of effective teaching and learning drawn from research and best practice, under the custody of the SSAT, the programme has greatly expanded.
- TeachMeets: Perhaps unknown to many, this is the underground revolution of teacher training. Curated and delivered by classroom teachers, these gatherings collate and broadcast great ideas that work in the classroom, further afield than any other national institute I know!
- Teaching School Alliances: No school should labour alone. TSAs are groups of schools and other partners, designed to bring teachers together for the express purpose of CPD, in regions where it matters most: their home turf.
- Professional organisations: Whether unions, subject associations or the new Chartered College of Teaching, membership organisations provide networking and learning opportunities for teachers that can only enhance their engagement with their profession.

INSET days will continue to be a poisoned chalice as long as education policy is constantly changing. So, we must find alternative mechanisms for sharing top-down policies to protect teachers' time for the benefit of schools and their communities. For policy-makers reading this, is it so inconceivable that any major changes to the curriculum, inspection or examinations be accompanied by extra time to manage these changes? Not only would teacher development be protected, but perhaps more thoughtful policy might emerge from such a commitment.

Fundamentally, we must enable teachers to be able to translate CPD content into the classroom, implementing what they have learnt into the classroom the very next day. We should certainly set aside time for staff to get to grips with whole-school priorities, as well as their CPD needs, with time to reflect and action personal learning plans as a direct outcome of appraisal, self-review, personal and professional goals and departmental, whole-school and student needs.

> The government has no coherent strategy for the development of teachers' professional capabilities once they enter the classroom.
>
> (RSA, 2014)

A BERA (2014) report states teachers' experience of professional development in most parts of the UK is "fragmented, occasional and insufficiently informed by research", in high contrast to internationally well-regarded education systems such as Finland, Canada and Singapore.

Why? Well, workload for starters. England's teachers work the longest hours and get paid one of the worst salaries in OECD countries: a barrier to professional development (Sellen, 2016). We know enquiry-based (or 'research-rich') environments are the hallmark of high-performing education systems, but how can this be the hallmark of every school and every teacher when professional development during the working week is an afterthought?

BERA and the RSA recently highlighted that "too often, schools' ability to make a long-term commitment to creating a research-engaged workforce is undermined by a target culture and short-term focus on exam results" (BERA, 2014, p. 12). What time is there for the humble teacher? Full-time teachers will rarely become 'teacher–researchers' under the current system. Instead, we may have to settle for *teaching* becoming research-rich, but not teachers themselves, who will increasingly rely on information being shared with them – partial, mediated and politicised. Unless schools are provided with the necessary cash to free their teaching staff from a 90% contact ratio, and until headteachers can focus less on 'what the DfE/Ofsted want', teachers can only really hope to become richer in research through carving out more from their own time.

> A striking contrast between the teaching profession in different countries is its status and the calibre of its recruits. Successful countries have shown how a workforce that assumes a high level of responsibility is rewarded and can attract some of the best graduates into a teaching career.
>
> (Schleicher, 2011, p. 61)

We can already see this evidence in TeachMeets and conferences up and down the UK. Teachers are organising themselves and coming together in the evenings and at weekends to share and to learn from each other. Of course this is beneficial, but why is it fast becoming the norm for teachers to undertake professional development in their own time, often without recognition or support from their schools?

Sadly, the research-informed movement is still in the hands of those outside of the classroom. Without a system-wide reform of teachers' time commitments, how can we hand teachers back the professional responsibility for their own careers?

Future-proof solutions

I dream of a day when CPD is part of every teacher's daily reality; when accumulating a fine-feathered cap of personal development is the norm, not a goal for a determined few or a gift for the privileged. I dream of a profession where development becomes so ingrained and so necessary that we cannot secure jobs, promotions, pay rises or credibility without an accurate log of our reflective journey, perhaps even a national development portfolio.

Dear reader, can you recall your CPD over the past five years? Is it accessible to you, to your current and prospective employers, your partners, such as universities, local schools or colleagues? If your answer is 'no', do you think like me that something is still missing? I dream of a profession that provides all teachers with a forum for making learning feasible within the working day, transparent and accessible, and not something that happens at weekends, or is limited to five days a year, imposed and effectively hidden.

We should strive for professional kudos, and the Chartered College of Teaching — a new beginning for teachers in England at least — provides an alternative to the de-professionalised system that continues to unfold before us. We need a "process where the 'voice' of teachers is given a meaningful place, whereas before it was considered just noise" (Evers and Kneyber, 1999, p. 7).

Too often we do not speak up collectively against government pressures and regulations that affect both our professional and personal lives, but perhaps we can find the solidarity we need in speaking up *for* something, and perhaps that something is *time* to learn together.

References

BERA (2014). *Research and the teaching profession: building the capacity for a self-improving education system*. [online] Available at https://www.thersa.org/globalassets/pdfs/bera-rsa-research-teaching-profession-full-report-for-web-2.pdf. Accessed 6/7/17.

Brighouse, T. and Moon, B. (2013). It's time to give teachers the skills and respect they deserve. *Guardian*. [online] Available at https://www.theguardian.com/teacher-network/2013/jan/29/teachers-professional-development-national-body-england. Accessed 6/7/17.

DfE (2016). *Government evidence to the STRB: the 2017 pay award.* December. [online] Available at https://www.gov.uk/government/uploads/system/uploads/attachment_data/file/575587/strb27evidence_accessible_final.pdf. Accessed 6/7/17.

Evers, J. and Kneyber, R. (2016). *Flip the System: Changing Education from the Ground Up.* Abingdon: Routledge.

RSA (2014). *UK "lacks coherent plan for teacher research and development", finds report.* [online] Available at https://www.thersa.org/about-us/media/2014/05/uk-lacks-coherent-plan-for-teacher-research-and-development-finds-report. Accessed 6/7/17.

Schleicher, A. (2011). *Building a high-quality teaching profession: lessons from around the world.* Paris: OECD.

Sellen, P. (2016). *Teacher workload and professional development in England's secondary schools: insights from TALIS.* Education Policy Insitute. [Online] Available at https://epi.org.uk/wp-content/uploads/2016/10/TeacherWorkload_EPI.pdf. Retrieved 03/10/2017.

Teacher Development Trust (2015). *Developing great teaching: lessons from the international reviews into effective professional development.* [online] Available at http://tdtrust.org/wp-content/uploads/2015/10/DGT-Summary.pdf. Accessed 6/7/17.

Weale, S. (2016). Thousands of schools stand to lose out under new funding formula. *Guardian*, 14 December. [online] Available at https://www.theguardian.com/politics/2016/dec/14/england-school-funding-formula-justine-greening-education-secretary. Accessed 6/7/17.

Wiliam, D. (2010). *Teacher quality: why it matters, and how to get more of it.* Speech delivered at The Spectator Schools Revolution conference. Transcript. [online] Available at http://www.dylanwiliam.org/Dylan_Wiliams_website/Papers_files/Spectator%20talk.doc. Accessed 6/7/17.

Chapter 13

Accountability and agency in a Scottish school

George Gilchrist

"I want teachers with adaptive expertise, not 'milkmen.'"

There is no doubt that both accountability and agency have roles to play in achieving our goals for Scottish education. As a headteacher, I believe that the balance is in danger of tipping too greatly in favour of accountability and damaging education in Scotland. While I work to protect my staff from the worst effects, it is likely to become increasingly difficult to do so unless there is a change of direction.

Accountability in education has been described by Figlio and Loeb (2011, p. 384) as "the process of evaluating school performance on the basis of student performance measures." They acknowledge how broad the concept *can* be, but point out that high-accountability systems narrow their focus to student performance in the form of test scores, with teachers reduced to 'deliverers.' By contrast, agency is concerned with teachers' ability to be active participants in their role as professionals. It casts them as autonomous, reflective professionals with high degrees of adaptive expertise. Accountability tells teachers what to do and how to do it; agency trusts them to know and take the right actions.

Where we are now

The two main national aims expressed by the Scottish Government in their National Improvement Framework (NIF) are to ensure that every child "achieves the highest standards in literacy and numeracy" and "has the same opportunity to succeed, with a particular focus on closing the poverty-related attainment gap" (NIF, 2016a, p. 3). This has been further refined to 'excellence and equity.' It would be difficult to argue with either. Indeed, one would hope these principles to be so self-evident in education as to make their repetition vacuous.

When Nicola Sturgeon became First Minister of the Scottish Parliament in 2014, she quickly pinned her colours to the mast of educational reform. 'Judge me on education' became her mantra as she set out her stall for reform by looking at what had worked in other countries. She seemed to look to England and the USA first, and, liking what she saw, to look no further, despite their questionable results over time (if not in terms of attainment, at least in terms of equity). Indeed, Pasi Sahlberg identifies both as subject to the Global Educational Reform Movement (or GERM) that seeks to apply business models to education with a concomitant reduction in teachers' agency and professional status.

Sahlberg (2017) writes that "the Finnish education system has remained quite uninfected [by] viruses of what is often called the *global education reform movement* or GERM. And the reason for that is clear: professional strength and moral health of Finnish schools." The Scottish Government have decided to learn instead from systems high on accountability, performativity, and underpinned by high-stakes standardised testing and narrow curricular focus. The two, it would seem, are incompatible. Many Scots and outside observers had been encouraged by our direction of travel with Curriculum for Excellence. Yet much of the current agenda goes against that curriculum's aims and vision, and runs counter to what sound educational research tells us works.

The First Minister's new agenda ratcheted up quickly. In January, the NIF laid out the Government's priorities. The document and accompanying rhetoric lauded thorough stakeholder consultation despite its great similarity to the pre-consultation draft. "Key drivers" to meet its objectives were identified as: "school leadership, teacher professionalism, parental engagement, assessment of children's progress, school improvement and performance information" (Scottish Government, 2016a, p. 9). Little prominence was given to curriculum, learning and teaching, or the promotion of teacher agency, and references to all the drivers were couched in accountability language – standards and expectations. The Scottish Government used an OECD commission visit late in 2015 as further justification for its plans. The fact that the OECD had been invited in and commissioned to oversee this strategic plan was largely ignored and, unsurprisingly perhaps, the report, *Improving Schools in Scotland: An OECD Perspective*, broadly supported the direction of travel (OECD, 2015). Andy Hargreaves, part of the OECD team, pointed out that Scottish education was at a watershed – it could go on to be truly world class or slip backwards in comparison to more progressive and innovative systems.

In May 2016, John Swinney was appointed Cabinet Secretary for Education, a move widely seen as symbolic of the Government's commitment to its reform programme. By June, he had unveiled his Education Delivery Plan – a timeline to improve performance and raise attainment, accompanied by comments from him and the First Minister about proposed changes to school governance arrangements, more direct funding and control to headteachers, and commitment to national testing as an accountability measure. They reportedly began consulting with groups interested in setting up their own schools or taking schools out of local authority control. This will sound very familiar to teachers in England and elsewhere, especially as it was accompanied by reassurances that teachers' professional judgement would have primacy in assessment procedures.

In August 2016, Mr Swinney delivered his first paper as part of the 'new narrative' recommended by the OECD report on Curriculum for Excellence (Education Scotland, 2016). Ironically, whilst it sought to allay teachers' fears over the amount of bureaucracy associated with CfE, its publication missed the Delivery Plan deadline (Scottish Government, 2016b). This paper, and Mr Swinney's accompanying letter, were unusually aimed directly at teachers, bypassing local authorities and school leaders. Mr Swinney set out his desire to "maximise precious teacher time.. He set clear expectations and even encouraged teachers to challenge school leaders about practices that lacked relevance "to the learner's journey." The rest of the paper provided clear messages about what to do and what to avoid and is to be applauded in its attempt to give teachers more agency. It certainly gave teachers 'permission' to focus on aspects of their practice that would enhance learning and improve learner outcomes. Unfortunately, it was accompanied by 99 pages of benchmarks for literacy and numeracy that teachers were encouraged to apply in assessing pupils. Education Scotland and Mr Swinney failed to recognise the dissonance at the heart of their communiqué.

In line with this imbalance, much of what we have heard from Mr Swinney and his representatives since has been about accountability, systems, and structures, and little about teacher agency. Professor Stephen Ball, speaking in Glasgow in 2016, had warnings for Scottish education's trajectory (Gilchrist, 2016). He pointed out that system reforms in England, the USA, Australia, and Sweden had all started out with the intention to raise attainment and close equity gaps. All had seen the opposite happen. He worried that many of these systems had also initially spoken of the primacy of teacher professionalism, but quickly lost sight of that in favour of ever increasing, narrow accountability measures. Stagnating or falling results lead to more reform, and so the cycle of failing schools and systems continues until such time as someone steps in to halt it.

Has that time come already for Scotland? Yes. The inception of the NIF and the evidently disproportionate attention given to accountability over agency demands it. What will we replace it with? I believe firmly that any new system must start and finish with the goals of promoting and supporting teacher professionalism and agency. I am not alone in this belief, and there is a raft of research and evidence from across the globe to support this approach. From the work of Helen Timperley in New Zealand and Australia, Michael Fullan and Andy Hargreaves in Canada and the USA, Alma Harris and Michelle Jones in Malaysia and elsewhere, and going back to the work of Lawrence Stenhouse in the 1970s, we have ample evidence of the positive impacts of teacher agency.

I have personally used Marilyn Cochran-Smith's work on practitioner enquiry to inform teacher development in the schools I lead (Cochran-Smith and Lytle, 2009). Through this approach, teachers develop as reflective practitioners who take control of their own professional development.

In my experience, changes to practice are most impactful and sustainable when identified by teachers themselves, rather than by others and 'done to' them. I want teachers with adaptive expertise, not 'milkmen,' as Professor Mark Priestley calls them (2013). So, I believe, do parents and children. If 'System Leadership' is the development of a self-improving system, then I see teacher agency and adaptive expertise creating the self-improving teacher (Gilchrist, 2015), and I believe neither is possible without the other. We have shown it in my schools; this approach delivers wins for all: teachers, learners, schools, and system. Top-down, imposed accountability, and over-standardisation fail more learners than they help. We need a culture of support, trust, and professional dispositions – all of which are currently systemically hampered.

We have a number of different approaches to school improvement in the individual nations of the UK, but all have similar high aspirations for their schools and learners, to raise attainment and to close equity gaps. What is clear to me is that the success or failure of any system is largely determined by the quality and professionalism of the teachers within it. Like many, I share Alma Harris's frustration; we are "tired of hearing teachers are the problem. They are the solution" (Harris, 2015). Belying the much vaunted power of Twitter, little has changed, though this sentiment is oft repeated. It is time the alternative was heard in Scotland and across the UK: only when teacher agency is given the same status as accountability will we get the best out of our education systems.

References

Cochran-Smith, M. and Lytle, S. L. (2009). *Inquiry as Stance: Practitioner Research for the Next Generation*, Teachers College Press, Boston, MA.

Education Scotland (2016). *Curriculum for Excellence: A Statement for Practitioners from HM Chief Inspector of Education*, available at https://www.education.gov.scot/Documents/cfe-statement.pdf, accessed on 12/05/2017.

Figlio, D. and Loeb, S. (2011). *School Accountability*. In Hanushek, M. S., Machin, S. and Woessmann, L. (eds.) *Handbooks in Economics, Vol 3*, North-Holland, the Netherlands.

Gilchrist. G. (2015). *Headteachers and System Leadership*, available at http://gg1952.blogspot.co.uk/2015/02/headteachers-and-system-leadership.html, accessed on 12/05/2017.

Gilchrist, G. (2016). *Stephen Ball Looks at the NIF and Gives Scotland a Few Warnings about the Future*, available at http://gg1952.blogspot.co.uk/2016/02/stephen-ball-looks-at-nif-and-gives.html, accessed on 22/05/2017.

Harris, A (2015). *I Am in Too. Tired of Hearing Teachers Are the Problem. They Are the Solution. They Need to be Celebrated & Respected*, 22 November, available at https://twitter.com/AlmaHarris1/status/668313576386379776, accessed on 12/05/2017.

OECD (2015). *Improving Schools in Scotland: An OECD Perspective*, available at http://www.oecd.org/education/school/Improving-Schools-in-Scotland-An-OECD-Perspective.pdf, accessed on 12/05/2017.

Priestley, M. (2013). *Milkmen or Educators? CfE and the Language of Delivery*, available at https://mrpriestley.wordpress.com/2013/04/15/milkmen-or-educators-cfe-and-the-language-of-delivery/, accessed on 14/05/2017.

Sahlberg, P. (2017). *Global Education Reform Movement Is Here!*, available at https://pasisahlberg.com/global-educational-reform-movement-is-here/, accessed 12/05/2017.

Scottish Government (2016a). *The National Improvement Framework*, available at http://www.gov.scot/Resource/0049/00491758.pdf, accessed on 12/05/2017.

Scottish Government (2016b). *Delivering Excellence and Equity in Scottish Education: A Delivery Plan for Scotland*, available at http://www.gov.scot/Resource/0050/00502222.pdf, accessed on 12/05/2017.

Chapter 14

Flip the system? Get organised!

Howard Stevenson

"The state has consistently sought to marginalise the collective voice of teachers."

When teachers feel the need to self-organise around a project called *Flip the System*, it should be obvious that something deep within our education system is wrong. That this project first developed outside of the UK, and received support from Education International (the international teacher union federation with more than 170 affiliates from over 400 countries), highlights that the issues are global in scope and not unique to the UK. That said, it is important to recognise that England (and not the UK) can be considered to be in the vanguard of a 'reform' movement in which democratic control of education is being removed, whilst power is being centralised in the hands of a tiny number of politicians and their powerful, but largely unelected, friends. There may be a language of autonomy, but the reality is very different, with decentralisation often used as a smoke screen to break up a public system and hand assets to the private sector. England has become the world's laboratory for this global experiment.

Where are we now?

That the English school system is one that is not at ease with itself is best illustrated by an examination of the labour market. Markets are not good ways to provide high quality, high equity public services, but as signals of the relative attractiveness of particular jobs and occupations, labour market data tells a story that cannot be ignored. Teaching is struggling to recruit new entrants (TES, 2016); it is really struggling to retain those who enter the profession (Schools Week, 2016a), and very few people in the system want to take on senior leadership roles within it (Schools Week, 2016b). It seems as though the current approach to these problems is to adopt a 'bring in – burn out – replace' (and repeat as necessary) model to teacher supply (see England's data in TALIS 2013). This is systemically unsustainable and morally indefensible. A more sustainable approach will only be adopted when the root causes of the problem are tackled.

The first problem that needs to be addressed is workload. Pay is clearly a factor, but it is workload that is the key problem in the pay-for-effort exchange. A super-competitive school system, combined with an inadequate employment contract, means that there is a relentless pressure to drive workload up, and too few safeguards to keep it down. The result is a workload that offers no realistic prospect of securing a decent work–life balance. Too often young teachers look to the future, see no prospect of change and decide to bail out whilst their skills have value in other labour markets (Lee-Potter, 2016).

However, the issues are more complex than workload (and pay) alone. Teachers also experience their work as an endless series of policy impositions from above, whereby they have little or no opportunity to influence decisions key issues - for example relating to curriculum, pedagogy and assessment. Sometimes these impositions come from government, other times from within teachers' own schools, as senior leadership teams try to second-guess what Ofsted wants, and impose it across the school in the name of 'consistency' (witness the debacle that is 'triple-marking').

All of this takes place in a context where education policy is more and more driven by the needs of the globalised economy. We have lost sight of education as a public good, with ambitious aspirations for all and underpinned by democratic values. Rather, students must be educated for the market, by a school system that looks like a market. In due course, the trajectory is an incremental shift towards a fully privatised system in which tax payers' money funds private sector for-profit providers in a system that is public in name only.

This is the political project that has characterised over 30 years of education 'reform' in England. One of its objectives has been to weaken the collective voice of teachers, thus making the pathway to privatisation easier to pursue. This is why the state has consistently sought to marginalise the collective voice of teachers, and why it has favoured conflict over consensus in relation to the development of policy. If teachers want to flip the system, this must start from an alternative narrative about what is possible, and how teachers can be engaged in change.

What is the alternative?

There are many aspects of education that must be addressed here, but I want to focus on a way of thinking about teacher professionalism that may be considered as fundamental to 'flipping the system'. At the heart of this approach to professionalism is the concept of agency – a complex concept when discussed fully, but for my purposes explained as the ability to exercise judgement, make decisions and act in ways that bring about change. In other words, to have, and experience, *control*.

For agency to be considered meaningful in respect of teachers and their work, it is important to think about the concept in relation to different aspects of teachers' professional lives. Most obviously, it is in relation to the learning conditions of students and the working conditions of teachers, but it is vital to understand these also with regard to different system 'levels' – recognising that teachers need to be able to assert influence and control in their own classroom and institution as well as at higher levels in the system such as local authority, Academy Trust or Government. In a globalised system, we might also think of agency in relation to international bodies such as the OECD. In a system where teachers have little control over their work, they are reduced to 'implementers' of ideas and initiatives developed by others: what Harry Braverman (1974, p. 79) described as the "separation of conception from execution". Nowhere is there a clearer illustration of the de-professionalisation of teaching than the impetus of top-down change, which many don't question openly for fear of the impact on their career (Stevenson, 2016).

Secondly, it is fruitful to think about questions of agency and control in relation to professional knowledge and professional learning. Being involved in framing the knowledge base that underpins teaching, and having control over one's own professional learning, can be considered core aspects of teacher professionalism. However, too often teachers feel they have no time to engage with pedagogical knowledge, whilst they feel they have no control over their own professional learning. Rather, this is driven by institutional imperatives and then pushed through the system in the form of performance management. Even teachers' own learning becomes instrumental and target focused.

It is vital we see agency in relation to both of these aspects of teachers' lives and work. To focus on one without addressing the other fails to give a holistic vision of teacher professionalism. For me, 'flipping the system' means, simply, that as a teacher I feel I can exercise agency in relation to both aspects of my work identified above. This is why agency is central, but it cannot be conceived of purely in individual terms ('*my* agency'). Rather, it is essential to recognise that I both acquire individual agency, and assert it, by acting collectively. Indeed, without collective agency, my individual agency is likely to be hugely circumscribed. This is precisely why so many teachers today are quitting. Not only do they not experience individual agency, but not enough see the possibility of exercising it collectively.

How to get from where we are to where we want to be?

It follows from the argument above that, if teachers are to assert their professional agency, they need to (re)discover the power of collective action. Some teachers see this power being exercised through social media, and there is no doubt that social media as a means of networking teachers is an exciting development. One teacher, well known through her tweets and blogs, recently went so far as to assert "Twitter is the only place ordinary teachers can have a powerful voice" (@HeyMissSmith, 2016). This is some claim, and there may be some element of truth in it. Social media is exciting, fast, engaging. It is also individualised, dispersed and unrepresentative. For those who live in the

Plato's cave that is Twitter, it can be hard to remember that the vast majority of teachers do not. Moreover, precisely because it is individualised and unaccountable, it is open to co-option – witness the way Michael Gove and Nick Gibb have sought to use their favourite Twitterati to convey support for their ideas. This is not to deny the power of social media, but it is to caution against viewing Twitter, or other forms of social media, as the way we flip the system.

Others may see new bodies, such as the College of Teaching, as providing a voice for teachers, and thereby offering the possibility of collective agency. Again, I can see merit in such an initiative, particularly under its current CEO, Alison Peacock. However, it remains important to be alert to its limitations. Whilst the idea may be a good one, and sincere people in the profession will claim its independence, there can also be no denying that the College is a body that has been actively encouraged by a political party which, on at least four occasions in relatively recent history, abolished bodies where teachers could claim to have a genuinely independent voice. (I developed these arguments in a blog for *The Conversation* – see Stevenson, 2014).

If teachers want to assert their collective agency, then that is best achieved through bodies that are independent, democratic and inclusive of all the profession. Those bodies already exist, and are the unions that represent the overwhelming majority of teachers (NFER, 2012). Teacher unions are not the only bodies that need to be involved in 'flipping the system', but teachers must recognise there can be no flipping the system without them.

Given the scale of the challenges that confront teachers, and all those working in schools, then there is a particular responsibility on unions to lead this project, but, if this is to happen, unions themselves must rise to their own challenges. First, and most importantly, they must help articulate a different vision of how education can be. Unions must speak for teachers across all the dimensions of professional agency set out in this chapter. Governments often want nothing more than to see unions pigeon-holed into a narrow 'working conditions' remit (hence the promotion of the College of Teaching as an alternative pole for 'professional issues'). Restricting unions to pay-and-conditions issues gives governments free rein on the bigger questions, which ultimately shape all else, *including* working conditions. There can be no escaping the reality that the professional in education is always political.

Second, teacher unions must create the broadest possible alliances amongst teachers, across all those working in education and across all those with an interest in education, including parents. Working with others is also much more difficult than we like to think. It requires listening to others at least as much as talking to them.

Finally, if unions are to become the mass-participation organisations they need to be (rather than the mass-membership organisations they are) they must work hard at creating cultures that welcome engagement, value participation and offer invigorating spaces to develop collective agency. This in part requires unions to recognise the diverse interests and experiences of their members.

Unions are necessarily about forging unity, but that also has to be based on a recognition of diversity – of interests and identities.

At this point, and in relation to all the above points, there can be no doubt that the formation of a new union, the National Education Union, marks a significant and exciting opportunity. If ever there was a moment for teachers who have not previously engaged with their union to get involved, now is that time. A union of nearly half a million educators will be a very powerful voice.

Of course, teacher unions are no more than an organisational shell in which individuals come together to assert collective agency. If teachers want to flip the system, then they must flip it themselves. Teachers must organise, and unions provide the vehicle for that – independent, democratic and inclusive. We must all face up to our responsibility to get involved, participate and bring about change. As long as we say we don't *have time*, we will have less and less of it. As teachers, we must *make time* to act collectively and say enough is enough.

Flipping the system opens up the possibility of system transformation in which teaching is experienced as a sustainable career – balanced, creative and making a difference to young people's lives without having to sacrifice one's own. There is nothing worth fighting for that is not gained without a struggle. When teachers organise and engage with their unions to assert their collective agency, flipping the system shifts from possibility to reality.

References

Braverman, H. (1974) *Labor and monopoly capital: The degradation of work in the twentieth century*. New York: Monthly Review.

Lee-Potter, E. (2016) I dropped out of teaching after six months – so I'm not surprised other teachers are leaving in their droves. *The Independent*, 1 March. [online] Available at http://www.independent.co.uk/voices/i-dropped-out-of-teaching-after-six-months-so-im-not-surprised-other-teachers-are-leaving-in-their-a6905346.html. Retrieved 04/06/2017.

NFER (2012) NFER Teacher Voice Omnibus November 2012 Survey: Understanding union membership and activity. [online] Available at https://www.nfer.ac.uk/publications/99936/.

Schools Week (2016) *Highest teacher leaving rate in a decade – and 6 other things we learned about the school workforce*. [online] Available at http://schoolsweek.co.uk/highest-teacher-leaving-rate-in-a-decade-and-6-other-things-we-learned-about-the-school-workforce/.

Schools Week (2016a) *Non-teachers should be hired to plug school leader shortage, says report*. 11 November. [online] Available at http://schoolsweek.co.uk/non-teachers-should-be-hired-to-plug-school-leader-shortage-says-report/. Retrieved 04/06/2017.

Schools Week (2016b) *Highest teacher leaving rate in a decade – and 6 other things we learned about the school workforce*. 30 June. [online] Available at http://schoolsweek.co.uk/highest-teacher-leaving-rate-in-a-decade-and-6-other-things-we-learned-about-the-school-workforce/. Retrieved 04/06/2016.

Stevenson, H. (2014) *Why teachers should be sceptical of a College of Teaching*. [online] Available at http://theconversation.com/why-teachers-should-be-sceptical-of-a-new-college-of-teaching-35280. Retrieved 04/06/2017.

Stevenson, H. (2016) Challenging school reform from below: Is leadership the missing link in mobilization theory?, *Leadership and Policy in Schools*, *15* (1), 67–90.

TES online (2016) *Bleak outlook: Teacher shortages loom in almost all secondary school subjects, says expert*. 16 May. [online] Available at https://www.tes.com/news/school-news/breaking-news/bleak-outlook-teacher-shortages-loom-almost-all-secondary-school. Retrieved 04/06/2017.

@HeyMissSmith (2016) *Twitter is the only place ordinary teachers can have a powerful voice. That is important.* [online] Available at https://twitter.com/HeyMissSmith/status/770568085963177984. Retrieved 04/06/2017.

Chapter 15

The Chartered College of Teaching

Professional learning without limits

Alison Peacock

"**When this voice, our voice, is universally recognised, then, and only then, will we celebrate what it truly means to be part of a powerful, autonomous profession.**"

As a teacher and researcher, I have contributed to a range of studies of leadership and pedagogy. Three books have been published about the philosophy of *Learning without Limits*, researching classroom practice and whole-school development that resist notions of fixed 'ability'. These studies illustrate how liberation from accepted norms can enable inclusive, trusting environments where teachers and young people experience a fulfilling sense of individual and collaborative agency. The second study, *Creating Learning without Limits* (2012), charted a dramatic and sustained improvement process in one primary school. The dispositions we uncovered at the heart of its leadership were:

1 Openness to ideas.
2 Questioning, restlessness and humility.
3 Inventiveness allowing for creativity.
4 Persistence and professional courage.
5 Emotional stability enabling risk-taking.
6 Generosity that welcomes difference and diversity.
7 Empathy offering mutual supportiveness.

My hypothesis is that these dispositions, combined with the core principles of trust, co-agency and inclusion, enable inclusive, ambitious pedagogy to flourish. I believe these dispositions could usefully be applied across the education system. When teacher members are routinely offered opportunities to engage in sustained research-informed scholarship that is of direct relevance to their daily experience of classrooms, this can only foster a greater sense of professional empowerment. In turn, this offers an unparalleled opportunity to build respect and a society-wide positive perception of teachers in England.

Beyond the General Teaching Council to a Chartered College

Few teachers understood or embraced the enforcement of a General Teaching Council during 2000–2012. The unpopular imposition of the GTC on our workforce meant that teachers resented its existence. They were right to – despite enforced membership of over 400,000 teachers and guaranteed significant annual income for the organisation, its influence was hardly felt. Against this backdrop, we now have an emerging Chartered College of Teaching with a small amount of initial funding from government, which seeks to establish itself as a voluntary membership body. It is easy to dismiss this development as irrelevant or doomed to failure. Some fear it will become an exclusive club for the keenest teachers or, worse still, that it will replace the GTC as an organisation with de facto enforced membership. Some parody the audacity of its supporters, whilst Ministers have warned of the potential for too much interest from those who could be portrayed as 'enemies of promise'. The Chartered College has to forge a new path. It is not a union, nor a professional association, neither a think-tank nor a campaign group. There is no route map for an organisation like this, and as such it must be courageous, innovative and responsive to democratic membership. In the words of Muriel Strode's poem (Strode, 1903):

> I will not follow where the path may lead, but I will go instead where there is no path, and I will leave a trail.

Consider the potential impact of a portal for online pedagogical scholarship routes available for teachers regardless of setting, a virtual network with global reach that puts teachers in touch with national events, research findings and regional hub meetings tailored to their phase, interests and specialism. The Chartered College is developing capacity to become an online membership body offering the chance for teachers to engage in dialogic exchange with colleagues about classroom reality, whilst recording the impact of research on their practice. As teachers embrace this vision, their College will become powerfully influential. This will not be achieved through campaigning, but through a quiet, steady insistence on providing evidence of impact whilst maintaining a dialogic questioning stance that refuses to accept norms or the status quo. When this voice, our voice, is universally recognised, then, and only then, will we celebrate what it truly means to be part of a powerful, autonomous profession.

Setting our own standards

Within a self-improving profession it follows that we should seek a move away from a culture of top-down judgement towards one of collective ambition. We need this culture to flourish within schools and networked communities where the focus is on uncovering and sharing excellence, rather than cowering away from punitive attitudes. Fear leads to closed-down, risk-averse behaviour contrary to the openness to new ideas necessary to adapt and enhance the impact of our teaching. Instead of leaders investing in the overall intellectual development of teachers, professional training has too long been seen as instrumental in nature. Training companies have profited hugely from schools scared about the latest centralised diktats, habitually sending teachers to one-off events to glean survival strategies for changing inspection requirements, examination frameworks or safeguarding regulations. This is what CPD has become.

Fresh expectations for professional learning?

Aware of the need for the school-led system to support teachers' continuous learning, the DfE (2016) has published a set of standards for professional development. As a headteacher, I contributed to these standards along with colleagues from across the education landscape. I see them as a starting point rather than a set of absolutes. Along with the teaching standards (DfE, 2011), we should use documents such as these to adopt a professional identity that overtakes recommended standards, using them as a baseline from which exceptional practice can develop. In other words, we should set our own standards, and they should be higher.

How refreshing it will be when the norm is for teachers, presenting to colleagues, to lead conferences themselves – teachers who can explain in detail the planning, teaching and assessment of their subject or phase and offer rich examples of children's work from their classrooms. This will provide compelling and meaningful professional learning that other colleagues can learn from immediately. It is not sufficient to talk the language of high ambition for all without illustrating how this is achieved day after day in classrooms. The Chartered College of Teaching aims to enable this vision of professional learning to become a reality.

Openness to ideas

Teaching is a conservative, risk-averse profession in the main. Teachers doggedly hold on to practice that has held them in good stead for years. We need convincing very strongly to change classroom practice with a glad heart. It can be exhausting to change what we do when we are working so hard, and past experiences of unsustained change, enforced through well-meaning but poorly informed or badly incentivised leadership, comes to bear for many. The central tenet of this book is that we risk nothing by considering other ways of working, provided that decisions are teacher-led and teacher-centred.

The art of professionalism is to combine knowledge, experience and intuition with openness to evidence that may lead to new practice. Teachers who become members of the Chartered College of Teaching will be eligible to apply to join a Chartered Scholarship route through which colleagues will engage with others, including a mentor, about the impact of their teaching. The intention is to encourage enhanced pedagogical practice and receptivity to new ways of thinking via engagement with educational research. Members will be able to share practice via video, writing or podcast, offering a window into their classroom for truly collaborative, teacher-led CPD. These shared learning experiences will be situated within related research evidence by the College's curators, thereby stimulating further interest and debate.

Achieving Chartered Teacher Status as part of a career trajectory beyond early qualification, and onwards to master's level or PhD work within universities, will raise the bar of teacher professionalism. Work will take place with learned societies and subject associations to ensure that their important contribution to teacher development is celebrated and enhanced still further. Part of the success of a profession-led system will be reflected in the numbers of post-doctoral colleagues employed to teach within our schools.

Questioning, restlessness and humility

A profession formed of colleagues that recognise the value of restless questioning and self-reflection resists mediocrity. Currently, whenever educational issues present, there is a tendency towards obstructive polarisation. It is my contention that informed dialogue in a trusted environment is a useful means to expand ideas and practice. Too often in education, the loudest or most powerful voices hold sway. The value of the Chartered College of Teaching will be to present a diverse range of informed opinion, underpinned by sound evidence rather than by ideological standpoint.

For too long, politicians and others have sought silver bullet solutions to school improvement. As professionals, we need to accept that although there are no easy answers, research in fields like cognitive psychology is beginning to contribute very powerful and useful evidence to support effective teaching. The aim of the Chartered College is to raise the bar of expectation for reflective practice. Contending with still-developing evidence is part of the challenge of being a great teacher. To be a true professional is to celebrate ongoing lifelong reflection and study, with openness and readiness to mentor others.

Technology now allows us to conceptualise ways of taking big research ideas and 'polluting' them through classroom practice. Such polluted research can then be reframed and explored further through the benefit of classroom reality. When teachers are research literate, they are capable of healthy cynicism; a combination of both evidence and day-to-day classroom reality forms a powerful mix. This is the bridge between research and practice that we finally need to build. No longer should it be the case that educational research is detached from teachers' experience. Nor should it be the case that those outside the classroom lead on the next generations of research questions and design. Greater partnership is needed, in order that English schools may gain global recognition for their openness to innovation, fuelled by relentless ambition to find a way through for every learner. Enhanced teacher expertise is the solution to the so-called 'standards' debate.

Inventiveness allowing for creativity

Within schools and colleges, too much fear of external accountability threatens to wring the neck of creativity. Schools, colleges and universities must reclaim an ethos of endless possibility. Our education system needs to become far more open and permeable. It would be energizing and transformative if school buildings became much less about keeping students in, and much more about welcoming communities to learn alongside students. New formations of all-through schools are becoming more common and open up greater possibilities for teachers to work across phases and to learn from their peers in diverse settings.

Schools as lifelong centres of scholarship at the heart of communities offer hope and endless possibilities. One such is the newly built University of Cambridge Primary School, which seeks to offer opportunities for children of differing ages to learn alongside each other within the wider context of a university community. The prospect of PhD students engaging in dialogue about specific aspects of the curriculum with young children is interesting and important. Similarly, the University of Birmingham Secondary School is working to link secondary pedagogy with university practice. The richer our opportunities to collaborate, the more likely it is that we will build a cohesive, informed and authoritative profession.

The digital Knowledge Platform of the Chartered College of Teaching will be populated with thematic research studies alongside compelling examples of school-based practice. This provides the energizing prospect of teachers learning from each other both within and across schools – to offer teachers the experience of witnessing the impact of innovation on practice.

Importantly, it is planned in the longer term to establish regional funds to form a resource for bids from individual teachers for secondment, sabbatical or international study. An independent, co-operative fund for the profession presents a hugely liberating opportunity to build teacher agency and wellbeing. When local and national organisations, individuals and community groups can be persuaded to invest in these regional funds, society will send a powerful message to the education system about how much teachers are valued and supported in their ambition to engage in further study. This would serve as a generous long-term investment in the wellbeing and flourishing of our young people.

Persistence and professional courage

Moving away from a blame culture means moving into an opportunity culture, where groups of colleagues and clusters of schools can seek to enhance quality through collaboration without reference to league tables. Membership of the

Chartered College of Teaching will enable individuals in schools across the country to experience the collective courage achieved from an influential and powerful network.

Self-regulation and peer review within and between schools offers a meaningful alternative to routine external inspection by Ofsted. Within a more courageous education system, my vision is that we would be braver about sharing examples of innovative impactful pedagogy. External inspection could be reduced to a body that intervened in exceptional circumstances with an expectation that local solutions would be found through collaboration and support rather than blame. Turning accountability on its head in response to a self-managing system would relieve the burden of fear and release energy for collective improvement. This opens the possibility of schools routinely gaining recognition for ambitious approaches that go beyond test scores towards building a life-changing, non-deterministic culture of high expectations.

Emotional stability enabling risk-taking

We need a humane approach to supporting leaders, teachers and pupils. This requires us to shift the narrative of teaching and learning away from a deficit model. Telling a positive story about the profession starts with the way we view ourselves. Within staffrooms, corridors and at conferences we are too reluctant to celebrate success and more likely to discuss worries and concerns. When the Chartered College of Teaching has established the benefits of opening classrooms to showcase achievement, classroom practice will become a shared art rather than a lonely performance. Sharing is the antidote to isolation and wellbeing is enhanced when we feel appreciated.

Recently, Research Schools have been announced across England in addition to over four hundred teaching schools. The increasing expectation that teachers will organize professional learning, mentor trainee teachers and offer school support is a welcome way of building confidence and recognition that the means for improvement lie within schools and colleges themselves.

Research partnerships with universities offer another rich seam of information to help teachers understand how they can engage with school-based enquiry to examine and refine practice. These developments work most effectively when teachers know they are valued and trusted to engage collaboratively with enquiry. Examples of this have notably occurred across the country as groups of colleagues have gathered together to determine local assessment policies and strategies to report curricular progress. Confidence leads to questioning, to debate and to greater capacity to challenge assumptions and accepted norms of behaviour.

Generosity that welcomes difference and diversity

Teaching is a complex and challenging role that deserves recognition and respect. There are no easy solutions to the range of workload issues that dominate teachers' lives, but working within a profession where colleagues are respected and trusted would go a long way to improving the experience of teachers as they progress through their careers.

We belong to an unequal society, living and working in communities that are hugely diverse and complex. No two schools or classrooms are the same, but they have much in common. Teachers benefit from opportunities to plan, teach and assess collaboratively. The Chartered College aims to provide opportunities to work together both virtually and face to face within regions, nationally and internationally. The advantage of technology is that no teacher need ever feel isolated in her practice.

As we necessarily shift from traditional white, male, middle-class images of those who hold sway in education, movements to empower women and BAME teachers and leaders in education can only be better supported through the new networking possibilities the College presents.

Empathy offering mutual supportiveness

The final *Learning without Limits* disposition of empathy is powerful in the essential move beyond blame towards a collective endeavour for system-wide success. Stories of individual children, teachers, schools and networks achieving excellent outcomes need to become much more prominently celebrated. The groundswell of Saturday conferences across the UK organised for mutual benefit rather than profit is testament to the impact of teacher agency. Improvement achieved through collective ambition and shared expertise has the potential to build empowerment. Within enabling environments, leadership teams learn to expect the best, instead of fearing the worst.

In schools that have moved away from 'monitoring' towards shared high expectations of professionalism, research lesson study often provides a helpful structure for triads of teachers to build targeted strategies to support individual pupils within a class. Models of collaborative lesson study such as this provide a means for colleagues to share their collective knowledge to help each other, instead of grading each other. This powerful shift away from judgement to collective enquiry focusing on impact on pupils' learning is a welcome means to shift educational discourse away from labels towards expertise.

Too idealistic?

An alternative vision for our profession that builds on the principles and dispositions of *Learning without Limits* is necessarily optimistic and radically different. Does this mean it is too idealistic or impossible to achieve? Our profession is made up of a vast body of colleagues who arrive in school every day wanting to work with young people to help them learn as much as they possibly can. It is time we enabled our profession to be inspired and supported – to be treated this way, too. As the new leader of the Chartered College of Teaching it is my aim to create an organisation that begins to shift the culture away from blame towards celebration, away from fear towards hope and away from despair to delight. This cannot be achieved by one organisation alone, but I believe we can begin to link with others to illustrate what can be achieved through profession-led collaboration in the spirit of a collective endeavour that goes far beyond politics and policy. Only by enabling teachers to do what they love as informed experts can we truly enable every child to achieve their full potential. Our teaching profession deserves to be liberated; indeed, we deserve, just as our pupils do, to be expected to learn without limits.

References

DfE (2016) *Standard for Teachers' Professional Development*. [online] Available at https://www.gov.uk/government/publications/standard-for-teachers-professional-development. Retrieved 03/06/2017.

DfE (2011) *Teachers' Standards Guidance for School Leaders, School Staff and Governing Bodies*. [online] Available at https://www.gov.uk/government/uploads/system/uploads/attachment_data/file/301107/Teachers__Standards.pdf. Retrieved 03/06/2017.

Hart, S., Dixon, A., Drummond, M. J., & McIntyre, D. (2004) *Learning without Limits*. Maidenhead: Open University Press.

Peacock, A. (2016) *Assessment for Learning without Limits*. London: McGraw-Hill International.

Swann, M., Peacock, A., Hart, S., & Drummond, M. J. (2012) *Creating Learning without Limits*. Maidenhead: McGraw-Hill International.

Strode, M. (1903) Wind-Wafted Wild Flowers, in *The Open Court: Devoted to the Science of Religion, the Religion of Science, and the Extension of the Religious Parliament Idea*, Volume 17, Number 8 (August). Reprint. London: Forgotten Books, 2016.

Part III

The teachers' manifesto

Ethical agency

JL Dutaut and Lucy Rycroft-Smith

Despite the connotations of a manifesto, this book has aimed throughout to stay above Left/Right divides. This manifesto is equally suited to the collective, grassroots tendency of Leftist politics and to small-government principles of the Right. Equally, we have steered a course that transcends the traditionalist/progressive rift of educational philosophy. It calls on the empowerment of all teachers, regardless of their persuasion in this regard. Chiefly, if we have achieved these aims at all, it is because our stance is one of pluralism and our objective is to make education more democratic, which supersedes the strictly political and promotes a philosophical pragmatism.

As we have argued so far, flipping the system must be founded on the empowerment of every teacher as an evidence-informed and collaborative professional. The third dimension of this professionalism is an ethical agency, an active stance towards the forces that shape education. Teachers, as professionals, are or ought to be engaged with educational purpose as much as they are with its outcomes. Indeed, how else to evaluate outcomes except in the context of a stated purpose? But if we are to be a profession, then we must have agency in determining these purposes (for they are, in fact, plural).

The politics of change

With regards to political forces, **d'Reen Struthers** explores the deleterious effect upon teachers of being trapped between a state of resistance – opposing mandated practices that bring no benefit to themselves or their students – and one of resilience – acquiescing to those same practices to focus their efforts on managing their effects on workload and students. As a teacher–educator, d'Reen describes the disempowerment felt by many as they qualify to become teachers, and the hope that qualification will bring a change.

Phil Wood goes on to describe the dromological pressure created by the political cycle, and to offer school-based solutions to slow down time through lesson study. In this way, he argues, at least at school level, new policies and initiatives can be implemented thoughtfully and sustainably.

Headteacher **Rae Snape** reflects d'Reen's and Phil's concerns as she describes how constant political reform brings precious little positive change in teachers' professional status, and precious little time to manage change in teachers' mandated practices. She urges her colleagues in leadership to protect their staff by investing in their professional development and putting the school's ethos at the forefront of its practice.

The philosophy of action

In philosophy, an action is always performed by an agent, with intention. In a sort of Cartesian turn, **Simon Gibbs** explores the beliefs teachers hold about themselves as agents, and about their students, and the impact these have on their work and students' outcomes. Having shown the importance of self-efficacy beliefs, Simon suggests that the current paradigm of reform focused on performativity is a case of the treatment killing the patient.

Ross Hall offers an alternative: an education founded on principles of empowerment and wellbeing, with schools returned to their communities to be more adaptive, more inclusive, more human. In her view from a pupil referral unit, **Jackie Ward** charts the effects of failing to change course, with rising exclusions and dwindling resources for support.

Simon Knight shows us what we can learn from special schools – from their innate ethos of inclusivity, and from their necessary embrace of both progressivism and traditionalism to meet each student's needs. Simon shows that schools and school systems need not mandate a philosophical direction. On the contrary, he argues, our philosophical direction must emanate from the students themselves, and professionalism comes from remaining flexible in our thinking and in our practices.

With examples from their work through the HertsCam Network, **David Frost**, **Sheila Ball** and **Sarah Lightfoot** round off this section by showing how an ethos of non-positional teacher leadership offers a practical means to bring about change at the institutional level through greater professionalism.

Demand ethical agency

The teachers' manifesto demands that teachers engage and be empowered to engage in the political and philosophical dimensions of their work, with the power to choose and amend their actions accordingly. This must include:

- Teacher engagement with professional ethics, including the creation of an ethical code of practice;
- Qualifying and professional standards that require evidence of engagement with educational purpose;
- Working conditions that make possible the continued attainment of such standards;

- Teacher engagement at every level in the design and implementation of policy that requires any change in:
  - The political or philosophical framing of their practice;
  - Measures impacting on workload and cognitive load;
  - The manner of their being held accountable for their performance.
- Accountability measures for all stakeholders and policy-makers at all levels that require a commitment to, and the monitoring of performance in, upholding the professionalism of teachers with regard to their ethical agency as defined above.

Chapter 16

Professional resilience and wellbeing

d'Reen Struthers

"We should be aspiring to a situation where teachers are encouraged to take ownership of their professional position and wellbeing to 'thrive in' rather than simply 'survive' the profession."

As a teacher educator observing the challenges faced by primary student teachers out in schools on teaching placements or on employment-based routes, it is worrying to see that even in their initial year of 'training' [sic] there are signs of doubt about teaching as a profession; time and time again, their resilience and wellbeing are tested. I watch as new entrants struggle with authoritarian regimes in schools that demand accountable performance of them, measured via the output of their pupils. One minute, the school wants every pupil to have evidence in their books from a lesson (the rumoured advice for Ofsted visits), and the next, a new maths scheme is to be introduced, in the full knowledge (presumably) that there is book monitoring next week. All the while, the phase leader is changing the scheme for reading and there is the pressure of spelling and phonics testing trickling down to pupils to also perform to the test. And so, life in a primary school goes on …

This exercise in plate-spinning, which also includes completing assignments to demonstrate that they are meeting the standards expected to achieve qualified teacher status, leads many of these young graduates to struggle. Their health and work–life balance is often at risk. I work regularly with people perplexed at what they experience as poor leadership and management in schools. They find themselves caught in the trap of wanting to protect their pupils from the consequences of these demands, while feeling the pressure to be compliant and accountable for their actions. Yet, they continue to perform at the necessary standard consistently across the year to be accepted into teaching, in the hope that professional status will eventually free them from this incessant performativity. These are moral dilemmas, experienced daily by new teachers who feel torn between maintaining a job and maintaining their professional integrity. These experiences of stress are described by Zukas (2011), as "crossing, transitioning, translating" role-defined boundaries. In essence, they are part of the process by which trainees learn to identify as 'real' teachers, but are they necessary?

Once considered part of the classical professions, teachers' domains of work have traditionally (1) had an orientation towards the promotion of human wellbeing – what I shall term 'othering' and will return to later; (2) drawn on a highly specialised body of knowledge and skills; and (3) been contextualised in relation to concepts of authority and trust (Freidson, 1994). It is easy to see how this definition applies to traditional professionals (doctors, lawyers, priests), and why, over time, there have been moves to make the professions more democratic and accountable, including in the field of education. Perhaps uniquely, though, the neoliberal language, values and practices perpetuated by the free-market and competitiveness-at-all costs economy (Apple, 2000; Hursh, 2007) have led to a prevailing policy view of teaching as a technical craft, easily learnt on the job, without need to engage with a critical theoretical body of knowledge. There has been a 'policy turn' away from "a predominant focus on specifying the necessary knowledge for teaching, toward specifying teaching practices that entail knowledge and doing" (McDonald et al., 2013, p. 378). Authority and trust have been eroded too, so that with the marketisation of education, students or pupils have become clients, knowledge a commodity to be 'transferred' and all sight of the 'public good' dismissed in favour of global economic considerations. Biesta (2016) reminds us that turning schools into small businesses distorts what education is about and significantly undermines the ability of teachers to be teachers and of schools, colleges and universities to be educational institutions (p. 87).

Still further, externally imposed school accountability systems have become a common element of the UK education system, with central government-led policies tied closely to the OECD's PISA data. With test scores disaggregated to students, teachers and schools, there is evidence that they directly affect the morale of teachers exponentially (Dworkin, 2009). This disaggregation of results frequently means that praise or blame can be ascribed to individual teachers and schools. Underlying assumptions suggesting that low student achievement is a product of incompetent teachers have led to high-stakes accountability initiatives to end failing schools; a narrative of raising teacher 'quality' has impacted directly on policy approaches to teacher recruitment, training and curricula, resulting in increases in teacher workloads (Hargreaves, 1994) and what Apple (1987) termed the 'deskilling' of teachers. However, to attract high-quality teachers, recruitment drives the promotion of the job as 'inspirational', a chance to 'give something back' and an effort in social justice (DfE, 2017), while brushing aside the significant everyday challenges teachers face. Despite the rhetoric, the latest figures suggest attracting new teachers into the profession with such promises is not working (Ward, 2017).

With the tension between what is healthy and sustainable for individual teachers increasingly set against the needs of the institutions they work in, teacher educators must also grapple with resilience's counter-concept: resistance. The question for my colleagues and me is whether we teacher educators should be seeking to prepare teachers for the way schools are (adapting to institutions) or focus on preparing new professionals for the ways schools could and should be (transforming institutions)?

Evidently, an overemphasis on resistance could leave teachers and teachers-to-be unable to find or hold a position in schools (Ingersoll, 2001). At a time of concerns about teacher retention and sustainability, this is of vital significance. Certainly, there are concerns that the hyper-focus on resilience within international teacher education research and practice is detrimental to both individual teachers and the teaching profession as a whole (MacBeath, 2012). Surely what we want are teachers who can both work in the current teaching profession *and* improve it: this calls for a clarity about how we use the terms 'resilience and wellbeing' and requires us to create and engage in opportunities to go beyond the mere replication of practice to a more critical engagement with the *contexts* of practice.

Ratner (2013), drawing from the field of cultural psychology, describes this as a macro–micro phenomenon, where conditions that are often perceived to be intra-psychological (e.g. stress and depression) are actually rooted in social and institutional structures and processes. It is evident that already too much focus, responsibility and blame is placed on teacher characteristics, and not enough on the power of the environment, structure and the array of situational factors that impact the work of teachers.

Specifically, teacher burnout and resilience can be viewed from two different perspectives. The clinical (or psychological) approach argues that some teachers have better coping skills or personalities that allow them to resist the negative effects of stress. Burnout is seen as a personal malady resulting from the inability to cope with stress and the stressors associated with the role. What arises from the tendency to 'blame' the victim of burnout is the need to suggest ways to enhance coping skills, offering stress management, holistic health care and even yoga (Celoline, 1982; Pines, 1993). By contrast, the sociological approach considers how not only structural and organisational variables themselves can serve as stressors to induce burnout, but also that change in structures and organisations may be necessary to promote teacher resilience. If burnout is seen as a form of work role alienation, then ways schools as organisations can mitigate stress and facilitate coping might seem a more strategic response. However, school environments can diminish teachers' perceived self-efficacy, threatening wellbeing (Johnson et al., 2014), especially when educational reforms mandate excessive conformity (Alexander, 2011).

When seen as an umbrella term for the ability to bounce back and manage conflicts, adaptability, commitment, flexibility, motivation, positivity and optimism, teacher *resilience* can easily become the goal of teacher retention. However, when over-emphasised by teacher educators and system leaders, this definition can too easily be presented as a set of coping mechanisms to promote wellbeing, while in fact it primarily benefits the institution at the expense of the teacher, leading to unsustainable professional tensions. When resilience is explained as "positive adaption despite adversity" (Bottrell, 2009), almost inevitably, individualised explanations of human problems and their suggested amelioration, as a consequence, lead us to psychologise and patholo-gise human problems. For the purpose of this article, I use the definition from Pemberton (2015, p. 2), who describes resilience in relation to human behaviour as

> the capacity to remain flexible in our thoughts, feelings and behaviours when faced by a life disruption, or extended periods of pressure, so that we emerge from difficulty stronger, wiser and more able.

Significantly, here is explicit reference to positive change for the betterment of the individual, as opposed to compliance to the status quo for the needs of the institution.

Teacher wellbeing, too, can be viewed from both an individual and social perspective. While wellbeing can be associated with an innate desire to reach one's full potential (Ryan and Deci, 2001), it has also been noted that indi-vidual satisfaction and wellbeing can influence others, contributing to a more collective, inclusive sense of the concept (ibid.). The psychological concept of wellbeing is often accompanied in education by an emphasis on physi-cal, emotional, mental and spiritual fulfilment. Mental wellbeing, specifically, is linked to a limited conceptualisation of perceived stimulation in teachers' professional lives.

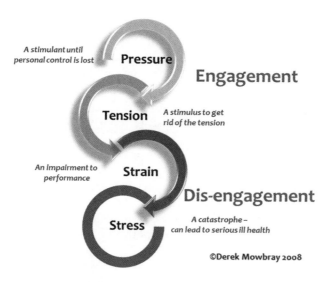

Figure 16.1 Psychological distress is at the wrong end of deteriorating psychological wellbeing (Mowbray, 2008).

The possibilities for teachers and teacher educators

The challenge for teacher educators is *how* to support and promote teacher wellbeing: should they encourage teachers to own their professional responsibilities or support them to manage and cope with them? Often, it can feel like suggesting the compartmentalisation of the 'professional' and 'personal' selves, which runs the risk of teacher burnout, of physical and emotional exhaustion, coupled with a mental distancing from one's professional life. This is relevant to the English context, where educational reform initiatives demand excessive conformity from teachers, supplanting efforts to continually renew the practice of teaching (Alexander, 2011). There are now a plethora of routes into teaching, with a predominance of school-led programmes of ITE. By implication, this means the focus is on inducting a new teacher into a particular school culture and habitus, rather than the teaching profession more generally, as offered by the traditional university routes (Struthers, 2013). Thus, the ultimate determinants of a teacher's success and the implied expectations of a professional educator remain malleability and resilience, while any focus on their work situation is effectively negated. This typically exemplifies instances where "teachers are expected to manage their professional responsibilities rather than developing their own professional judgement" (Margolis et al., 2014, p. 394).

We should be aspiring to a situation where teachers are encouraged to take ownership of their professional position and wellbeing to 'thrive in' rather than simply 'survive' the profession (Johnson et al., 2010). Underlying this approach is the belief that teachers need to develop their 'voice' and to have more agency in their workplace. While there are clinical strategies to support teachers to adopt a sense of agency and to depersonalise negative experiences, which usually involve one-to-one approaches to the development of coping skills, many teacher educators would not be trained for this work; nor does this approach attack the organisational or structural problems that teachers experience in school. More cost effective would be for schools to introduce social support networks and practices that did not stifle teacher enthusiasm. Perhaps changing the measure of school accountability to a more value-added approach rather than using test pass rates could be one approach, especially as we know that some pupils do less well on standardised tests. However, what is obvious is that blaming and holding teachers to account for shortcomings in the learning outcomes of their pupils ignores the reality that factors outside the control of the schools often exert a significant effect upon pupils' knowledge acquisition. While teacher educators can support this, ultimately the school as the employing institution may not choose to engage with their workforce in these ways, instead feeling the pressure to put their best teachers with those pupils who are struggling, further impacting on teacher morale.

From Australia, a *Framework of Conditions Supporting Early Career Teacher Resilience*, arising from research with new teachers and coordinated from across the continent, offers a refreshing social constructionist approach to resilience by disrupting and diverting attention away from concerns over early career teachers' individual problems. Instead, it takes a positive view about what it is that enables professional competence to develop, looking at the "factors and transactions of individual experience and tracing their constitution in social relations, societal discourse and ideological positions" (Johnson et al., 2010, p. 533). There is also an explicit challenge to the normative criteria used to assess so-called resilience in newly qualified teachers. The framework identifies five themes: policies and practices, teachers' work, school culture, relationships and teacher identity. Both teacher educators and teachers can therefore contemplate the way a teacher's reality is located in the context of policy and ideological demands, and framed by teachers' own moral qualities, which drive their interactions with their pupils.

To understand why this is an important step in the right direction, it is necessary to return here to the idea of 'othering' as a fundamental aspect of teaching as a profession. Like healthcare workers, priests and counsellors, the job of teaching involves putting the interests of others at the forefront, scaffolding the learning and development of pupils. Framing teaching in a technocratic context poses a moral challenge to teacher–pupil relationships, and restricts individuals' ability to make informed, professional judgements drawn from research-informed practice. When teacher agency is silenced and, as shown in Figure 16.1, the stimulant pressure shifts beyond personal control to become an overwhelming stress, not only is it harder to employ individual strategies to solve problems, but even when deployed, these strategies are less effective. Collective practice, through professional learning communities, peer groups, mentoring, coaching and other forms of social networks, can offer useful support, and hint at the kind of system within which professionalism in education can thrive.

In this context, it is evident that school–university partnerships are necessary for the development of a rigorous academic framework to develop innovative programmes of initial teacher education. Such programmes should take as a starting point the link between individual and institutional wellbeing. They must make critical engagement with the very idea of professionalism in education a consistent aim and give more prominence to transition. Finally, their focus must be unwaveringly on developing pedagogies consistent with sustainable workload and long-term effectiveness. Only such criticality has the power to unite voices in mutually supportive networks, and to protect education from policy decisions and political agendas whose purpose or effect might be to undermine the purpose of education in a democracy.

References

Alexander, R. (2011). Evidence, Rhetoric and Collateral Damage: The Problematic Pursuit of 'World Class' Standards. *Cambridge Journal of Education*, 41, 265–286.

Apple, M. (1987). The De-skilling of Teachers. *In:* Bolin, F. S. & Falk, J. M. (eds.) *Teacher Renewal: Professional Issues, Personal Choices.* New York: Teachers College Press.

Apple, M. (2000). Between Neoliberalism and Neoconservatism: Education and Conservatism in a Global Context. *In:* Burbles, N. C. & Torres, C. A. (eds.) *Globalization and Education: Critical Perspectives.* London: Routledge.

Biesta, G. (2016). Good Education and the Teacher: Reclaiming Educational Professionalism. *In:* Evers, J. & Kneyber, R. (eds.) *Flip the System: Changing Education from the Ground up.* Oxon: Routledge.

Bottrell, D. (2009). Understanding 'Marginal' Perspectives: Towards a Social Theory of Resilience. Qualitative Social Work, 8, 321–339.

Celoline, A. L. (1982). *Job Burnout in Public Education: Symptoms, Causes and Survival Skills.* New York: Teachers College Press.

DfE (2017). *Get in to Teaching* [online]. Available: https://getintoteaching.education.gov.uk/life-as-a-teacher [accessed March 2017].

Dworkin, A. (2009). Teacher Burnout and Teacher Resilience: Assessing the Impacts of the School Accountability Movement. *In:* Saha, L. & Dworkin, A. (eds.) *International Handbook of Research on Teachers and Teaching.* New York: Springer Science.

Freidson, E. (1994). *Professionalism Reborn: Theory, Prophecy, and Policy.* Chicago, IL: University of Chicago Press.

Hargreaves, A. (1994). *Changing Teachers, Changing Times: Teachers' Work and Culture in the Postmodern Age.* London: Cassell.

Hursh, D. (2007). Assessing No Child Left Behind and the Rise of Neoliberal Education Policies. *American Educational Research Journal,* 44, 493–518.

Ingersoll, R. (2001). Teacher Turnover and Teacher Shortages: An Organizational Analysis. *American Educational Research Journal,* 38, 499–534.

Johnson, B., Down, B., Le Cornu, R., Peters, J., Sullivan, A. M., Pearce, J. & Hunter, J. (2010). Conditions that Support Early Career Teacher Resilience. *In:* Paper, R. (ed.) *Australian Teacher Education Association Conference.* Townsville, Qld.

Johnson, B., Down, B., Le Cornu, R., Peters, J., Sullivan, A., Pearce, J. & Hunter, J. (2014). Promoting Early Career Teacher Resilience: A Framework for Understanding and Acting. *Teachers and Teaching,* 20, 530–546.

MacBeath, J. (2012). *The Future of the Teaching Profession.* Brussels: Education International Research Institute and the University of Cambridge, Faculty of Education.

McDonald, M., Kazemi, E. & Kavanagh, S. (2013). Core Practices and Pedagogies of Teacher Education a Call for a Common Language and Collective Activity. *Journal of Teacher Education,* 64, 378–386.

Margolis, J., Hodge, A. & Alexandrou, A. (2014). The Teacher Educator's Role in Promoting Institutional Versus Individual Teacher Well-being. *Journal of Education for Teaching,* 40, 391–408.

Mowbray, D. (2008). *Building a Psychologically Healthy Workplace. The Manager's role in resilience.* (Presentation). [Online]. Available at https://www.iosh.co.uk/~/media/Documents/Networks/Branch/Midland/East%20District/Past%20events/D%20Mowbray%20The%20managers%20role%20in%20resilience.pdf. Retrieved 03/10/2017.

Pemberton, C. (2015). *Resilience: A Practical Guide for Coaches.* Berkshire: Open University Press.

Pines, A. (1993). Burnout: Existential Perspectives. *In:* Schaufeli, W. B., Maslach, C. & Marek, T. (eds.) *Professional Burnout: Recent Developments in Theory and Research.* Washington DC: Taylor and Francis.

Ratner, C. (2013). Macro Cultural Psychology: Its Development, Concerns, Politics, and Direction. *In:* Gelfand, M., Chiu, C. & Hong, Y. (eds.) *Advances in Culture and Psychology*. New York: Oxford University Press.

Ryan, R. & Deci, E. (2001). On Happiness and Human Potentials: A Review of Research on Hedonic and Eudaimonic Well-being. *Annual Review of Psychology*, 52, 141–166.

Struthers, D. (2013). (Disturbing) New School–University Partnerships. *In:* Beckett, L. (ed.) *Teacher Education Through Active Engagement; Raising the Professional Voice*. London: Routledge.

Ward, H. (2017). Recruitment Fears Increase as Number of Teacher Trainees Drops by Almost 7 per cent. *TES* [online]. [Accessed 26th March 2017].

Zukas, M. (2011). Making a Mess of Boundaries: A Tale of Doctors, Blue Forms and Educational Research (Keynote). *Australian Association for Research in Education Conference*. Hobart.

Chapter 17

Lesson study

An approach to claiming slow time for professional growth

Phil Wood

"Teaching's intellectual nature has been replaced by a simplistic, technical one – to deliver predetermined and packaged materials created by others."

Introduction

Over the past 15 years, policy development in English education has seen an ever-more acute acceleration. This acceleration was first identifiable under New Labour and 'deliverology', an ideology which demanded ever-faster rises in national examination results. Driven by this need for higher attainment, increasing numbers of complex policy initiatives were developed, including school self-evaluation, personalised learning, curriculum innovation and diplomas. Since 2010, government has continued to accelerate policy development. Much of the educational landscape has seen radical change, sometimes untried and untested, sometimes not even making it to final implementation before being abandoned or changed. This chapter begins by arguing that more time is needed to encourage 'slow thinking' through professional discussion, curriculum and pedagogic development. Lesson study is then outlined as a potential vehicle for such slow work, based on collaboration and debate and focused on improving teacher practice.

Paul Virilio, urbanist and cultural theorist, defines social and political acceleration, particularly relating to technology, as 'dromology' (literally 'the logic of speed'): a compression of time as a consequence of changes in geopolitics, technology and the media. Virilio sees greater generation and use of data as a recipe for disinformation and confusion. Politicians are able to hide, embed or control issues, as "speed is power itself" (Virilio, 1999, 15). As policy generation compresses over time, those outside of government are in a constant state of reaction, attempting to understand and analyse new sets of ideas as the next policy is already being announced. By instigating reform at a very fast pace, a Secretary of State essentially creates a 'power-grab' – the sheer velocity of change eroding debate, ensuring less resistance and short-circuiting the democratic process. In addition, the media become the dromological troops of politicians (Eriksen, 2001), feeding off the accelerated context in which they work.

Eriksen reflects on the dromological impacts of modern society by arguing that what he calls 'fast time' increasingly drives out 'slow time'. The former is in part characterised by a need to react to, and prioritise, increasing flows of information. The latter allows for deliberation, thought, debate and reflective ways of working, which are integral to the educative process, yet are slowly disappearing from our education system. Eriksen identifies six problems with this shift. Speed is addictive. It leads to over-simplification and a loss of precision in favour of Taylorist assembly-line processes. Paradoxically, speed demands space (consider your email inbox!), so it saves no time. As a result, it spreads like a contagion, killing off slow time.

In education, these effects are all too obvious. Recourse to ever-more complex data systems allows rapid generation of targets and tracking sheets, as a result of which quantitatively tracked 'learning' and 'progress' have in some instances displaced professional dialogue and reflection. Data systems are 'fast' processes; they give simplified snapshots of a complex process, but from a process philosophical perspective, this leads to the problem that a series of flows are collapsed into simplistic 'events'. The consequence of these developments is that the acceleration of education has in part gone hand-in-hand with ever greater reliance on numeric data, both internal and external.

The dromological impact of social and political change might lead us to believe that we need to make faster, better decisions and changes. The constant speeding up of reform, demands for rapid progress and an increasing focus on the short-term have served to blunt critical capacities, to surrender professional and community debate to ever more rapid production of – and enslavement to – numeric data. This analysis supports Hargreaves and Fullan's (2012, p. 14) description of the 'business capital' model of education. They argue that the focus on data and adherence to an 'outputs' model of education may lead to a view of teachers and teaching which assumes that good teaching:

- may be emotionally demanding, but it is technically simple;
- is a quick study requiring only moderate intellectual ability;
- is hard at first, but with dedication can be mastered readily;
- should be driven by hard performance data about what works and where best to target one's efforts;
- comes down to enthusiasm, hard work, raw talent, and measurable results;
- is often replaceable by online instruction.

The business capital model makes sense of teaching's de-professionalisation: its intellectual nature has been replaced by a simplistic, technical one – to deliver predetermined and packaged materials created by others.

Hargreaves and Fullan (2012) offer an alternative view of the process of education, both in school and at policy level, through the concept of 'professional capital'. This educational perspective is based on seeing teachers as valued professionals who require time and resources to develop and perfect their professional skills and thinking. This approach is developed through the exercise of particular approaches to professional learning, which includes the emergence of collaborative endeavour. Professional capital is not driven by a top-down model dictated by senior leaders fulfilling their own agendas or those of government, but is facilitated by senior leaders giving teacher groups the space to exercise their own professional judgement. In short, it is a dialogic approach which attempts to make great pedagogy a community asset, overcoming the deadening hand of 'pedagogic solitude' (Shulman, 1993), where teachers work independently and rarely discuss pedagogy with others. From this perspective, data are still important, but act as the starting point for discussion and development, not as a numeric yoke under which teachers are expected to toil.

Teachers need to operate in fast time – it is inherent to the job – but they also need significant opportunity for periods of 'slow time' to act individually and collaboratively to affect positive change in the contexts in which they work. There are a number of different ways in which the utility of slow time can be realised: creating professional learning communities, coaching and mentoring or practitioner investigation. Here, I explore lesson study as one possible approach to utilising slow time, using focused, collaborative activity to develop professional practice and pedagogic literacy (Cajkler and Wood, 2016), rather than pressuring individual teachers to perform better, often to a prescribed formula.

The case of lesson study

Lesson study is an approach for improving student learning and teacher pedagogy through the collaborative development of lessons (Dudley, 2011; Fernandez et al., 2003; Lewis, 2009; Lewis et al., 2006). The basic method centres on a group of teachers working together to identify a learning challenge faced by students, which then becomes the focus for improving teaching and learning in that area, opening up the "pedagogic black box" (Cajkler and Wood, 2015) for discussion, reflection and evaluation.

Lesson study originated in Japan over 100 years ago, and developed as an approach to pedagogic development. Initially, it remained unknown beyond Japan but has since developed across the world as a teacher-led method for gaining pedagogic insights and developing expertise (Stigler and Hiebert, 1999). It is now widely used in Hong Kong, Singapore, China, Malaysia, Indonesia, the USA and many parts of Europe. There is no single, correct way to carry out lesson study, as even in Japan variations emphasise different parts of the process. However, some core aspects of the method appear to be invariant and necessary. These include the idea of collaborative work, deep consideration of learning and pedagogy, the productive use of observation and opportunity to evaluate both the process and evidence for changes in student activity and learning. Figure 17.1 shows an outline of the stages of a basic lesson study cycle.

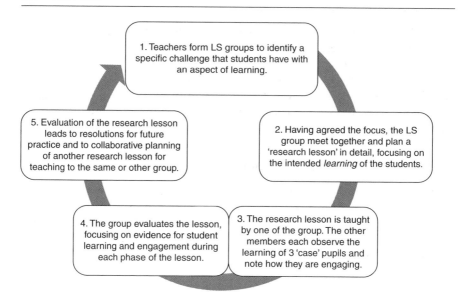

Figure 17.1 Stages of the lesson study cycle.

This basic lesson study cycle can be altered for use in different contexts and with different age groups. Our own research has covered work with colleagues from primary, secondary, college and university contexts. In each case professional and learning cultures differ, and as such, the detail of the process changes to fit those cultures. However, central to the use of lesson study is the opportunity for teachers to work together to understand and develop learning, based on collaborative endeavour and dialogue. Importantly, the cycle often occurs over several weeks, and as such allows for reflection and debate; it is a process which establishes the opportunity to operate in slow time and thus open up opportunities to extend human capital, through a decisional and collaborative focus. This brings with it the opportunity for greater professional agency in developing understanding of student learning through greater decisional capital in planning and evaluative work.

The research carried out by the Lesson Study Research Group at the University of Leicester has shown several positive impacts emerging from teacher engagement with lesson study.

Making space and time for discussion about learning and teaching

In a system that constantly relates work to data and outcomes, critical space and time for teacher-determined discussion of teaching and learning can be lost. Establishing regular opportunities for reflection and development – unhindered by performative narratives – can have high value, allowing for deeper critical engagement with pedagogic issues. Because the emergence of new insights within lesson study can take place over an extended period, multiple ideas are shared by different members of the group. The collaborative meetings, central to planning and evaluation, allow for rich dialogues to occur, leading to sharing good pedagogic practice beyond the specific approaches finally chosen for the lesson. Participants in our research regularly comment on the positive impact that having time to discuss pedagogy, focused on a point of common interest, has had on their wider practice.

Reasserting a sense of professionalism and agency

The acceleration and volume of work in schools can result in a feeling of reduced agency and professionalism as teachers become passive recipients of rapid and constant changes in policy, often filtered and mediated by senior leadership teams. The use of approaches such as lesson study can begin to redress this balance to a degree by devolving to teachers more opportunities for decision making, especially in identifying challenges faced by their students. In turn, these insights act as the basis for professional discussions concerning planning, execution and evaluation. This greater professional freedom helps, over a period of time, to build greater pedagogic expertise and allows new insights relevant to practice to emerge. Crucially, as the value of these insights is realised, so the process is reinforced and leaders disincentivised from interfering. Any decay in decisional capital to meet organisational requirement rather than pedagogic need will erode the process. Conversely, effective lesson study erodes leadership by diktat.

Making formative and positive use of observation

Recent changes within the school system and Ofsted have led to a move away in (some) schools from linking classroom observation to performance management. However, there is still widespread use of observations focused on teachers and teaching. There is no doubt that this can be important in helping colleagues develop practice, and can be both positive and supportive, particularly as part of mentoring and coaching frameworks. Lesson study, however, uses an almost diametrically opposed approach to observation, with learning and student activity being at the core of the process. As such, it is a basis for the growth of both human and social capital.

In some of the schools we have worked with, the introduction of lesson study has brought a wider cultural shift in the perception of observation, even when lesson study is not being used. Where previously teachers were reticent towards observation, having mainly experienced it as a performative tool, many have come to see it as a formative opportunity to discuss and support colleagues. The use of observation, in these schools, has become far more discursive, more reflective and more focused on improving practice, rather than as a tool for measurement.

Affective impacts on teacher groups

Across a number of the projects we have worked on, a recurring theme has been the affective impact the use of lesson study has had as a slow education process. There is anecdotal evidence of more general teacher talk concerning pedagogy in informal times and spaces, and a greater feeling of 'togetherness' as shared interests and approaches begin to develop.

Opening up the pedagogic black box

Within a lesson study approach, teachers are not only afforded the opportunity to engage with colleagues in a deep and consistent dialogue about learning, but are also encouraged to offer suggestions, leading to a legitimate and active input to the development of the pedagogy for research lessons. In this way, lesson study is a process which opens up the 'pedagogic black box', identifying and discussing pedagogy as a complex, emergent, holistic set of processes, better understood through in-depth discussion between collaborating teachers, each of whose experience and ideas are afforded credibility and potential.

Challenges

As the reflections above suggest, lesson study as a vehicle for pedagogic development – conceived as slow time for professional reflection and discussion – is an effective way to develop professional capital. However, whilst these positive impacts have been reported by teachers, it is no panacea. There are a number of issues of sustainability and approach which present challenges to using lesson study.

Firstly, across all our research, the issue of time is a recurring theme. Lesson study is not a quick process; this is one of its key strengths. It takes time to identify an area for development, to develop a collaborative approach, to carry out the resultant lesson and evaluate it. With the time pressures inherent in the English education system, this can make using the approach problematic. If lesson study is to thrive, there needs to be full support from a school's leadership team to protect this time and space for such debate and development. This requires an initial effort of professional trust, and where lesson study is at its most successful is where it has been embedded into the culture of the school progressively.

Another potential problem which traditional lesson study may suffer from is an over-reliance on observation as a tool for capturing and understanding the process of learning in a lesson. In the basic cycle outlined above, the majority of the evidence for an evaluation comes from observation of students during the lesson, and whilst some practitioners and researchers attempt to develop research lessons which will make the learning process 'visible', much will remain hidden. As Nuthall (2007, p. 158) argues,

> how students learn from classroom activities is not simply a result of
> teacher-managed activities, but also the result of students' ongoing

relationships with other students, and of their own self-created activities or use of resources.

As a consequence, we always advise participants in lesson study to triangulate their observations with other sources of evidence. Where possible, either informal or formal interviews with students are a useful source of information – stimulated-recall interviews the most useful – but even this approach is imperfect. Student work and attainment remain the all-important benchmark. With this caveat in place, the technique can still open up useful reflections on the processes undertaken by students.

The third, and perhaps most important challenge for lesson study, is embedding it into the culture of a school. Perhaps one of the reasons the process appears to offer so much in schools in Japan is because it is an embedded element of the school system. When new initiatives are presented by government, lesson study groups often play a role in establishing the changes at school level in a coherent fashion. Teacher professionalism and slow time are integral to the Japanese education system in a way that they aren't in England.

Conclusion

Education in England has been under dromological pressure at least since the inception of the National Curriculum in 1988, with more and more policy used as a lever to bring faster and faster change. But how far has this brought us in terms of increased academic achievement? With ever greater incursion of private interests into education too, the education system is breaking apart organisationally, professionally and politically. We are accelerating into an uncertain future, with little reasoned debate or consensus-building. At such a juncture, when the only clear message is that reform is needed, it is important that we provide time for teachers to gain sustained opportunities for professional growth, that we invest in their professional capital. To do this well, we need to expand the amount of slow time available for focused reflective and constructive activity. When so much of the work in schools is carried out by necessity in fast time, it is the investment in slow time and professional growth which will give firm foundations for action. This approach will not feed an event-hungry political class, and it does not promise increased examination outcomes in a matter of weeks, but if developed through the adoption of frameworks, of which lesson study is but one example, it will form a better basis for our country's education system than anything dromology has to offer.

References

Cajkler, W., and Wood, P. (2015). Lesson Study in Initial Teacher Education. In P. Dudley (ed.), *Lesson Study: Professional Learning for Our Time*, pp. 107–127. London; New York: Routledge.

Cajkler, W., and Wood, P. (2016). Lesson Study and Pedagogic Literacy in Initial Teacher Education: Challenging Reductive Models. *British Journal of Educational Studies*, 64(4), 503–521. Available at http://www.tandfonline.com/doi/abs/10.1080/00071005.2016.1164295

Dudley, P. (2011). *Lesson Study: A Handbook*. Available at http://lessonstudy.co.uk/wp-content/uploads/(2012)/03/Lesson_Study_Handbook_-_011011-1.pdf [accessed 20 January 2017]

Eriksen, T. H. (2001). *Tyranny of the Moment: Fast and Slow Time in the Information Age*. London: Pluto Press.

Fernandez, C., Cannon, J., and Chokshi, S. (2003). A U.S.–Japan Lesson Study Collaboration Reveals Critical Lenses for Examining Practice. *Teaching and Teacher Education*, 19(2), 171–185.

Hargreaves, A., and Fullan, M. (2012). *Professional Capital: Transforming Teaching in Every School*. London: Routledge.

Lewis, C. (2009). What Is the Nature of Knowledge Development in Lesson Study? *Educational Action Research*, 17(1), 95–110.

Lewis, C., Perry, R., and Murata, A. (2006). How Should Research Contribute to Instructional Improvement? The Case of Lesson Study. *Educational Researcher*, 35(3), 3–14.

Nuthall, G. (2007). *The Hidden Lives of Learners*. Wellington: NZCER Press.

Shulman, L. S. (1993). Teaching as Community Property: Putting an End to Pedagogical Solitude. *Change*, 25(6), 6–7.

Stigler, J., and Hiebert, J. (1999). The Teaching Gap: Best Ideas from the World's Teachers for Improving Education in the Classroom. New York, NY: The Free Press.

Virilio, P. (1999). *Politics of the Very Worst*. New York: Semiotexte.

Chapter 18

Only connect

Resisting the winds of change

Rae Snape

"Rather than being Lemmings of Despair, we must be Flamingos of Hope."

I have been a member of the Primary Headteachers' Reference Group at the Department for Education since 2010. This has been an incredible privilege which has allowed me some insight into how policy is created. I joined the last time Government was in purdah, a strange limbo land between educational paradigms. When waiting for Headteacher colleagues to arrive from across the country and for the reference group meeting to start, it is always interesting to look at the photographic chronological display of the Secretaries of State for Education going back to 1964, and to think about what each brought with them; which fresh biases, what new edicts to impose on teachers and schools. Each name conjures up something different: Thatcher, Williams, Joseph, Clarke, Baker, Blunkett, Morris, Balls, Gove, Morgan. With each term in office lasting on average only a couple of years, and with each Minister having the mandate to introduce their own educational priorities, this creates a constant upheaval in our schools and our profession. I have never understood why a more efficient cross-party agreement can't be reached as to what makes a happy and successful education for young people in our country. A consensus approach could be sustained for longer periods, and would bring stability and security to the nation's teaching workforce and its young people.

With all the continual chopping and changing, teachers have become so destabilised that they are constantly looking outward for the magic medicine, without realising they are not even sick in the first place. For this reason, I feel we should resolve to be the positive antidote for educators, children and society. Rather than being Lemmings of Despair, we must be Flamingos of Hope. Advocating for happiness, humour, hope, creativity, connection, psychological safety and optimism are key. If we are going to encourage others to join our noble, elegant and rewarding profession, we must manifest schools as exciting, brilliant, joyful, beautiful and unpredictable places that celebrate the uniqueness of the individual.

When the school I am headteacher of had their last Ofsted visit, along with a number of encouraging things, the senior inspector said that The Spinney was "forward thinking and outward reaching." We have built on this mantra over the years, proactively connecting with national and international organisations as a means to improve learning outcomes and opportunities not only for our pupils, but for the teaching team, too. This has ensured that both our curriculum and professional development are as leading edge and innovative as possible. The huge range of Spinney partnerships have included Cambridge Primary Review Trust, Whole Education, Mind Up, Random Acts of Kindness, STEAM Co, Cambridge University Faculty of Education, PEDAL, EmpathyLab and Anglia Ruskin University, as well as Ashoka Changemaker Schools and Schools as Learning Communities in Europe.

The Spinney became an Ashoka Changemaker School in 2015, and in doing so joined the biggest global network of social entrepreneurs, and over 200 other Changemaker schools. The aim of the network is to identify, connect and support innovative schools that are empowering young people with the skills and confidence to make the world an even better place. There are 14 other Ashoka Changemaker Schools in England; a large wall display in the Spinney manifests our shared aims to promote change-making through a curriculum that encourages compassion, curiosity, communication, creative and critical thinking, innovation and making, collaboration and local and global citizenship.

> At the Spinney, we know that our curriculum must be thoughtfully designed because it is a gift we give our pupils to take into the future, a gift we will never see them fully open.

The Spinney's curriculum is well-rounded, holistic and creative; however, we are equally aware that since English children are among the most tested in Europe, we need to give them the skills and knowledge to ace the tests. We describe ourselves as pragmaticians: we train for the test and we teach for life. The world can be a complex, challenging, chaotic place; our aim at The Spinney is to give our young people the knowledge, capabilities and virtues to confidently navigate an uncertain future and to follow their dreams.

Sir Ken Robinson, co-author of Creative Schools, is one of the supporters of the Ashoka Changemaker Schools global network. This is his take on education:

> The aim of education is to enable students to understand the world around them and the talents within them so that they can become fulfilled individuals and active, compassionate citizens.
>
> (Robinson and Aronica, 2015)

The Spinney is also a pathfinder school for SEAS4ALL which, in partnership with Barcelona University and CREA (Community of Researchers on

Excellence for All), supports Schools as Learning Communities in Europe. This partnership has also had a positive and profound impact on our curriculum and pedagogy. Led by Professor Ramón Flecha, SEAS4ALL builds on the evidence of other educational researchers and philosophers, including Max Weber, Jürgen Habermas, Lev Vygotsky, Pierre Bourdieu and, in particular, Paulo Freire's Pedagogy of Hope.[1]

> Education must begin with the solution of the student–teacher contradiction, by reconciling the poles of the contradiction so that both are simultaneously teachers and students.
>
> (Freire, 1993, p. 72)

The principle of Schools as Learning Communities is based on the successful implementation of a number of key educational activities, underpinned by fundamental human values. The values (including humanity, kindness, equity, democracy, cooperation and solidarity) prompt us to reflect deeply about how we can best organise our curriculum to promote pro-social skills, and future-proofed learning, as well as securing high standards and optimal academic outcomes so that all our pupils succeed. An example of one of these successful educational actions is dialogic literary gatherings. A DLG is a whole class activity which requires the group to pre-read an extract or chapter of an adapted classic text such as *The Odyssey*, *Don Quixote* or *The Tempest*, and assemble in a circle to discuss, debate and share ideas and opinions.

As the children and teachers have become more familiar with DLGs, the quality of their egalitarian dialogue has improved wondrously – relationships have been strengthened and comprehension and reading skills have improved simultaneously. Classic texts prove a stimulating prompt for the children to discuss the human condition, and they have explored a wide range of themes such as love, body image, fear, television culture, relationships and death.

Despite constant revisions, I remain excited and optimistic about the future of education as more and more teachers and schools are encouraged to move from isolation to connection, to authentic meaningful collaboration, and through this to realise the honest art of being human.

> We want an education system based on hope not fear, one that appreciates the humanity of human nature.
>
> —Professor Yong Zhao[2]

The winds of policy change may be inevitable and relentlessly blow strong, but, though we may bend a little in the breeze, we must not uproot the tree. Rather, we must branch out to connect with others and for the sake of the children and our colleagues send our roots down further to ensure our beliefs, vision and values prevail and sustain us in uncertain times.

#OnlyConnect

Notes

1 For more information on the SEAS4ALL project, see Freire, P. (1993) *Pedagogy of the Oppressed*. New York: Continuum Books.
2 Quoted by Helena Marsh (@HelenaMarsh81) on Twitter. Available at https://twitter.com/HelenaMarsh81/status/818559130147364869. Retrieved 04/06/2017.

References

Flecha, R. (Ed.) (2015) *Successful Educational Actions for Inclusion and Social Cohesion in Europe*. New York: Springer Briefs in Education.
Robinson, K. and Aronica, L. (2015) *Creative Schools*. London: Penguin.

Chapter 19

Inclusion and teachers' beliefs in their efficacy

Simon Gibbs

"Beliefs that teachers hold (both about themselves and their students) are important, are vulnerable to influence, and [...] significant differences follow in terms of classroom practice and outcomes for the children."

Introduction

What we believe about ourselves affects what we do and how we do it. What we succeed in doing today affects our beliefs about what we can do in the future: our sense of self-efficacy (Bandura, 1997; Simmons et al., 1999). What we believe we can or should do is also partially determined by our psychological environment (Cho & Shim, 2013; Gibbs & Powell, 2012; Roeser, Midgley, & Urdan, 1996). Further, and despite some illusions that we are sole determinants of our actions, whatever we do, we do not do alone. We are part of interlinked human, social systems, interacting and in dialogue with others. Others help create the selves that we believe we are and are able to be (Sampson, 2008).

In this chapter, I set out some of the parameters for teachers' beliefs, and relate what is known about key aspects of the nature of teachers' beliefs, motivations and practices to the psychological environments for teaching. In doing so, I will draw attention to the potential constraints or inconsistencies between what teachers might believe is their core purpose or capability and what is actually permitted or encouraged (with reference to the work of Festinger, 1962; and Seligman, 1972). What teachers believe is possible for them to do affects what they do, the nature and quality of the education they provide and their motivation and determination to succeed – or otherwise. The chapter is grounded in concerns about teachers' well-being, the evidence of the likely causes and consequences of teachers' stress (Kokkinos, 2007; Skaalvik & Skaalvik, 2011, 2016), as well as a wish to support the development of educational practices that are more inclusive of difference and diversity. The main purpose of the chapter is, therefore, to examine how teachers' beliefs about what they can do to achieve specific educational outcomes (their self-efficacy as teachers) are influenced by their psychological and organisational contexts (Goddard & Goddard, 2001; Ross & Gray, 2006).

Amongst the most relevant and immediate contexts for teachers' practices are government policies regarding education and schools, and the yet more immediate contexts of individual schools. Further, while the effects of stress factors for teachers and consequent attrition are not unique to the UK, the focus here is on issues that are particularly pertinent in the UK, and England in particular.

Teachers' efficacy beliefs

We may hope and assume that all who train to be teachers truly want to teach and educate young people – albeit for varying reasons (Klassen, Al-Dhafri, Hannok, & Betts, 2011; Tang, Cheng, & Cheng, 2014). It is also evident that teachers who are strongly motivated to develop and improve their practice are likely to inculcate similar motivations in their students (Schiefele & Schaffner, 2015). Teachers with positive beliefs in their efficacy, believing they know what is necessary to achieve specific desired outcomes, are more likely to achieve these outcomes for the children in their classrooms (Caprara, Barbaranelli, Steca, & Malone, 2006; Tournaki & Podell, 2005). Teachers' efficacy beliefs have been shown to be positively related to superior outcomes in specific subject areas (see, for example, Tschannen-Moran & Johnson, 2011) as well as teachers' survival in the profession (Schwarzer & Hallum, 2008; Skaalvik & Skaalvik, 2014, 2016). Teachers' beliefs in their efficacy are also associated with the development of more inclusive practice in mainstream classes by, for example, accepting greater responsibility for the education of children with identified and significant special needs, reducing segregation or exclusion because of problematic behaviour and, in general, accepting and understanding diversity (Ekins, Savolainen, & Engelbrecht, 2016; Gibbs & Powell, 2012; Savolainen, Engelbrecht, Nel, & Malinen, 2012).

In addition to the substantial body of work devoted to understanding the nature and effects of individual teachers' efficacy beliefs, conceptual and empirical research has shown how the collective efficacy beliefs of school staff are closely associated with the ethos of schools, the development and transformational effects of leadership and beneficial outcomes in terms of motivation, attainment and well-being for both students and staff (Goddard, Kim, & Miller, 2015; Moolenaar, Sleegers, & Daly, 2012).

Teachers (individuals and staff groups) gain their efficacy beliefs mainly from experiences of success (direct first-hand experience, as well as observed (vicarious) experience (Bandura, 1997, 1998; Wolters & Daugherty, 2007), and within environments that foster professional reflection and transformational learning that generate changes in the learner beyond expectation (Angelle & Teague, 2014; Black, 2015; Gibbs & Miller, 2012; Kurt, Duyar, & Çalik, 2011). Of course, it is something of a truism that success breeds success, but if we start with the premises that teachers want to be successful and that successful education depends on successful teachers, we do then need to think about what helps teachers be successful and what, if anything, hinders that. One of the answers offered to this question refers to teachers' perceptions of the environment for education; another answer that is sometimes offered refers to the perceived 'nature' and background of children.

Education for all: inclusivity

There is an apparently natural and insatiable need (in Western cultures at least) to objectify, classify and categorise phenomena – and people. There are a number of factors (several enshrined in legislation and policy) that influence and encourage categorisation within education. In the UK (but by no means only in the UK), children may find themselves categorised in a number of ways that affect where and how they are taught. (It might also be remembered that until the early 1970s in the UK, it was not required that all children could/should be educated. Up to the passing of the 1970 Education (Handicapped Children) Act, children who were, on the basis of a medical examination, considered to be 'mentally deficient', were not fully entitled to education.) Children's age, 'ability', gender and religious faith may be used to determine the type of school they attend. The labels that are used to categorise them (ostensibly often to describe their perceived 'special' educational needs) can also influence how and where they are taught and what teachers believe they can to do to help them. Such categorisation of children continues to influence teachers' conceptualisation of their role and competency with regard to certain groups. Thus, it has been found that teachers may hold firm views about whether or not they know how, or are prepared, to teach children with specific 'disabilities' (Jordan & Stanovich, 2003). Such beliefs can be easily influenced. It has, for instance, been known for some time that teachers' expectations of children generate self-fulfilling outcomes. Thus, in an experiment when children were arbitrarily described as being more likely to do well, they achieved better outcomes than their peers who had not been assigned that label (Friedrich, Flunger, Nagengast, Jonkmann, & Trautwein, 2015; Harris & Rosenthal, 1985; Rosenthal & Jacobson, 1968). More recently, we found that just the arbitrary use of a particular label ('dyslexia' vs 'reading difficulties') created significant differences in teachers' beliefs about the essential nature of children's educational difficulties and their efficacy beliefs about being able to intervene significantly with such children (Gibbs & Elliott, 2015).

So, in summary, it is important to recognise that the beliefs that teachers hold (both about themselves and their students) are important, are vulnerable to influence and that significant differences follow in terms of classroom practice and outcomes for the children. So what of the current educational environment and context, how may these affect the beliefs teachers hold and what may be the effects of these 'environmental' and systemic factors in practice for teachers and children?

Government policies: context and consequences

The UK is currently home to one of the biggest gaps in the world between the earnings and wealth of the richest and poorest in society (Dorling, 2014, 2015; Wilkinson & Pickett, 2010). It has been estimated that some 3.7 million (28%) children are living in poverty in the UK (CPAG, 2015). It is evident that the socio-economic status of families can profoundly affect children's readiness for school, ultimate levels of attainment, employment prospects and life-span (Hills, 2015). However, despite a lack of evidence to warrant their value as means of ensuring greater social mobility and inclusion, current government policy appears to be to promote educational structures and systems that in reality only perpetuate social and economic stratifications (Ayscue & Orfield, 2016; Hattie, 2009; Piketty, 2000; Tranter, 2012; Triventi, 2013) that, *inter alia*, will generate or reinforce expectations about the educational potential of groups of children. As I write, the new Conservative government under Theresa May's leadership is ardently promising the development of new grammar schools. These, we are told, are intended to promote 'social mobility'. The available evidence suggests it is more likely to enhance the 'Matthew Effect' – the rich get richer and the poor get poorer.

In pursuit of government policy, schools continue to be subject to intense scrutiny, competition and increasing pressure from marketisation (Allen, 2015; Bunar & Ambrose, 2016; Wright, 2012). For teachers (and schools), the culture of performativity adversely affects the quality of professional relationships and yields self-serving compliance (Ball, 2003; Hardy & Lewis, 2016; Jeffrey, 2002; Perryman, 2006). The regular and frequent inspection of schools by Ofsted often generates more heat than light, and for many schools and teachers serves only to perpetuate a fear of failure. Interestingly, in this respect at least, the government seems to recognise the potentially adverse effects of labelling. Thus, schools that 'fail' are most often closed and rebranded (else who would want their child to attend – who would want to work in – a school that was labelled as a failure?) (Gorton, Williams, & Wrigley, 2014; Nicolaidou & Ainscow, 2005). As one commentator has noted of Government strategies that are publicly intended to raise standards in schools:

> Those factors that impede improvement are constant outside interference, and detailed external control and inspection. Factors which help improve standards include teachers' feelings of ownership and responsibility over change, and the sense of the school as a centre of change, changes that happen over time rather than at once.
>
> (Cullingford, 2013, p. 3)

Currently, therefore, it seems likely that factors that impede school improvement prevail over factors that might be more beneficial for schools, teachers and young people. There is evidence that external inspection is more likely to have negative than positive effects for teachers, both as individuals and as members of staff teams. Thus, the pressure to perform for Ofsted is too often "damaging emotionally and professionally … [and] may reduce trust, inhibit discussion of difficulties and diminish honest self-evaluation" (Hopkins et al., 2016, p. 59).

There is a growing consensus that the determination of recent UK governments to push through their reforms "leaves a demotivated teacher workforce, [and] a possible impending teacher recruitment crisis" (Allen, 2015, p. 36). Psychologically, a persistent fear of failure and the perception that there is little that individuals or groups can do to avert failure can lead to a sense of passive helplessness that is often associated with professional burn-out and depression (Fincham & Cain, 1986; Maier & Seligman, 2016; Schonfeld & Bianchi, 2016). The phenomenon of 'learned helplessness' was first reported by Seligman (1972), who in a series of experiments on animals and humans showed how when repeatedly unable to control unpleasant circumstances ('aversive stimuli'), participants typically become passive, depressed and 'helpless', unable to do anything to change or avoid the unpleasant situation. It is not hard to see how being unable to avoid repeated inspections could leave teachers feeling depressed and 'helpless'.

But what, also, of experiences of the teacher who is required to subject themselves to repeated inspection (with no formative feedback) whilst knowing in their heart it is valueless? Such 'cognitive dissonance' (Festinger, 1962) induces stress and a motivation to minimise the dissonance. At the least, this is likely to confirm that either the teacher's own views are not recognised or valued, or to deny that inspections have no merit.

Perhaps, in extremis, one of the few viable solutions for many teachers, the only apparent escape from the helplessness and dissonance, is to stop being a teacher? In fact, there is already cumulative evidence that the recruitment and retention of teachers is a significant cause for concern. Department for Education data in the academic year 2014–15 indicate that although just over 25,000 newly qualified teachers entered the profession, 43,000 qualified teachers left (DfE, 2016). Further, of those entering the profession, current trends suggest that within three years about 22% will have left teaching (DfE, 2016). Absenteeism is also a concern. In the same period (2014–15), 56% of teachers had at least one period of sickness absence, with an average of 7.6 days lost in the year for each of these teachers. Absence rates such as these (higher than the national average of 5.3 days for all employees (EEF, 2016)) are financially and educationally costly, entailing interruptions to the predictable programme for children's education and the cost of employing additional staff to cover for absent colleagues.

Counter-measures

The evidence summarised above does not lend credence to a view that the regime of inspection, accountability and performativity contributes positively to maintaining an effective and well-motivated teaching workforce – in fact, quite the reverse. It is, therefore, easy to suggest what we might *stop* doing. However, what does appear to be effective in sustaining the motivation and positive belief of teachers in the importance of teaching and education includes: high-quality leadership and management of schools, high quality teacher development, an emphasis on supportive dialogue within staff teams and between teachers and students and regular opportunities for collaboration and joint problem-solving (Brown, Gibbs, & Reid, in preparation; Gibbs & Miller, 2012; Mulholland, McKinlay, & Sproule, 2016). I will address each of these in turn – though none can stand alone. These are interdependent aspects of educational practices that benefit teachers, children and societies. For me, however, the golden thread that runs through them all and should, I suggest, be at the heart of the curriculum for all, is the quality and understanding of human relationships.

Leadership

There is now a substantial body of evidence demonstrating how leadership practices in schools and school systems not only help ensure good outcomes for students but also ensure the ongoing professional development of teachers and professional learning communities (Hallinger & Heck, 2010; Harris et al., 2013; Hopkins, Stringfield, Harris, Stoll, & Mackay, 2014). Cross-cultural comparisons also make available a radically different vision of the cultural importance and leadership of education (Hargreaves, Halász, & Pont, 2007) in which leadership and purpose are nationally shared values. Thus, in Finland for instance, "public education is seen as vital to the country's growth and security, and the shared high regard for educators who are seen as central to this generational mission, draws highly qualified candidates into the teaching profession" (Hargreaves et al., 2007, p. 14). This makes it clear that the leadership of schools is no simple vacancy-filling exercise but should be a matter of national concern for both social and economic reasons, now and in the future. As indicated and empirically validated, this requires that the leadership and management of schools be a shared and collaborative sociocultural enterprise that is in a reciprocal relationship (and dialogue) with its immediate and distal contexts (Hallinger & Heck, 2010). It may be argued that only in such circumstances can teachers professionally and personally prosper.

Collaborative work

It is implicit in the above that staff collaborate and take shared responsibility for the benefits to their professional community (Hallinger & Heck, 2010; Moolenaar, 2012; Wahlstrom & Louis, 2008). In the past, therapeutic insights have been found helpful in developing teachers' responsiveness and collaboration (Hanko, 2002), and Gibbs and Miller (2012) indicated how the collaborative work of psychologists as facilitators of teachers' understanding has been beneficial. However, an understanding of the nature of collaboration, joint exploration and learning also requires a reformulation of the nature of schools as learning organisations that are democratic, fluid and transformative (Riveros, Newton, & Burgess, 2012). This also implies that all involved in education, all those with an investment in education, need to recognise themselves as 'learners'. This underlines the centrality of dialogue as a process that enables learning about the nature of learning, about society and each other (Biesta, 2015; Sampson, 2008). Given the social, economic and cultural schisms both within our (UK) society and internationally, we need to heed the evidence about intergroup prejudice (Tajfel, 1969, 1982) and put in place educative processes that enable the development of mutual inter-group and cross-cultural understandings (see, for instance, Stephan & Stephan, 2013; Verkuyten & Thijs, 2015).

Staff development

In order to develop schools and teaching practices that provide some immunity to the corrosive effects of economic and social policies on education, and their divisive effects for children and families, staff need support to reflect and learn. There is evidence that enhancing teachers' individual and collective efficacy beliefs is productive. Schools in which staff espouse higher collective efficacy with respect to learning and behaviour have been found to buck the typical trend of exclusion, lowered attainment and minority segregation found in other schools in similar circumstances, where staff perceptions of their efficacy are depressed (Belfi, Gielen, De Fraine, Verschueren, & Meredith, 2015; Brown et al., in preparation; Gibbs & Powell, 2012). So, when staff believe and understand how they may work collaboratively with their neighbourhood communities, this helps reduce outcomes often associated with economic or social disadvantage. Whilst some responsibility for developing the ethos and culture in which efficacy beliefs can grow lies with organisational leadership, the importance of dynamic, mutually respectful and legitimating reciprocal relationships between team members and leaders cannot be underestimated in developing learning organisations (Benlian, 2013; Thomas, Martin, Epitropaki, Guillaume, & Lee, 2013; Valcea, Hamdani, Buckley, & Novicevic, 2011). In Bandura's terms, such endeavours represent 'group enablement' (1997, p. 477) that enhance organisations' staff collective efficacy.

Summary

In this chapter, I have outlined evidence about the effects of teachers' beliefs in themselves as professional practitioners. This has been contextualised by consideration of social, economic, cultural and psychological factors that have been found to affect teachers' beliefs and practices. In considering alternatives to what may restrict educational beliefs, policies and practices, I have put forward some evidence of how dialogue and better understanding of human inter-relationships might provide the foundations of an alternative schema for educa-tion – one based on the principle that a good education is profoundly rooted in humanity and relationships, and in caring for both young people and teachers, for the future of education and of society.

References

Allen, R. (2015). Education policy. *National Institute Economic Review, 231*(1), R36–R43. doi:10.1177/002795011523100105

Angelle, P. S., & Teague, G. M. (2014). Teacher leadership and collective efficacy: Teacher perceptions in three US school districts. *Journal of Educational Administration, 52*(6), 738–753. doi:10.1108/JEA-02-2013-0020

Ayscue, J. B., & Orfield, G. (2016). Perpetuating separate and unequal worlds of educational opportunity through district lines: School segregation by race and poverty. In P. A. Noguera, J. Pierce & R. Ahram (Eds.), *Race, Equity, and Education* (pp. 45–74). Switzerland: Springer.

Ball, S. J. (2003). The teacher's soul and the terrors of performativity. *Journal of Education Policy, 18*(2), 215–228. doi:10.1080/0268093022000043065

Bandura, A. (1997). *Self-efficacy: The exercise of control.* New York: Freeman.

Bandura, A. (1998). Exploration of fortuitous determinants of life paths. *Psychol. Inq., 9*, 95.

Belfi, B., Gielen, S., De Fraine, B., Verschueren, K., & Meredith, C. (2015). School-based social capital: The missing link between schools' socioeconomic composition and collective teacher efficacy. *Teaching and Teacher Education, 45*, 33–44. doi:10.1016/j.tate.2014.09.001

Benlian, A. (2013). Are we aligned … enough? The effects of perceptual congruence between service teams and their leaders on team performance. *Journal of Service Research,* doi:1094670513516673

Biesta, G. J. J. (2015). *Good education in an age of measurement: Ethics, politics, democracy.* Abingdon: Routledge.

Black, G. L. (2015). Developing teacher candidates' self-efficacy through reflection and supervising teacher support. *In Education, 21*(1), 78–98.

Brown, C., Gibbs, S., & Reid, A. (in preparation). Creating opportunities for responsibility taking: The relationship between school leadership, staff collective-efficacy beliefs and educational outcomes.

Bunar, N., & Ambrose, A. (2016). Schools, choice and reputation: Local school markets and the distribution of symbolic capital in segregated cities. *Research in Comparative and International Education, 11*(1), 34–51. doi:10.1177/1745499916631064

Caprara, G. V., Barbaranelli, C., Steca, P., & Malone, P. S. (2006). Teachers' self-efficacy beliefs as determinants of job satisfaction and students' academic achievement: A study at the school level. *Journal of School Psychology, 44*(6), 473–490. doi:10.1016/j.jsp.2006.09.001

Cho, Y., & Shim, S. S. (2013). Predicting teachers' achievement goals for teaching: The role of perceived school goal structure and teachers' sense of efficacy. *Teaching and Teacher Education, 32*, 12–21. doi:10.1016/j.tate.2012.12.003

CPAG. (2015). Child poverty facts and figures. Available at http://www.cpag.org.uk/child-poverty-facts-and-figures [accessed 13th January 2016].

Cullingford, C. (2013). *An inspector calls: Ofsted and its effect on school standards*. London: Routledge.

DfE. (2016). *SFR 21/2016: School workforce in England: November 2015*. (SFR 21/2016). London: DfE.

Dorling, D. (2014). *Inequality and the 1%*. London: Verso Books.

Dorling, D. (2015). Income inequality in the UK: Comparisons with five large Western European countries and the USA. *Applied Geography, 61*, 24–34.

EEF. (2016). Health – the key to productivity: Sickness absence survey 2016. Available at www.eef.org.uk [accessed July 2017].

Ekins, A., Savolainen, H., & Engelbrecht, P. (2016). An analysis of English teachers' self-efficacy in relation to SEN and disability and its implications in a changing SEN policy context. *European Journal of Special Needs Education, 31*(2), 236–249. doi:10.1080/08856257.2016.1141510

Festinger, L. (1962). *A theory of cognitive dissonance*. Stanford, CA: Stanford University Press.

Fincham, F. D., & Cain, K. M. (1986). Learned helplessness in humans: A developmental analysis. *Developmental Review, 6*(4), 301–333. doi:10.1016/0273-2297(86)90016-X

Friedrich, A., Flunger, B., Nagengast, B., Jonkmann, K., & Trautwein, U. (2015). Pygmalion effects in the classroom: Teacher expectancy effects on students' math achievement. *Contemporary Educational Psychology, 41*, 1–12. doi:10.1016/j.cedpsych.2014.10.006

Gibbs, S., & Elliott, J. (2015). The differential effects of labelling: how do 'dyslexia' and 'reading difficulties' affect teachers' beliefs. *European Journal of Special Needs Education, 30*(3), 323–337. doi:10.1080/08856257.2015.1022999

Gibbs, S., & Miller, A. (2012). Teachers' resilience and well-being: A role for educational psychology. *Teachers and Teaching, 20*(5), 609–621.

Gibbs, S., & Powell, B. (2012). Teacher efficacy and pupil behaviour: The structure of teachers' individual and collective efficacy beliefs and their relationship with numbers of children excluded from school. *British Journal of Educational Psychology, 82*(4), 564–584. doi:10.1111/j.2044-8279.2011.02046.x

Goddard, R., & Goddard, Y. L. (2001). A multilevel analysis of the relationship between teacher and collective efficacy in urban schools. *Teaching and Teacher Education, 17*(7), 807–818. doi:10.1016/s0742-051x(01)00032-4

Goddard, R., Goddard, Y. L., Kim, E. S., & Miller, R. (2015). A theoretical and empirical analysis of the roles of instructional leadership, teacher collaboration, and collective efficacy beliefs in support of student learning. *American Journal of Education, 121*(4), 501–530.

Gorton, J., Williams, M., & Wrigley, T. (2014). Inspection judgements on urban schools: A case for the defence. *The Urban Review, 46*(5), 891–903.

Hallinger, P., & Heck, R. H. (2010). Collaborative leadership and school improvement: Understanding the impact on school capacity and student learning. *School Leadership and Management, 30*(2), 95–110.

Hanko, G. (2002). Making psychodynamic insights accessible to teachers as an integral part of their professional task. *Psychodynamic Practice, 8*(3), 375–389. doi:10.1080/1353333021000018980

Hardy, I., & Lewis, S. (2016). The 'doublethink' of data: Educational performativity and the field of schooling practices. *British Journal of Sociology of Education*, 1–13. doi:10.1080/01425692.2016.1150155

Hargreaves, A., Halász, G., & Pont, B. (2007). *School leadership for systemic improvement in Finland*. Paris: Organization for Economic Cooperation and Development.

Harris, A., Day, C., Hopkins, D., Hadfield, M., Hargreaves, A., & Chapman, C. (2013). *Effective leadership for school improvement*. London: Routledge.

Harris, M. J., & Rosenthal, R. (1985). Mediation of interpersonal expectancy effects: 31 meta-analyses. *Psychological Bulletin, 97*(3), 363–386.

Hattie, J. (2009). *Visible learning: A synthesis of over 800 meta-analyses relating to achievement*. Abingdon: Routledge.

Hills, J. (2015). *Good times, bad times*. Bristol: Policy Press.

Hopkins, D., Stringfield, S., Harris, A., Stoll, L., & Mackay, T. (2014). School and system improvement: A narrative state-of-the-art review. *School Effectiveness and School Improvement, 25*(2), 257–281.

Hopkins, E., Hendry, H., Garrod, F., McClare, S., Pettit, D., Smith, L., … Temple, J. (2016). Teachers' views of the impact of school evaluation and external inspection processes. *Improving Schools, 19*(1), 52–61. doi:10.1177/1365480215627894

Jeffrey, B. (2002). Performativity and primary teacher relations. *Journal of Education Policy, 17*(5), 531–546. doi:10.1080/02680930210158302

Jordan, A., & Stanovich, P. J. (2003). Teachers' personal epistemological beliefs about students with disabilities as indicators of effective teaching practices. *Journal of Research in Special Educational Needs, 3*(1), n.p. doi:10.1111/j.1471-3802.2003.00184.x

Klassen, R. M., Al-Dhafri, S., Hannok, W., & Betts, S. M. (2011). Investigating pre-service teacher motivation across cultures using the Teachers' Ten Statements Test. *Teaching and Teacher Education, 27*(3), 579–588. doi:10.1016/j.tate.2010.10.012

Kokkinos, C. M. (2007). Job stressors, personality and burnout in primary school teachers. *British Journal of Educational Psychology, 77*(1), 229–243.

Kurt, T., Duyar, I., & Çalik, T. (2011). Are we legitimate yet?: A closer look at the casual relationship mechanisms among principal leadership, teacher self-efficacy and collective efficacy. *Journal of Management Development, 31*(1), 71–86.

Maier, S. F., & Seligman, M. E. P. (2016). Learned helplessness at fifty: Insights from neuroscience. *Psychological Review, 123*(4), 349–367.

Moolenaar, N. M. (2012). A social network perspective on teacher collaboration in schools: Theory, methodology, and applications. *American Journal of Education, 119*(1), 7–39.

Moolenaar, N. M., Sleegers, P. J. C., & Daly, A. J. (2012). Teaming up: Linking collaboration networks, collective efficacy, and student achievement. *Teaching and Teacher Education, 28*(2), 251–262. doi:10.1016/j.tate.2011.10.001

Mulholland, R., McKinlay, A., & Sproule, J. (2016). Teachers in need of space: The content and changing context of work. *Educational Review, 69*(2), 181–200. doi:10.1080/00131 911.2016.1184131

Nicolaidou, M., & Ainscow, M. (2005). Understanding failing Schools: Perspectives from the inside. *School Effectiveness and School Improvement, 16*(3), 229–248. doi:10.1080/ 09243450500113647

Perryman, J. (2006). Panoptic performativity and school inspection regimes: Disciplinary mechanisms and life under special measures. *Journal of Education Policy, 21*(2), 147–161. doi:10.1080/02680930500500138

Piketty, T. (2000). Theories of persistent inequality and intergenerational mobility. *Handbook of Income Distribution, 1*, 429–476.

Riveros, A., Newton, P., & Burgess, D. (2012). A situated account of teacher agency and learning: Critical reflections on professional learning communities. *Canadian Journal of Education / Revue canadienne de l'éducation, 35*(1), 202–216.

Roeser, R. W., Midgley, C., & Urdan, T. C. (1996). Perceptions of the school psychological environment and early adolescents' psychological and behavioral functioning in school: The mediating role of goals and belonging. *Journal of Educational Psychology, 88*(3), 408–422.

Rosenthal, R., & Jacobson, L. (1968). Pygmalion in the classroom. *The Urban Review, 3*(1), 16–20. doi:10.1007/BF02322211

Ross, J., & Gray, P. (2006). Transformational leadership and teacher commitment to organizational values: The mediating effects of collective teacher efficacy. *School Effectiveness and School Improvement, 17*(2), 179–199. doi:10.1080/09243450600565795

Sampson, E. E. (2008). *Celebrating the other: A dialogic account of human nature.* Chagrin Falls, Ohio: Taos Institute Publications.

Savolainen, H., Engelbrecht, P., Nel, M., & Malinen, O.-P. (2012). Understanding teachers' attitudes and self-efficacy in inclusive education: Implications for pre-service and in-service teacher education. *European Journal of Special Needs Education, 27*(1), 51–68. doi:10.1080/08856257.2011.613603

Schiefele, U., & Schaffner, E. (2015). Teacher interests, mastery goals, and self-efficacy as predictors of instructional practices and student motivation. *Contemporary Educational Psychology, 42*, 159–171. doi:10.1016/j.cedpsych.2015.06.005

Schonfeld, I. S., & Bianchi, R. (2016). Burnout and depression: Two entities or one? *Journal of Clinical Psychology, 72*(1), 22–37. doi:10.1002/jclp.22229

Schwarzer, R., & Hallum, S. (2008). Perceived teacher self-efficacy as a predictor of job stress and burnout: Mediation analyses. *Applied Psychology, 57*, 152–171. doi:10.1111/j.1464-0597.2008.00359.x

Seligman, M. E. P. (1972). Learned helplessness. *Annual Review of Medicine, 23*(1), 407–412. doi:doi:10.1146/annurev.me.23.020172.002203

Simmons, P. E., Emory, A., Carter, T., Coker, T., Finnegan, B., Crockett, D., … Labuda, K. (1999). Beginning teachers: Beliefs and classroom actions. *Journal of Research in Science Teaching, 36*(8), 930–954. doi: 10.1002/(SICI)1098-2736(199910)36:8-930::AID-TEA3-3.0.CO;2-N

Skaalvik, E. M., & Skaalvik, S. (2011). Teacher job satisfaction and motivation to leave the teaching profession: Relations with school context, feeling of belonging, and emotional exhaustion. *Teaching and Teacher Education, 27*(6), 1029–1038. doi:10.1016/j.tate.2011.04.001

Skaalvik, E. M., & Skaalvik, S. (2014). Teacher self-efficacy and perceived autonomy: Relations with teacher engagement, job satisfaction, and emotional exhaustion *Psychological Reports, 114*(1), 1–10.

Skaalvik, E. M., & Skaalvik, S. (2016). Teacher stress and teacher self-efficacy as predictors of engagement, emotional exhaustion, and motivation to leave the teaching profession. *Creative Education, 7*(13), 1785.

Stephan, W. G., & Stephan, C. W. (2013). Designing intercultural education and training programs: An evidence-based approach. *International Journal of Intercultural Relations, 37*(3), 277–286. doi:10.1016/j.ijintrel.2012.05.001

Tajfel, H. (1969). Cognitive aspects of prejudice. *Journal of Biosocial Science, 1*(S1), 173–191.

Tajfel, H. (1982). *Social identity and intergroup relations.* Cambridge: Cambridge University Press.

Tang, S. Y. F., Cheng, M. M. H., & Cheng, A. Y. N. (2014). Shifts in teaching motivation and sense of self-as-teacher in initial teacher education. *Educational Review, 66*(4), 465–481. doi:10.1080/00131911.2013.812061

Thomas, G., Martin, R., Epitropaki, O., Guillaume, Y., & Lee, A. (2013). Social cognition in leader–follower relationships: Applying insights from relationship science to understanding relationship-based approaches to leadership. *Journal of Organizational Behavior, 34*(S1), S63–S81. doi:10.1002/job.1889

Tournaki, N., & Podell, D. M. (2005). The impact of student characteristics and teacher efficacy on teachers' predictions of student success. *Teaching and Teacher Education, 21*(3), 299–314. doi:10.1016/j.tate.2005.01.003

Tranter, D. (2012). Unequal schooling: How the school curriculum keeps students from low socio economic backgrounds out of university. *International Journal of Inclusive Education, 16*(9), 901–916. doi:10.1080/13603116.2010.548102

Triventi, M. (2013). Stratification in higher education and its relationship with social inequality: A comparative study of 11 European countries. *European Sociological Review, 29*(3), 489–502. doi:10.1093/esr/jcr092

Tschannen-Moran, M., & Johnson, D. (2011). Exploring literacy teachers' self-efficacy beliefs: Potential sources at play. *Teaching and Teacher Education, 27*(4), 751–761. doi:10.1016/j.tate.2010.12.005

Valcea, S., Hamdani, M. R., Buckley, M. R., & Novicevic, M. M. (2011). Exploring the developmental potential of leader–follower interactions: A constructive-developmental approach. *The Leadership Quarterly, 22*(4), 604–615.

Verkuyten, M., & Thijs, J. (2015). Multicultural education and inter-ethnic attitudes. *European Psychologist, 18*(3), 179–190.

Wahlstrom, K. L., & Louis, K. S. (2008). How teachers experience principal leadership: The roles of professional community, trust, efficacy, and shared responsibility. *Educational Administration Quarterly, 44*(4), 458–495.

Wilkinson, R., & Pickett, K. (2010). *The spirit level: Why equality is better for everyone.* New York; London: Penguin UK.

Wolters, C. A., & Daugherty, S. G. (2007). Goal structures and teachers' sense of efficacy: Their relation and association to teaching experience and academic level. *Journal of Educational Psychology, 99*(1), 181–193. doi:10.1037/0022-0663.99.1.181

Wright, A. (2012). Fantasies of empowerment: Mapping neoliberal discourse in the coalition government's schools policy. *Journal of Education Policy, 27*(3), 279–294. doi:10.1080/0 2680939.2011.607516

Empowering teachers to empower young people to live for the common good

Ross Hall

"To improve our wellbeing, we can no longer afford to do what we have always done, or follow the rules without question, or be blindly compliant."

Universal wellbeing

Embracing ideas of *happiness* and *flourishing*, striving for *universal wellbeing* must become the central purpose of education systems everywhere; a purpose which includes, but reaches far beyond, the prevailing focus on academic attainment, employment and economic contribution. Universal wellbeing is a bigger idea than the more narrowly economic standard of living, and should be thought of holistically as the aggregate of a complex set of inextricably interdependent factors that include economic, social, cultural, political and personal wellbeing – the wellbeing of all humans, of other species and of the planet at large.

Our wellbeing is permanently in flux and unfolds from moment to moment through every single human action. *Everyone* determines the quality of life.

As we move around this world and as we act with kindness, perhaps, or with indifference or with hostility toward the people we meet, we are setting the great spider web atremble. The life I touch for good or ill will touch another life, and that in turn another, until who knows where the trembling stops or in what far place and time my touch will be felt.

(Buechner, 1969)

Transformation

Striving for universal wellbeing is perhaps humanity's highest purpose: a task made increasingly urgent by unprecedented transformations we are now experiencing in almost every aspect of life. Fuelled by explosions in population growth, urbanisation and technological advancement, life today is subject to the massive forces of accelerating volatility, complexity and hyper-connectivity, forces which make our intractable tangle of human and environmental problems *everyone's* problems and increasingly difficult to address.

The ancient Greeks had two words for the concept of time: *chronos* – sequential, quantitative, chronological time – and *kairos* referring to the extraordinary periods when culture transforms qualitatively and profoundly … We are now in the midst of a *kairos* moment at the level of our entire species on a planetary scale. Transformation is inevitable and already underway.

(Wahl, 2016)

It is clear that to improve our wellbeing, we can no longer afford to do what we have always done, or follow the rules without question, or be blindly compliant. We cannot rely on an elite few to command the rest. As a matter of urgency, we need to empower *everyone* to improve our collective wellbeing. We need to empower everyone *to live for the common good*. We must fundamentally transform the *practice*, *experience* and *idea* of education.

Being and becoming empowered

Being empowered to live for the common good (sometimes called *changemaking*) involves taking responsibility, taking the lead and collaborating with others to make life better for yourself – *and* your family, friends and community – *and* humanity – *and* other species – *and* the planet. It is about the way you live your life, your choices, and the actions you take from moment to moment. Living for the common good is a way of *being* in the world. It involves *being* empathic and thoughtful, *being* curious and creative, *being* resilient and effective.

Becoming empowered to live for the common good, then, is a process of becoming *equipped* with – and *inclined* to use – a complex array of *inner powers* (inherent potentialities that are expressed through a person's actions, including the things that are variously called knowledge, understanding, skills, capabilities, competencies, capacities, strengths, qualities, dispositions, traits, habits, preferences, passions, values, beliefs, attitudes, hopes, aspirations, expectations, intuitions and so on).

Education, then, is not simply seen as the acquisition of knowledge and the development of skills, but also in terms of the development of vast and powerful potentialities inherent in the very nature of every human being.

(The Ruhi Institute, 2017)

Experience

Within the limits imposed by our genes, the *extent* to which we develop our inner powers – the extent to which we become empowered – is determined by the *experiences* we have throughout childhood and adolescence: the environments we spend time in; the people we spend time with; the things we sense, feel, think and do.

But nurturing these inner powers is rarely the focus of our attention when we are working with young people or otherwise influencing their experience. Commercial and cultural influences often pull in opposite directions. Despite good intentions, parenting is typically ill-informed and improvised. For most people, the experience of school reflects narrow conceptions of human potential and success, reveals highly individualistic and economic ambitions and reinforces compliance with the status quo.

Ecosystems

To improve our collective wellbeing – for the new world to become a *better* world – *every* young person must be provided with experiences that are:

- explicitly intended to empower them to live for the common good;
- woven together inside and outside of school;
- systematically scaffolded throughout childhood and adolescence.

We need to re-cast education systems as *learning ecosystems* in which whole communities work together to provide experiences for *every* young person in the community that ensure they become empowered to live for the common good. These ecosystems will be continuously adaptive: innovations, ideas and information will flow; communication and collaboration will be central; participation and decision-making will be open, inclusive and widely distributed. These will be *human, emergent* ecosystems.

They will leverage existing resources but will not be constrained by traditional school models. Classrooms, subjects and timetables will be more flexible; young people will have a greater voice in the system; parents will be engaged; universities will prioritise changemaking experience in their admissions practices, and provide empowering learning journeys to their students; policies will create time, space and incentives for empowering experiences. Student assessments will help young people become empowered to contribute positively; evaluations will judge the quality and success of schools and educators in terms of their effectiveness in helping young people become empowered; research will be applied effectively to mainstream innovation and good practice; technologies will maximise access to – and the effectiveness of – empowering learning experiences; and teachers will be empowered to empower young people to create a better world.

Empowering teachers

Teachers and other out-of-school educators (referred to collectively here as *teachers*) will be instrumental to imagining, building and continuously adapting these new learning ecosystems. But teachers must be better selected, trained and supported if they are to take on – and succeed in – these demanding new roles. They must be empowered *themselves* to empower young people – an idea that is in direct opposition to what many regard as a systematic *dis*-empowerment of teachers sweeping the world – and a major challenge where teacher shortages are chronic. To empower teachers at scale, we need to make wideranging changes, including:

1   Paying more attention to – and ensuring – the wellbeing of teachers;
2   Improving the status of teachers and the attractiveness of teaching;
3   Creating more routes into the teaching profession;
4   Ensuring selection and licensure of teachers are rigorous;
5   Reinventing pre-service and in-service professional learning and development to ensure that every teacher develops the knowledge, skills and inclinations they need to empower young people to live for the common good;
6   Training teachers to research, innovate and nurture better ecosystems;
7   Allowing teachers ownership of their collective professional standards, ensuring high standards and holding teachers accountable;
8   Paying fair compensation;
9   Creating career pathways that give teachers opportunities to grow professionally;
10 Trusting teachers and providing them with time and space to collaborate extensively, and to improve ecosystems.

Mechanisms and mindsets

To effect these critical changes – and to perpetuate systemic improvement – transformative innovations will be needed. New policies, rules and incentives will be required. So too will new infrastructures, processes and resources. But transformation will not come about through mechanistic changes alone – we need to shift behaviours and mindsets.

> Paradigms are the sources of systems. From them come goals, information flows, feedbacks, stocks, flows … People who have managed to intervene in systems at the level of paradigm have hit a leverage point that totally transforms systems.
>
> Meadows (1999)

Leading change

In shifting mindsets and mechanisms, teachers *must* take a lead role. But the teachers that step up to take the lead cannot do it alone and must be joined in their efforts by other change leaders from across the ecosystem – from teacher unions, teacher training institutions, universities, policy-making organisations and so on. Collective impact and collaborative professionalism will be at the heart of change.

We need to invest in building *communities* of change leaders who are fully committed to:

- Modelling the change we need to see;
- Bringing the vision to life and campaigning for change;
- Thinking and planning eco-systemically;
- Collaborating on projects with shared impact goals, impact plans, processes and resources;
- Monitoring, measuring and communicating impact and progress;
- Advancing our understanding of ecosystems, experience, becoming, being, living for the common good and universal wellbeing;
- Learning, adapting and improving together;
- Distributing participation in system change, recruiting new change leaders and growing the profession of change leadership.

It will take courageous change leaders to take on this difficult work while battling the demoralising forces that are so dominant in current systems. It would be easy to think that this will never happen. But it is already happening. Around the world, teachers and other change leaders are organising themselves with the explicit goal of empowering teachers to empower young people to strive for universal wellbeing. We have reason for hope.

References

Buechner, F. (1969). *The Hungering Dark*. New York: Harper Collins.

Meadows, D. (1999). Leverage Points: Places to Intervene in a System. The Sustainability Institute: Hartland. [online] Available at http://donellameadows.org/wp-content/userfiles/Leverage_Points.pdf. Retrieved 05/07/2017.

The Ruhi Institute (2017). *Statement of Purpose and Methods*. [online] Available at http://www.ruhi.org/institute/. Retreived 5 July 2016.

Wahl, D.C. (2016). *Designing Regenerative Cultures*. Axminster: Triarchy Press.

Chapter 21

Making a difference
The view from a PRU

Jackie Ward

"**A system that leaves starfish gasping on the beach is ineffective. A system that tells teachers to leave them there is unethical.**"

When I think about my time at my primary PRU, I am put in mind of the Loren Eiseley story (Eiseley, 1977) about a wise man who saw a younger man dancing along on the beach, throwing starfish into the water. "I must ask, then, why are you throwing starfish into the ocean?" asked the somewhat startled wise man. The younger man replied: "The sun is up and the tide is going out. If I don't throw them in they will die". "But young man, do you not realise that there are miles and miles of beach and there are starfish all along every mile? You can't possibly make a difference!" At this, the young man bent down, picked up yet another starfish and threw it in the ocean. As it met the water, he said: "It made a difference for that one".

Here we have a lyrical analogy for the perfect storm that is educational policy in England. The wise man of government decrees the fate of the little fish swimming in our educational waters, counted, labelled and packaged into mainstream, special, private; as high fliers, middling, under-achievers, non-achievers; destined for higher education, employment, the dole or NEET. All are at the mercy of deeper currents in top-down policy, with some, sadly, swimming against the tide. And what happens to those who are then washed up on the beach? Who, like the younger man, cares enough to help them back into the sea despite all incentives to the contrary?

Exclusions in my community are rising, like a flood, year on year – and we at the PRUs are like King Canute, unable to stem the tide, but hopping wildly around to pick starfish out of the sand and return them to the teeming waters of our troubled schools. Why troubled? Well, how else to describe a system that routinely casts out those who struggle in the nets of conformity? To continue with the sea imagery, mainstream schools are like commercial trawlers; they keep the uniform specimens who are biddable, get results and reflect well on the institution, but reject the differently adjusted, the challenging, those with undiagnosed needs – such as ADHD, ASD, ODD and mental health issues – often refusing to see that, for these children, these conditions exist.

When I first arrived at the PRU over eight years ago, we had a mixture of placements. Children who came on short respite often successfully returned to their mainstream schools; permanently excluded students were in the minority. Now, it is a very different story: there are no shortcuts, no Education, Health and Care Plans – and no specialist placements. Mainstream schools are beleaguered and struggle to get the specialist help that would make a difference to these children's lives; Educational Psychologists, Speech and Language specialists and CAMHS are extremely difficult to get hold of and, more and more, schools are expected to buy in provision privately, putting a massive strain on budgets. Sadly, when the end of the line is reached, and schools feel they have no alternative but to permanently exclude, this is still the cheapest option and removes the 'problem' without redress or responsibility on their part. Successive Green and White Papers have sought to make schools more accountable for their decisions, but these have remained paper-based and our most vulnerable children remain in the shadows of society and on the fringes of life itself. There needs to be a massive culture change in how we manage inclusive practices in our schools, because this cannot continue – unless we are happy to build more PRUs, more Alternative Provision, to segregate our starfish even further.

Headteachers regularly call for more of this type of provision even though it is extremely expensive for the taxpayer. A typical PRU will have approximately thirty-two children at primary level and a similar number at secondary, with no more than eight children and, at least, one teacher and one TA to a class. Realistically, more staff are needed due to the nature of the needs of our most complex children, and some require high-needs funding beyond that. I speak to many teachers who struggle on the ground to meet the needs of their pupils, and the reasons are many and varied. Ofsted is the most oft-cited, followed swiftly by 'results'. There is always a grim flurry of exclusion activity around SATs time. Then there is a lack of coordinated school support and recognition of problems by senior managers, often underpinned by a disjointed behaviour policy with different practice going on throughout the school. Most children who come to the PRU are highly anxious and struggle with any form of transition; they benefit from a structured approach which consolidates firm rules and boundaries. Our PRU has an excellent early intervention service, with a good track record of preventing exclusion, but this has been torpedoed by financial restraints and short-sightedness. So, practically, what can teachers 'on the ground' realistically do?

Well, they can ask for help. And when they get help, they need to try everything that is recommended until all options are exhausted. Often, teachers will produce a litany of 'tried that', 'done that', 'didn't work', 'haven't got time' and so on. Many times, I have gone into schools and found that there are simple things which really *do* work and I often find underlying medical needs for intervention. One child who came to our PRU with 'nothing wrong' has been diagnosed with ADHD, communication difficulties and mental health issues; she is now going through for an EHCP. Professionalism means taking responsibility at every level.

There also needs to be much more emphasis on SEN and Behaviour at ITT/ITE level. The government needs to ensure that supportive mechanisms are in place for children who struggle and their teachers. There needs to be less emphasis from Ofsted on assessment and results and more focus on well-being and mental health; it is not good enough to just pay lip service to PSHE – it needs embedding in our curriculum and teachers need to be empowered to deliver the very best they can for their most vulnerable students. If we are going to flip the system, we need to flip it *for everyone*, top to bottom. A system that leaves starfish gasping on the beach is ineffective. A system that tells teachers to leave them there is unethical.

A report by the Children's Society as far back as 2011 identified that children with SEND are much more likely to be excluded due to associated educational or behavioural difficulties. The situation becomes more difficult due to funding cuts and external pressure on schools and headteachers to 'perform' or 'improve' in meeting demanding and shifting floor targets.

We live in a fast-paced society, but we cannot afford to leave the weak and vulnerable behind. We should be delivering a curriculum that suits *all* learners rather than trying to fit square pegs into round holes; the alternative is that we will continue to fail vast swathes of our young people. Our children need to be fully prepared to function in their future lives and contribute positively to society through relationships and work; anything less is a failure to educate on our part. Exclusion has a massive effect on our children. It seems that society loves, indulges and strives to protect our kids unless they are 'naughty' – then they are fair game for wholehearted condemnation.

For a recent conference, I got permission to interview a little eight-year-old boy from our PRU, who spoke movingly about leaving the only school he had ever known and about dearly missing his friends. This child had been diagnosed with ASD and is moving to special school. I will be honest and admit both his teacher and I cried buckets. Buckets, but not enough to wash him back into the ocean. When I retired before the summer, he wrote in my memory book (his teacher told him I was going it alone as a consultant): "Hope you help children get back to mainstream school".

I think of the starfish, and I hope to be able to carry on saying: "It made a difference for that one".

Reference

Eiseley, L., (1977), *The Star Thrower*, New York: Harvest.

Chapter 22

The progressive traditionalism of special education

Simon Knight

"The inability to independently apply what has been learned would potentially compromise the value of the education they have received. It would risk their education having no currency beyond school."

In his book of aphorisms, *The Bed of Procustes*, Nassim Nicholas Taleb reflects on the human desire to address the challenges presented by the limitations of our knowledge, through the suggestion that we are

> squeezing life and the world into crisp commoditized ideas, reductive categories, specific vocabularies, and prepackaged narratives.
>
> (Taleb, 2010, p. 1)

He goes on to observe that education systems are themselves Procrustean beds, in which we place the needs of the system first and compel the children (and teachers) to fit the structures that we have created. Within the United Kingdom, this elevation of the importance of the system is apparent in a variety of ways. A system based on chronologically determined comparative judgements of capability drives much British education policy, and the impact of this on learning outcomes and life opportunities is at times highly variable. One example can be found in the data related to the movement of learners as they approach their GCSE examinations, a subject explored by Philip Nye in *Who's Left: The Main Findings*, in which it is stated that:

> Our research leads us to conclude that, in some cases, pupils are being 'managed out' of mainstream schools before this point with the effect of boosting the league table performance of the school which the pupil leaves.
>
> (Nye, 2017)

Furthermore, Nye observes that:

> outcomes for each type of mover are worse on average than they are for pupils in general who finish their secondary education at a state mainstream

school (nationally about 57% of children in mainstream schools achieved five A*-C GCSEs or equivalent including English and Maths [...] in 2014/15).

(ibid.)

This system-first rigidity can also extend to local decision making with schools – and indeed individual teachers – advocating strongly for specific approaches, articulating a pedagogical certainty based on an interpretation of the available evidence or their preferred way of educating. In special education, however, the variability and complexity of the needs of those taught acts as a perpetual challenge to a singularity of thinking and uniformity of practice. Whilst consistent values and high expectations are key, the ability to respond to the needs of the individual requires a plurality of approaches that reflect a more responsive and flexible pedagogy.

One example of this difference can be found in the way special schools have approached the debate around 'traditional' or 'progressive' methodologies. I am aware that the very nature of what is defined as traditional or progressive is part of the debate itself, so for my current purposes, I have taken the definitions and comparative statements from Tom Sherrington's excellent blog *The Progressive-Traditional Pedagogy Tree*.

> Traditional: Leaning towards an emphasis on content, structures, ordered systems, formal learning, measurable outcomes.
>
> Progressive: Leaning towards an emphasis on processes, experiences, organic systems, informal learning, intangible outcomes.
>
> (Sherrington, 2014)

So, in my experience, what characterises a special educational approach? What are the key pedagogical elements and how do they interrelate with one another? And what can the rest of the education system learn from that?

In reflecting on this, there are two central areas of consideration. The first is the curricular structure of the school and how this adjusts from one age phase to another. The second is the way in which the acquisition, consolidation, generalisation and application of knowledge are approached.

One school in which I have worked has two distinct curricula, one for pupils up to the age of 16 and one which was for pupils within the post-16 department. These are broadly focused on two different educational priorities and reflect the only point in the school where there is a distinct shift in approach: a conscious decision, carefully managed, to reflect the transition into adulthood and life beyond the school. In the main part of the school the curriculum is essentially a concept-based structure within which the focus is on the developmentally progressive acquisition of knowledge, understanding and skills. Once pupils arrived in post-16, the focus becomes more closely linked to the successful application of existing knowledge within functional community-based contexts. This is not to say that the pre-16 curriculum failed to allow for application, or that once a child reached 16 new knowledge was abandoned, but rather that the emphasis was on a movement from acquisition towards application. This can be summarised as shown in Figure 22.1, which illustrates a change in the school structures, starting from a broadly progressive approach, through one characterised by more traditional methodologies and concluding with a return to progressive modes of delivery.

However, the methodologies used within those parts of the school, I would argue, are not definitively traditional or progressive, but rather a synthesis of the two. In the Early Years, staff are working with children as young as two, all of whom have some form of complex developmental need. The nature of these needs is not always clear, and as such one of the key roles of the staff in that part of the school is the formal assessment of existing capability, to establish which areas of cognitive need are developmental priorities. This is delivered in a traditional way – making use of direct instruction, expert knowledge and repeated testing to establish understanding. Yet the provision is not just looking at the nature of intellectual development, but also the sense of development of self – to what extent the children are aware of others, can interact effectively, can operate within social structures and understand how to behave in a way that won't leave them isolated. This requires the teacher to act as facilitator and interpreter, with elements of learning being flexible and self-directed. What the staff are trying to establish is an understanding of the wider socio-emotional development of the child, and that can be well served by a less formal structure. At the same time, behavioural guidelines are being established, and this is based on a causal relationship between behaviour and consequences that has more traditional elements.

As the children move into full-time education, there is a move towards a model that is more rooted in traditional pedagogies, with the main aim being to address gaps in development and improve attainment. This is highly

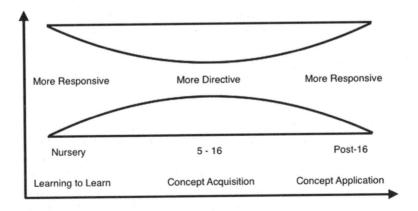

Figure 22.1 Curriculum map: from progressive to traditional and back again.

instructional and reliant on teacher expertise in both the identification of the developmental priorities and the specifics of delivery. There is a significant amount of one-to-one teaching, with the process of learning being very tightly defined and highly structured. Then, once the pupils reach Year 12 and move into the post-16 part of the school, the organisational structure has far more in common with progressive approaches, as does the way in which the staff work. There is no age-based grouping; lessons do not always have a consistently defined length, but instead can be process-based with a strong element of cross-curricular group work. For example: addressing the tasks necessary to decide what to eat, where to buy it, how to prepare it and then safely consume it. However, assessment of this is carefully structured, with tightly defined learning objectives for every young person, covering both subject-based learning and more generic personal development. There is a high level of co-construction, choice and group-based work, as the structures around learning begin to be broken down, to better reflect the contextual reality of applying the knowledge acquired and the skills learned within the wider world. This is something that many of the students within special school settings can find extremely challenging, and yet the inability to independently apply what has been learned would potentially compromise the value of the education they have received. It would risk their education having no currency beyond school.

So, in this example, the curricular and pedagogic models that have been developed reflect a movement between progressive ideas and traditional ones, making use of elements of both to best suit the needs of the pupils at any specific time and ensure the effective delivery of what is being taught.

Beyond this, it is also important to consider the pattern of learning from the point of view of the introduction of new concepts and skills. As mentioned above, this is initiated through detailed assessment of developmental need on a highly individualised basis. These individual learning needs are addressed directly by the teacher using a highly structured one-to-one approach. Once the agreed criteria for success have been reached, the teacher moves to less structured group work sessions, using varied resources and contexts to avoid conceptual understanding being tied to specific tools or activities. This is then taken further through extension work where pupils work with minimal adult intervention to ensure that what has been acquired can be applied with a high level of independence.

In many ways, the approach to teaching described starts with the traditional and becomes more progressive as the pupils demonstrate competency: a journey from traditional acquisition through to progressive application, within a curved curricular structure that starts off broadly progressive and becomes traditional before returning to the progressive. Teaching – as well as what is taught – has a fluidity that allows the teachers to maximise the potential of the exceptionally complex children that they work with. In short, it is an approach that is as progressive, or indeed traditional, as the pupils need it to be.

So, while an understanding of traditionalism and progressivism and the debates around them matter, what can be learned from special education is that they are not entirely exclusive, but complementary. A commitment to a more pluralistic approach in this example helps to ensure that not only is knowledge acquired effectively, but that it is also applied purposefully beyond the structures of formal education. After all, isn't that the real marker of a professional teacher, to engage in the debate and draw conclusions rooted in an intellectual relationship with what we do in the classroom? To put the needs of the children in front of us above our personal dogmas, to ensure that we don't place children in a pedagogical Procrustean bed.

References

Frank Wise School (2012). The Frank Wise School Curriculum Framework. (online) Available at: http://frankwise.oxon.sch.uk/school/ [Accessed July 2017].

Frank Wise School (2014). The Griffiths Centre Curriculum Framework. (online) Available at: http://frankwise.oxon.sch.uk/post-16/

Nye, P. (2017). *Who's Left: The Main Findings.* (online) Available at: http://educationdatalab.org.uk/2017/01/whos-left-the-main-findings/ [Accessed July 2017].

Sherrington, T. (2014). *The Progressive – Traditional Pedagogy Tree.* (online) Available at: https://teacherhead.com/2014/03/15/the-progressive-traditional-pedagogy-tree/ [Accessed July 2017].

Taleb, N. (2010). *The Bed of Procustes.* New York: Allen Lane.

Chapter 23

The HertsCam network

Supporting non-positional teacher leadership

David Frost, Sheila Ball and Sarah Lightfoot

"These teachers have developed the capacity to organise and create the infrastructure for school and teacher development."

HertsCam is a well-established network led by teachers themselves. It supports teachers in leading innovation in their own schools and building knowledge about teaching and learning across schools. Experienced teachers facilitate school-based support groups, teach a master's degree course and organise network activities. Participation enables teachers to lead collaborative development projects that improve the quality of teaching and learning. HertsCam's core activities include the Teacher Led Development Work (TLDW) programme, the MEd in Leading Teaching and Learning programme and the Networking programme, which includes international engagement.

The TLDW programme supports teacher leadership in primary, secondary and special schools by enabling teachers and other educational practitioners to plan and lead projects designed to develop the quality and effectiveness of aspects of teaching and learning in their own schools. Each participant designs and leads their own development project over the course of one academic year. Successful completion leads to the award of the HertsCam Certificate in Teacher Leadership. TLDW groups are facilitated by members of the HertsCam Tutor team, all experienced teachers.

Like TLDW, the MEd in Leading Teaching and Learning programme is designed, planned and taught entirely by practitioners. This two-year, part-time programme enables teachers to plan and lead development projects in their schools. The MEd differs from the TLDW programme in that it requires a high level of scholarship and critical analysis drawing on relevant literatures and domains of knowledge.

The Networking programme includes a series of six Network Events each year and the Annual Conference. Typically, between 50 and 150 teachers participate in each event by presenting their development projects or leading workshops. Towards the end of the academic year, the entire network comes together for the Annual Conference.

The concept of non-positional teacher leadership

HertsCam recognises the potential of all teachers to exercise leadership as part of their professional role. In 2014, a book arising from the work referred to above was published. *Transforming Education Through Teacher Leadership* (TETTL), edited by David Frost, contains 18 chapters: accounts of teacher leadership which, collectively, explicate a theory about teacher professionality and educational transformation through teachers' narratives and accounts of their leadership practice. The theory of non-positional teacher leadership is illustrated in Figure 23.1.

The rhetoric of teacher leadership was adopted by HertsCam as a way of transcending the limitations of concepts such as continuing professional development, practitioner research and action research. 'Teacher leadership' seemed to have the potential to be more empowering. In formulating our understanding, we were drawn to Fullan's argument that every teacher is an agent of change, and that such agency is part of being 'new professionals' (Fullan, 1993). This is expressed well by teacher Val Hill in TETTL:

> (we) propose that leadership could be a dimension of all teachers' professionality ... we argued for an approach to teacher leadership, which does not assume that leadership is linked with positions in the organisational hierarchy of the school. Instead it recognises the potential of all teachers to exercise leadership as part of their role as a teacher. [...] In HertsCam and the wider International Teacher Leadership (ITL) network, we argue that [leadership] should be seen as an essential part of teachers' professionality.
>
> (Hill, 2014, p. 58)

Figure 23.1 The theory of non-positional teacher leadership.

The vision portrayed in TETTL is of an inclusive and democratic approach that offers the means to enable any practitioner to develop their leadership capacity. Leadership in this context is conceptualised as influence, a defining characteristic of leadership practice (Yukl, 2010).

Facilitation

The defining characteristic of the HertsCam network is that it is self-supporting. The key to this is teachers' ability to facilitate, enable and empower other teachers. These teachers have developed the capacity to organise and create the infrastructure for school and teacher development. Anderson et al. (2014) are all members of the network's Tutor Team (currently 30 or so individuals), experienced practitioners who facilitate the TLDW programme. Tutors facilitate TLDW groups in their own schools by drawing from a common set of tools and techniques, including facsimiles, guide sheets, workshop protocols, formats for planning documents, prompt sheets for dialogue and so on. Tutors access these tools online; they select and adapt them when planning each two-hour school-based session. The fact that all activities are facilitated by network members means that the approach is self-sustaining and very low-cost.

Practice development through projects

A cornerstone of the non-positional teacher leadership approach is our focus on development projects. We define development work as strategic, focused and deliberate action intended to bring about improvements in professional practice. It takes the form of collaborative processes featuring activities such as consultation, negotiation, reflection, self-evaluation and deliberation, which take place in planned sequence.

Through designing and leading projects based on their own professional concerns, participants develop a strong sense of empowerment and voice – their agency is enhanced. Workshops enable them to reflect on their values and plan how to contribute to the development of practice in their schools. This tends to have the effect of mobilising and refreshing their sense of moral purpose, putting their professionality on a new level. They experience being taken seriously by colleagues and find themselves becoming influential, as described by Helen Foy:

> (My) project would enable colleagues to work collaboratively to share good practice and learn from each other. My aim was to ensure that all students would benefit from extensive and appropriate provision in PE that would inspire them to raise their aspirations. I planned to engage my colleagues in a process of development in which we would plan and refine our curriculum and teaching and learning practices to meet the needs of all our students.
>
> (Foy, 2014)

Helen was not the Head of Department. She was not designated as a 'teacher leader' at the time she carried out the project she writes about, but she acted strategically in a deliberate and planned way to achieve goals that she had clarified in consultation with colleagues. This is not informal; it is non-positional.

Extended professionality and educational transformation

The most obvious benefit of non-positional teacher leadership is that development projects can lead to school improvement. This is commonly understood as increased levels of student attainment, but HertsCam's focus tends to be on contributory factors rather than on results themselves.

The central assumption of TETTL is that it is possible to enable all teachers to extend their professionality to include a strong leadership dimension. The idea of extended professionality put forward by Eric Hoyle (1975) is often assumed to be about reaching beyond your own classroom to the wider world of ideas, research and professional development courses. By contrast, the non-positional teacher leadership approach aims to mobilise commitment and moral purpose.

Building professional knowledge

The most successful teacher-led development projects are those that lead to 'knowledge in situ', new norms of practice being shared and embedded. However, it is also important to enable teachers to contribute to what is known in the education system more widely. Publishing written narratives about developed work is helpful, but it is also vital to continuously enrich the professional knowledge shared within the networks to which teachers belong. Through networking, teachers build knowledge collectively, a live knowledge base rather than a codified body of explicit knowledge. (Nonaka, 1994)

It might be assumed that knowledge-building amongst teachers is all about passing on know-how, but there is another dimension which is essentially concerned with the inspirational value of what is shared, a moral knowledge that sits alongside the technical kind. This is particularly well exemplified by Marie Metcalfe's project.

> Over half of the pupils in Marie's school had English as an additional language, with 29 different languages being spoken by the school population. Marie was concerned that there was very little contact between the school and the families from these different ethnic groups and thought that a focus on the children's first languages might help with the learning of English and literacy skills in general. It seemed to Marie that raising awareness of the different languages spoken by pupils would help to affirm and celebrate the children's cultural background and promote their self-esteem.

Marie was also keen to reach out to the different language communities in the school and encourage their participation in school life.

(Metcalfe, 2014)

Marie died shortly after she led this project, but her story has been told in different ways in many parts of the world and continues to inspire other teachers to address matters of social justice. Advocacy for teachers and for good professional practice may come from academics, social activists and teacher unions, but in the long run, it is the voice of teachers themselves that must be heard. Non-positional teacher leadership offers a way to let them speak.

References

Anderson, E., Barnett, P., Thompson, L., Roberts, A. & Wearing, V. (2014) Teachers are doing it for themselves: knowledge-building in HertsCam, in D. Frost (ed.) *Transforming Education Through Teacher Leadership*, pp. 119–128. Cambridge: LfL.

Foy, H. (2014) Levelling the playing field: improving the quality of Physical Education, in D. Frost (ed.) *Transforming Education Through Teacher Leadership*, pp. 45–52. Cambridge: LfL.

Frost, D. (Ed.) (2014) *Transforming Education Through Teacher Leadership*. Cambridge: LfL.

Fullan, M. (1993) Why teachers must become change agents, *Educational Leadership*, 50 (6), 12–17.

Hill, V. (2014) The HertsCam TLDW programme, in D. Frost (ed.) *Transforming Education Through Teacher Leadership*, pp. 73–83. Cambridge: LfL.

Hoyle, E. (1975) Professionality, professionalism and control in teaching. In V. Houghton et al. (eds.) *Management in Education: The Management of Organisations and Individuals*. London: Ward Lock Educational / Open University Press.

Metcalfe, M. (2014) Marie Metcalf's story: raising awareness of language and cultural diversity at a London primary school, in D. Frost (ed.) *Transforming Education Through Teacher Leadership*, pp. 20–23. Cambridge: LfL.

Nonaka, I. (1994) A dynamic theory of organizational knowledge creation. *Organization Science*, 5 (1), 14–37.

Paige, C. (2014) Raising aspirations through dance education, in D. Frost (ed.) *Transforming Education Through Teacher Leadership*, pp. 13–16. Cambridge: LfL.

Steel, L. (2014) Strategies to develop literacy in science, in D. Frost (ed.) *Transforming Education Through Teacher Leadership*, pp. 9–12. Cambridge: LfL.

Yukl, G. (2010) *Leadership in Organisations* (6th edition). Upper Saddle River, NJ: Pearson Education.

Part IV

The teachers' manifesto

Political agency

JL Dutaut and Lucy Rycroft-Smith

Having defined teacher professionalism, the next stage is to develop how a flipped system might facilitate such cognitive, collaborative and ethical agency. Political decisions that affect teachers' working conditions are taken at every level – in schools, regionally, across partnerships and multi-school trusts, nationally and internationally – every day. We have found that the devolved nature of education policy across the UK's four nations provides helpful comparatives, but that trends toward marketisation of provision and de-professionalisation of teaching are constants. Unequal effects reflect differing stages of implementation. Within each nation, inequality of standards is effectively a consequence of the same process of combining commendable decentralisation with unnecessary competition.

Decentralisation without competition

Setting the parameters of what he perceives as a societal tipping point, **Andy Hargreaves** argues that education must adapt, as it will increasingly be called upon as a political lever for inclusion in an atomising age of identity. This adaptation impinges upon teachers assuming a fully fledged professionalism. Drawing on his experience as a teacher and as a writer for an exam board, **Darren Macey** demonstrates how top-down accountability can never provide the adaptability Andy says is necessary. Meanwhile, in Northern Ireland, headteacher **Gary Farrell** argues that while their system is more open to teacher input, much of his most effective work still happens despite government, not because of it. Many habits remain, he argues, from historically centralised Westminster bureaucracy, one **Julian Critchley** is familiar with. As a DfE civil-servant-turned-teacher, he exposes the multitudinous reasons education policy is poorly devised and implemented.

Back in Northern Ireland, **Tony Gallagher** describes the development of an initiative to bring schools together, circumventing traditional political challenges. So successful was this ground-up, teacher-led collaboration that it is now enshrined in law. Consider, by contrast, England's challenges in dispelling pernicious 'psycho-babble', as explored in Part I. **Gareth Alcott** suggests the key reason grassroots movements and Teaching School Alliances here have not yet created a full-scale flip to teacher-led professional development is lack of synergy. Further to her work on the Carter Review of Initial Teacher Education, **Sam Twiselton** echoes Gareth's call for synergy, this time between schools and universities, to circumvent the counter-productive polarisation that invariably results from politicisation.

Accountability without limits

Pulling on a host of contributions to this book, it is clear that one of the key drivers of poor policy is top-down accountability, which reduces those most directly involved in implementation to voiceless delivery agents. Teachers must, as we have argued, have agency with regards to the ethical dimension of their work, but that is not to say they can refuse to implement policy. Politicians are elected to set an ideological direction of travel and to deliver promises they have made to the voting public, to whom they are accountable. So far, so democratic. Regional Schools Commissioners, trust executives, headteachers, their deputies, assistants and middle leaders are appointed to oversee the continued provision of excellent education for each child in their charge. They are accountable for that to their managers and stakeholders. So far, so professional. Yet, in this model, accountability flows but one way.

As editors, we acknowledge a danger that the critique of top-down accountability permeating this book could be construed as a pie-in-the-sky wish for less, or no, accountability. In fact, our manifesto calls for smarter accountability – an accountability without limits, to borrow from Alison Peacock. There is only so much professionalism we can wrest back through demands, and anything we do can as easily be wrested back. To sustainably flip the system, for a better education environment for all, it is necessary both that we hold each other to account, and those who direct us. As professionals with collaborative agency, the former is ensured, but as long as our managers are not accountable *to us*, they will not be accountable *for us*, and even the best curriculum reform will continue to face the prospect of poor implementation. Top-down targets for teacher wellbeing, in this regard, are a mirage. Indeed, if such targets were imposed all the way down from the Secretary of State in a chain that reached our classrooms, it would only be as strong as its weakest link. It is necessary that we embed, across the education system, a philosophy and practice of reciprocal accountability. Only this will seal our professionalism and protect it into the future. Only this promises to slow the pendulum swing of education policy, and offers the prospect of better policy, better implemented.

Demand accountability

The teachers' manifesto demands that professionalised teachers be trusted and supported to make education policy at all levels. This must include:

- Teacher activism in the creation, implementation and evaluation of policy;
- Qualifying and professional standards for system leaders that require demonstration of reciprocal accountability with regards to policy implementation;
- Working conditions for system leaders that make possible the continued attainment of such standards;
- Teacher evaluation of leadership performance at every level with regards to:
    - Support for teachers to generate, implement and evaluate policy;
    - Consultation with teachers prior to, during and after top-down policy implementation;
    - Consideration for, and appropriate actions to support, teacher wellbeing.
- Accountability measures for all stakeholders and policy-makers at all levels that require a commitment to, and the monitoring of performance in, upholding the professionalism of teachers with regard to their political agency as defined above.

Chapter 24

Time for a flipping change

Andy Hargreaves

"We have urged cooperation among our pupils and teachers, but incited and incentivised schools and their head-teachers to compete against each other. Who are we as educators? What has become of us?"

The world is at a terrible tipping point.

Until 2015, one of the most prominent policy priorities for many countries was improving educational achievement and simultaneously making it more equitable. Education was the highest item on the policy radar. For many years, Tony Blair's three top priorities were "Education. Education. Education". Barack Obama took America on an educational Race To The Top. Nation after nation writhed in public about its own inadequacies when the OECD's international PISA results were published. The British and the Americans hung their heads in shame in comparison to the stellar educational results of Singapore, South Korea and China. Educational achievement grabbed the newspaper headlines and it drove international efforts for nations to become more competitive and secure less shameful results.

But except for a few days, here and there, now and again, educational performance no longer makes the headlines. We are faced with something much more sinister instead, and our educational systems and their leaders have yet to come to terms with it.

From 2000 to 2015, international educational policy almost everywhere was in an age of educational achievement and effort. We are now entering a very different and in some ways darker age of educational identity, wellbeing and engagement. The change agenda, inside and outside education, has flipped. What does this mean, and how can we flip it back?

The age of achievement and effort

From the 1990s, but especially from the start of this century, large-scale educational reform on a national and international scale has been driven by four compelling questions.

1   How are we doing?
2   How do we know?
3   How can we improve?
4   How can this benefit everyone?

Together, these questions have led many of us to think about educational performance, measurement, improvement and equity. They are important questions; we should not ignore them, and we haven't.

In the 1990s, England initiated a National Literacy and Numeracy Strategy designed to raise achievement in relation to measurable targets of educational performance according to standardised achievement tests. As results improved, debates raged about their statistical and educational authenticity, and criticisms mounted about the collateral damage on children's learning and whole development that was incurred by excessive testing and teaching to the test. At the same time, evidence began to accrue of the negative effects on teacher motivation, recruitment and retention that resulted from teachers' work becoming too standardised and leaving no room for professional judgment.

Many schools still improve their results with cynical, short-term methods. A 2016 report in the Harvard Business Review of 160 'failing' academies in England found that when "super-heads" were appointed from successful schools elsewhere, many short-term gains that were made did not last. Most "super-heads" stayed for only a year or two when they

> focused their changes on the school year and subjects used to assess performance, so they could make quick improvements, take the credit, and move on. In every case, exam results dipped after the "super head" left and only started improving three years later.
>
> (Hill et al., 2016)

The English system actually awarded higher salaries and bonuses to the school leaders who achieved temporary, but ultimately evanescent short-term results, compared to the leaders who built more sustainable improvements over time.

Over the past 15 years, though, there have also been more authentic efforts at improvement that have yielded positive results. My research colleagues and I have witnessed this in our own research in England (Hargreaves & Harris, 2009). The schools did not improve their performance by just tightening the ship, or by replacing people. Nor did they concentrate on the quick but questionable fixes of teaching to the test or concentrating disproportionate attention on pupils whose scores were just below the threshold for proficiency. Instead, there was a genuine emphasis on transforming teaching and learning.

We found similar patterns of what Dennis Shirley calls 'achievement with integrity' across two entire local authorities – Tower Hamlets and Hackney in London (Shirley, 2016). Both of them moved from being the very worst performing authorities in England to achieving well above the national average within a decade (Hargreaves, Boyle & Harris, 2014). These authorities refused to accept that poverty automatically equated with failure. They invested in teacher development and leadership development so that good educators stayed and grew within the authorities. They also insisted that schools helped one another even when they were competing for pupils, so that all schools in the community achieved success and families no longer sent their children to be educated elsewhere.

In the age of achievement and effort, for all its limitations, England has become a pioneer in how to build systems, cultures and expectations where schools work with schools to increase opportunities for pupils who come from families experiencing poverty and who traditionally have experienced little success. It has also spearheaded initiatives for local authorities to work together in the same way, too.

One striking example was the Greater Manchester Challenge, where ten local authorities were brought together in 2007/08 to improve educational outcomes over three years. Cooperation across local authority boundaries encompassed many strategies – including using recently turned-around schools to help other schools or asking schools with particular expertise to provide development for teachers in other local authorities. By 2011, GMC schools were above the national average on all standardised test measures, and secondary schools in the most disadvantaged communities had improved at three times the rate of the national average (Ainscow, 2015).

Unfortunately, over the last decade, for ideological and financial reasons, the UK government has deliberately weakened the democratic powers and community strengths of these and other authorities in favour of a national system of semi-private free schools and academies that have no proven record of superior success.

Meanwhile, Wales and Scotland have persisted with local authorities and community control of state education (OECD 2014, 2015). In response to an OECD review of its school improvement strategy, the Welsh education system established a *Pathways to Success* programme in 40 disadvantaged schools that has seen overall improvements in examination results, especially for students with special needs (Ainscow, 2015). The Scottish system has instituted a similar strategy of cross-school collaboration in nine of its 32 local authorities. The drive for greater equity and excellence through authentic strategies that concentrate on teaching and learning and that build collaborative professionalism within and across schools in the context of preserving strong communities and local democracy is alive and well in Scotland and Wales. Aspects of these strategies also still persist, though more unevenly, in the free-for-all educational system of free schools, academies and academy chains or trusts that England has mainly become.

The driving questions of the age of achievement and effort must stay with us. It is important that every child has opportunity, that the possibility of social mobility is there for everyone, and that schools and communities are relentlessly committed to all pupils' success. But even if excellence and equity could be accomplished perfectly, this would no longer be enough. The world is in turmoil, and our schools and school systems have to know how to respond.

The age of identity, engagement and wellbeing

The world is being plagued with a new set of problems of monumental proportions. The defining questions for our societies and our schools now are even more serious than ones of achievement, opportunity and competitiveness. They cut to the very core of who we are. There are three of them.

- Who are we?
- What will become of us?
- Who will decide?

When we think about pedagogy, we usually assume it means methods of teaching. But the Greek origins of pedagogy are to be found in how children were taught virtues of citizenship and becoming a person as they were escorted to school and back. In the midst of international tension and turmoil, many educators are turning to the idea of educating the 'whole child', as in the network of schools in the Whole Education Network in the UK. Social and emotional learning are receiving increasing attention alongside traditional academic learning.

Ontario, in Canada, has made child wellbeing one of its four system-wide priorities. The Scottish Curriculum for Excellence values not only traditional academic excellence but also the importance of children becoming confident learners and effective contributors. Why?

Many unsettling trends are converging. First, there is, it seems, a global epidemic of mental health problems among young people. In England, a report for Public Health England (Health Behaviour of School Age Children, 2015) has found that an in an average class of thirty 15-year-olds, three could have a mental disorder (Green et al., 2005), seven are likely to have been bullied (Langford et al., 2014) and six may be self-harming (Brooks et al., 2015).

Second, there is the unavoidable international refugee crisis, arguably one of the very worst since World War II. And when refugee children arrive in classes of the countries to which they flee, they have not merely been missing school, or face learning in a new language. Many have also been exposed to multiple incidents of post-traumatic stress involving death, loss and dislocation (see Natalie Scott's chapter).

Third, there are the negative effects of digital technologies on children's learning and lives. Several years ago, when I went into schools and asked teachers about technology, apart from worries about misuse of smartphones, they would point to the benefits of increased and independent access to information, capacity to network with experts and other schools, support for pupils with learning disabilities, and many other benefits. Now, the first issues that teachers typically mention are the anxieties that occur among adolescents because of cyber-bullying. They worry about short attention spans, distractibility and lack of depth arising from excess screen time – and they are increasingly concerned about the disinhibition that emerges in online interaction as insults abound and rage exceeds anything that might be said eyeball-to-eyeball, face-to-face.

Who are we? What will become of us? How do we understand and engage with people who are different from us? What are the limits that distinguish acceptable from unacceptable communication and behaviour? How are we responsible for the trucks that drove into holidaymakers in Nice and Christmas shoppers in Berlin; for the shootings of Muslims at prayer in a Canadian mosque; for repeated school shootings in America; for prejudice, hatred, violence and exclusion? As the Chinese philosopher Confucius pointed out, if others do noble things, we should emulate them. If they commit unworthy acts, we should look to ourselves and ask how we are responsible for them. When they were children, did we really teach them 'well'?

We have been emphasizing academic achievement at the expense of human development. We have elevated individual family choice above the needs of the community. We have urged cooperation among our pupils and teachers, but incited and incentivised schools and their head-teachers to compete against each other.

Who are we as educators? What has become of us? What can we now decide? The world has flipped. It's now time to flip the system in education. How?

Four ways to flip

Students should take their place at the centre

Technology experts and advocates have offered pupils more personalization of curriculum choices, in part by providing independent access to information and resources irrespective of the teacher. Deep learning and personalization capture apparently progressive and child-centred impulses among educators and hook them up to the inexorable imposition of more and more technology and to the language through which we think about it. Children aren't machines, and nor are their teachers. A flipped classroom isn't a digital classroom, necessarily. Children shouldn't be left on their own with digital devices but placed at the centre of a human system of learning, development and care that involves many skilled, caring and responsible adults.

In a project with one-seventh of the school boards in Ontario, Canada, we are placing students in the centre when they design and post display boards around the school in locations of their choosing that celebrate diverse student identities, including religious, ethnic and sexual identities – as a way to counter bullying and promote positive wellbeing. We are seeing students study indigenous women who have been murdered or who have disappeared, and then research their lives, even though there are no indigenous students in the school. We have seen a student mental health committee that consists of students who have had mental health issues in their lives or among their peers. We have also witnessed large conferences where students are not merely the targets of adult talks, or providers of entertainment at the beginning, but dynamic presenters on the stage about global issues in their own right. Flipping the system does not mean putting devices at the centre. It means placing pupils at the centre.

What is essential for some pupils is good for all pupils

Flipping the system also means moving away from a standardised curriculum for all pupils on the one hand, and a free-for-all of individual choice and personalisation that has no reference to core values and commitments on the other. An inspiring insight from our work with Ontario's special education strategy is that what is essential for some students may be good for everyone. A technological aid like a teacher's microphone for students with hearing impairments may also give everyone a front seat, with better audio all round. Teaching self-advocacy for students who have learning disabilities where they can talk to their teachers about how they learn best may also be good for helping all children become confident learners, as is a priority in Scotland. A student from a refugee family who has also suffered post-traumatic stress may need one-to-one attention from his teachers in school, but doesn't every child deserve some degree of personal attention, too – and won't that then help the newcomer child blend in more easily?

Twenty-first-century learning and curriculum should be matched by twenty-first-century assessment

Our push to develop more twenty-first-century learning with and without technology is being delivered through twentieth-century and even nineteenth-century assessments. The examination system invented in ancient Chinese bureaucracies still stifles creativity in many Asian education systems, including in China itself. In England, differentiated learning co-exists with standardised achievement tests. The negative effects of the tests are well known – narrowing of the curriculum, discriminatory effects on second language learners and their teachers, teaching to the test, anxiety among children during and before the tests and inflexibility in relation to a diverse student population. There is an epidemic of anxiety among adolescents today. Excessive testing isn't helping.

Extensive high-stakes testing belongs to the age of achievement and effort. Issues of identity, engagement and wellbeing call for other kinds of assessments. We can take more indicators of pupils' happiness, or engagement, of course, but more and more surveys will just inundate everyone with requirements to report what they are doing so they have less time for actually doing it. Ongoing self-assessments and peer assessments among students can enhance everyone's sense of how students are doing, even with instant and accumulated digital tools like emojis. But in the end, the challenge is how to create more consistency in teachers' professional judgments of students' learning – a challenge that countries like Scotland are now facing. Some of the answer to this question is technical – in terms of the quality of the data that inform teachers' judgments. But a lot is relational – about how teachers work together within and across their schools as communities who discuss, inquire into and make collective judgments about the work their pupils do.

There is no child wellbeing without teacher wellbeing

Whether we are parents, leaders or teachers, if we aren't healthy ourselves, we will probably be little use to other people. What example do we set if we are always the first to arrive at school and the last to leave? If we are emailing long after bedtime and we cannot then sleep, how much use are we to the people we teach or lead next day? If 600 teachers in a school district or local authority are taking online courses in mindfulness (as has occurred in one study we are conducting), is this a good development or a bad one?

The secret to teacher wellness is not to be found in more individual yoga classes or mindfulness exercises, though they can do no harm. It is in teachers' quality of work–life, and in their work–life balance. Teaching has to be a job that provides room for professional judgment and welcomes diversity of approach in pursuit of consistent high quality. It should be a job that doesn't expect teachers to be young, tireless and without other demands or interests in their lives. It should provide opportunities for professional collaboration on work that is of interest to teachers and of benefit to pupils. It's not a certainty, but the great likelihood is that if teachers are well, all will be well. It's in the basic wiring of teachers to always put themselves last, so leaders and others need to make an extra effort to put them first sometimes.

A new frontline

The world has already flipped. In a positive sense, it is now time for schools to flip what *they* do, before it is too late. Bullies and bigots are the product of our educational systems. So are the high school loners who exact their perverse retribution on others later on.

Engagement, identity and wellbeing are the new frontline of educational improvement. Disengaged students can easily turn into disgruntled adults. Those who are emotionally unwell can become dangers to all of us and to themselves if they then become psychologically unhinged. And if we turn people into outsiders, with null or negative identities, some of them will surely turn against us later on. These are not easy days for flipping the system, so it is important that we face them together. In the words of Helen Keller, "Walking with a friend in the dark is better than walking alone in the light" (Lash, 1980).

References

Ainscow, M., 2015. *Towards self-improving school systems: Lessons from a city challenge.* Abingdon: Routledge.

Brooks, F., Magnusson, J., Klemera, E., Chester, K., Spencer, N. & Smeeton, N., 2015. HBSC England national report: Findings from the 2014 HBSC study for England. Hatfield: University of Hertfordshire.

Green, H., McGinnity, A., Meltzer, H., Ford, T. & Goodman, R., 2005. *Mental health of children and young people in Great Britain, 2004.* London: HMSO.

Hargreaves, A. and Harris, A., 2009. *Performance beyond expectations.* Nottingham: National College for School Leadership.

Hargreaves, A., Boyle, A. & Harris, A., 2014. *Uplifting leadership: How organizations, teams, and communities raise performance.* San Francisco: John Wiley & Sons.

Health Behaviour of School Age Children. *Health behavior in school-aged children: World health organized collaborative cross-national survey.* [online] Available at: http://www.hbsc.org [Accessed 31st May 2017].

Hill, A., Mellon, L., Goddard, J. & Laker, B., 2016. How to turn around a failing school. *Harvard Business Review* [online] Available at: https://hbr.org/product/how-to-turn-around-a-failing-school/H02Z5P-PDF-ENG [Accessed 31st May 2017].

Langford, R., Bonell, C. P., Jones, H. E., Pouliou, T., Murphy, S. M., Waters, E., Komro, K. A., Gibbs, L. F., Magnus, D. & Campbell, R., 2014. The WHO Health Promoting School framework for improving the health and well-being of students and their academic achievement. *Cochrane Database of Systematic Reviews, [e-journal],* 4. DOI:10.1002/14651858.CD008958.pub2.

Lash J. P., 1980. *Helen and teacher: The story of Helen Keller and Anne Sullivan Macy.* New York: Delacorte Press/Seymour Lawrence.

Organization for Economic Cooperation and Development, 2014. *Improving Schools in Wales: An OECD Perspective.* Paris: OECD.

Organization for Economic Cooperation and Development, 2015. *Improving Schools in Scotland: An OECD Perspective.* Paris: OECD.

Public Health England, 2015. *Promoting children and young people's emotional health and wellbeing.* London: Public Health England.

Shirley, D., 2016. *The new imperatives of educational change: Achievement with integrity.* New York: Routledge.

Chapter 25

The only way is long-term

Darren Macey

"It would be hard to design a more inefficient system deliberately."

During my career as a teacher, I could never understand why most of the education policy directives seemed so ill-thought-out. Delivered as they were with alarming regularity from the DfE, via compliant leadership teams living in constant fear of Ofsted, I had little time to work it out as I laboured to implement them. I eventually made my bid for freedom after almost a decade in the classroom.

It took just a few weeks for my confusion about the chaos of educational policy to become a grudging understanding as I became acquainted with the process of qualification reform, a process begun by the (then) Education Secretary, Michael Gove, who, on assuming the role, set about decrying the all-pervasive Blob (the educational establishment). He then proceeded to castigate the quality of the current exam system, point out the iniquities of schools "gaming" the system of modular exams, and question the use of early entry of students.

I was a deputy head of maths in charge of Key Stage 4 when this began. Our school policy was to allow students to take their GCSE exam in the November series, and if they hit their target grade when the results came in January, they could stop attending maths lessons in order to focus on subjects in which they were behind or found more difficult. Far from being the 'gaming' that Michael Gove so feared, this was our way of supporting student progress across their range of academic subjects. For those students at the lower end of the ability spectrum who found mathematics lessons a form of cruel and unusual punishment, it provided an incentive to work hard and escape the perceived purgatory in which they had endlessly suffered. It was catastrophic when, just a few weeks ahead of an exam that our students had pinned their hopes on for 14 months, the green fields of maths-free school tantalisingly ahead of them, the DfE announced a change to the rules which meant that early entry did not count in league tables any more – with immediate effect. As a school under a high-stakes accountability regime that had been in Special Measures, our management felt there was no choice but to pull the exam entries, and it was left to class teachers to inform the students. The response was chaotic; there were tears, and of course students blamed their teachers for letting them down.

Despite the fact that as teachers we initially bore the brunt of the student malcontent, for a few brief and shining days, bottom–set Year 11 and their teachers had what felt like a common enemy, an *entente cordiale* with designs to march on Parliament and tear off the chains of league table-based bondage, or at least tweet their outrage while muttering angrily into bottles of energy drink and cups of tea respectively.

It was around this time that I began looking in earnest for opportunities outside of the classroom, the end of my tether reached at yet another example of a seemingly thoughtless approach to reforming education. Ministers clicked their ruby-slippered heels together three times, and instantly the system changes, leaving teachers to mend the yellow brick road as a fresh whirlwind sweeps through. I was lucky enough that my mutterings of "there's no place like the private sector, there's no place like the private sector, there's no place like the private sector" coincided neatly with my eventual employer initiating a hefty recruitment drive.

How is this being allowed to happen?

Ministers habitually cast a covetous eye over the education systems of countries that sit above us in international rankings, cherry-picking ideas that make good soundbites, but rarely looking at the timetable of change in those countries. Unfortunately, ministerial reputations are rarely built on a measured approach, particularly as a new government might be in place five years down the line when effective reforms begin to make an impact, and no sensible partisan minister wants the other lot to get the credit. While many countries roll out changes over a period of time without changing direction with every new government, in England, short-termism rules.

I would dearly love to see a realisation that consultations in education cannot work in the same way that they do in other government departments (although I am making the possibly incorrect assumption that they do work in other departments). As an example, let me explain how the content was decided for the new Maths A-Level.

The DfE created a committee called ALMAB (the A-Level Mathematics Advisory Board), to be made up of representatives from Russell Group universities. It did in fact include some teacher representation, albeit from highly performing and selective schools. ALMAB duly produced a list of content and outline priorities for the course that was put out to consultation, and Ofqual produced a set of rules around how the assessment questions should be balanced.

It is easy for working groups and responses to white paper consultations to be disproportionately dominated by special interests. This is in no small part due to the staggering workload of most teachers limiting their involvement in anything outside of the classroom unless specifically invited. There were of course some flaws in the content list produced. This is entirely understandable because the interrelation between the content is complex and exceptionally difficult to get right in one go. Following the completion of the consultation, some of the suggested amendments were actioned and the minister signed off the content. At this point, the content became fixed and no power known to humanity could change it. It is unfortunate that the fundamental basis of high-stakes assessment is locked down in this way before any opportunity to trial ideas and develop content is afforded. Even the best-laid plans rarely survive contact with the real world unscathed and it is inevitable that some fine tuning is necessary.

This process was also not consistent for all subjects. Some subjects had the content decided by a working group, led by the exam boards, rather than by an entirely independent panel, before submission to the DfE. The final sign-off was at the minister's prerogative.

A major iceberg was hit at this point. ALMAB, on behalf of the DfE, were responsible for both the content and the 'intent' for its use, while Ofqual were responsible for making sure the final qualifications clearly met these criteria. However, ALMAB was officially disbanded soon afterwards – as such groups often are – and had no further official role in the process. This left Ofqual tasked with regulating a qualification for which they had to interpret the wishes of a third party that no longer officially existed. Part of the problem was that although the content document contained some genuinely innovative and interesting ideas, many appeared to be intended to inform teaching and learning and not necessarily form part of the exam, and with such limited opportunities to extensively trial new ideas, the ethics of asking the first cohort to face innovative question styles in a high stakes terminal exam without knowing the effect are a little problematic. Unfortunately, these ideas were now officially in the content – and so Ofqual has a duty to make sure they do appear in the exams in some form regardless.

Irrationally, the content document has taken on the status of a semi-religious text that is both open to interpretation and in some cases not quite fit for purpose, but which cannot be altered, even though the regulator is sympathetic to the issues that it throws up. The exam boards have to go away and make something that works despite all this, and Ofqual have to do their best to meet the requirements of both regulation and common sense. Small wonder that fewer than 8 months from first teaching, no A-Levels in Mathematics had been accredited.

The awarding bodies have had to create assessment that impacts on thousands of students and teachers on a short timescale, from an imperfect template and with little opportunity to trial the new ideas contained within it, or to request any adjustments when some piece of content is found to be problematic. The outcome is unlikely to satisfy the teachers who are forced to rewrite their schemes of work, teaching a qualification for which they have no idea what the grade standard will be; and also unlikely to satisfy the DfE who will get a qualification that isn't quite what they intended. To an outside observer it must seem like the whole system is set-up to create conflict: the DfE think the exam boards are dumbing down and Ofqual are not accrediting fast enough; the exam boards want clearer guidance from the DfE and Ofqual in order to meet opaque-seeming requirements; Ofqual, with a huge volume of qualification accreditations to review, are having to apply strict regulations based on a third-party template while trying to meet the DfE's tough timetable, as first teaching looms ever closer. Meanwhile, ALMAB had to produce a framework for the content without opportunity for their ideas to be trialled first, and then take no further formal part in realising their vision. It would be hard to design a more inefficient system deliberately.

The structure of reform in education, from the viewpoint of both a teacher and an exam board, is currently too rigid, too short-term, and has no space for trialling ideas before they are implemented. This can only lead to organisations either playing safe and neutering the ideas of the reformers as much as possible, or taking gambles on untried and untested ideas regardless of consequence. Until we stop rushing through reforms in a single Parliament, systemic issues will remain and multiply.

So how to change things? Governments come and go, and ministers are in their roles but fleetingly. We don't allow tourists the right to make fundamental changes to beaches; we shouldn't allow politicians to do so to our schools either. Reformers should be looking to the people that are in it for the long haul – teachers and university education departments, for example – if we genuinely want a better system. Governments could and should take the radical step of positioning themselves as the stewards and cheerleaders of the experts and provide them a platform for both trialling and sharing the best ideas, rather than imposing a shifting ideology whose priorities change as often as the tides, and twice as dangerously.

Chapter 26

A Northern Irish perspective

Gary Farrell

"Whilst we must take cognisance of educational policy, we do not allow it to solely dictate what we do."

I have been the principal of the same school in Northern Ireland for almost fourteen years, and during that period I have witnessed significant changes in society which have impacted on the needs of our children. Unfortunately, these needs have not been reflected in a shift in educational policy and practice. However, becoming principal of a brand new school gave me the ability to influence in many ways the direction I felt we needed to go to ensure the needs of our children were being met.

With devolved government in Northern Ireland, we as a teaching body are ideally placed to exert influence on policy direction. I have been personally involved in a number of campaigns that I believe directly led to a shift in policy or policy review. I also believe that the Revised Curriculum in Northern Ireland has given a degree of autonomy to educators and allowed schools to set their own agenda. However, many historical policies are still impacting negatively on educational development in Northern Ireland – academic selection, End of Key Stage Assessment and the workings of the Educational Training Inspectorate, to name but a few.

A school perspective

Before ever hearing of Changemaker schools, our school community considered ourselves to be forward-thinking, progressive practitioners with an ethos of providing a very broad range of educational experiences to all our pupils. Central to achieving our vision is our ability to seek out new ideas, new initiatives and unique opportunities for our pupils, leading to our involvement in the Roots of Empathy Programme in Ireland, the Cross Border Dissolving Boundaries Project, Young Enterprise NI, Entrepreneurship Projects and our use of ICT in short filmmaking.

Having come into the Changemaker schools network in 2014, our mindset has evolved – looking to empathy, creativity, teamwork and leadership as our driving principles. Whilst we must take cognisance of educational policy, we do not allow it to solely dictate what we do. This 'sense of liberation' empowers our teachers, and the key aim for us is that we now focus more on giving our children the tool box they require to be able to maximise their contribution to society.

Van der Wateren and Beardsley (2016, p. 35) write: "we need to convince policymakers that it is also in their interest to move away from the current trend of narrow aims, central control and measurable outcomes and give teachers the freedom to develop their own new curriculum." This, I believe, is the key to unlocking the door for all schools. If we accept the notion that schools exist to serve and educate a community, and understand that each community is unique and complex, then we must accept that for a school to be effective it must be allowed the autonomy to develop policy and practice with and for its community.

In 2006 the Department of Education in Northern Ireland introduced a revised curriculum. This gave schools much more autonomy over curriculum detail, but probably even more important was the emphasis it placed on the development of the child's skills and attributes alongside subject knowledge. This is not to say that we have total freedom – parental demands, school competition, open enrolment, assessment regimes and pressure of school inspections still very much lead us to follow Department policy and directives, if only to convince the more conservative stakeholders that we are providing a top quality education.

A creative approach

Northern Ireland has a strong culture of 'Area Learning Communities.' These communities are comprised of groups of schools sharing practice and developing ideas to ensure that we are working effectively for the children we educate. One of the communities to which our school belongs contains one secondary school and nine partner primary schools. This allows for cross-phase work including planning, curricular development and professional development for teachers; the work of these learning communities is very much led by those from within, as the people who have the best understanding of the community and children they serve.

This culture of collective agency has allowed us to develop and introduce a 'Whole-School Mindfulness Programme' in response to mounting evidence that mental disorders are increasingly common among young people and that the behavioural symptoms of mental illness are becoming more apparent at an early age. It is estimated that three children in every classroom have a diagnosable mental health condition, a twofold increase from the 1980s to the mid-2000s (YoungMinds, 2016). The current system allows us to be much more proactive and creative in addressing these issues, as opposed to the old reactive strategies we once used.

Further, we are committed to our values of peace and care for others, and the flexibility in our curriculum allows us to engage in evidence-based activities to develop those values in our students. Recently, we have been involved in the much acclaimed Roots of Empathy programme. Originally developed by Mary Gordon, *Roots of Empathy* is aimed at young children and uses a young baby as a stimulus. Pupils observe and discuss the baby's growth both socially and emotionally over the period of one year of weekly visits to the class. As a follow-up, the children engage in work related to personal development. A recent evaluation by Queen's University Belfast tells us that the programme, when delivered successfully, leads to an increase in pro-social behaviour and a reduction in difficult behaviour, also citing an increased ability of participants to recognise others' emotions, to regulate one's own and show empathy (Centre for Evidence and Social Innovation, 2017).

Our success lies in our ability to identify programmes that we believe will have a positive impact on the children in our school. Through our own auditing of our provision, we then make a place within our curriculum to commit to them. The rationale for any new initiative is shared with our stakeholders, supported by concrete evidence of their effectiveness, and the results are shared widely with our community. The strength in Northern Ireland's education system is that it allows us the freedom to be responsive, and to be democratically accountable to the people who matter most – our pupils and their parents.

Owning our challenges

Of course, there will always be barriers to change and objections to new directions, but as a team of professionals, we collectively control the direction of our practice. We ask two types of questions. First, does the change in question fit the model of education our stakeholders demand? Will it impact on our overall achievements and standards? Will our curriculum become distorted? How will it be viewed by external bodies, e.g. the Education and Training Inspectorate? As we gather evidence and views in answer to these, the second set of questions we ask ourselves is whether the policy, initiative or project will benefit the children. What skills and attributes might they develop as a result to allow them as individuals to play a purposeful role in society?

If the answers to the latter questions are stronger than the reasons for not engaging in the process, then the direction we take is clear. It is never a decision taken lightly, and always involves consultation with staff, the school board of management and key stakeholders, backed by clear evidence of need and detailed success criteria. It is not always successful, but it is a process we own.

We work together as a whole school to ensure that initiatives like those described, and our immensely impactful, eight-year involvement with the charity Young Enterprise Northern Ireland, dovetail into our curriculum, as opposed to being an imposition from outside. Getting the balance between our core business of learning and teaching and our individual programmes is the key to our success. Indeed, this has been recognised at our school's two most recent inspections, where the Education Training Inspectorate concluded our school was very effective in all areas of provision, with achievements and standards awarded outstanding on both occasions.

Conclusions

The journey that we set out on was one that would lead to our pupils being well-rounded individuals with a skill set that would allow them to play a pro-active, innovative and leadership role within society. We have achieved this against the backdrop of uncertainties highlighted by some of our stakeholders and at times in defiance of what we perceive to be flawed Department of Education Policy. Becoming a Changemaker school has given us a new confidence to fight for what we believe in, and belonging to the Changemaker network affords us the opportunity to learn from and work with others inside and outside of Northern Ireland (in itself a significant opportunity for us).

Where we have succeeded, it has often been despite a system in Northern Ireland that, I believe, needs to go a step further to break away from the chains of the past – policy and practice that was driven by a central UK government. Continuing issues of contention such as the process of pupil assessment, the role and purpose of the Education and Training Inspectorate, lack of provision for teachers' continued professional development, lack of support for schools in relation to increasing numbers of pupils presenting with complex needs and increasing class sizes, all of which are compounded by rapidly decreasing school budgets, mean that education is heading into a very uncertain future.

As a teaching profession, we need to be strong in the face of such challenges. I believe that by building on our already established learning communities and connecting these with others both within the UK and beyond, we can create the catalyst for meaningful and effective change.

References

Centre for Evidence and Innovation (2017), A cluster randomised controlled trial evaluation and cost-effectiveness analysis of the Roots of Empathy schools-based programme for improving social and emotional wellbeing outcomes among 8–9 year olds in Northern Ireland, in *Public Health Research*. Awaiting publication. [online] Available at https://www.journalslibrary.nihr.ac.uk/programmes/phr/10300602/#/ [Accessed 27 June 2017].

Van Der Wateren, D. and Amrein-Beardsley, A. (2016), Measuring what doesn't matter: the nonsense and sense of testing and accountability, in Evers, J. and Kneyber, R. (eds.) *Flip the System: Changing Education from the Ground Up*, Abingdon: Routledge.

YoungMinds (2016), *YoungMinds Annual Report 2015–16*. [online]. Available at https://youngminds.org.uk/media/1233/youngminds-annual-report-15-16-final.pdf [Accessed 27th May 2017].

Chapter 27

How education policy-makers make mistakes

Julian Critchley

> **"In the British political system, Ministers like to talk about accountability, but rarely feel themselves accountable."**

For a scholarly – and entertaining – account of why Ministers make mistakes, one can do no better than to read the masterly study by Crewe and King, *The Blunders of Our Governments* (2014). Their broad categories of blunder-causation are a useful tool to apply to the particular failures, mistakes and cock-ups of English education policy. Compelling and humorous as this may be, it is not until we are able to transparently access and analyse educational policy mistakes that we can begin to do better. Here, I propose to do just that, following the structure Crewe (2014) provides for his general analysis of Government, and fleshing it out with a targeted look at the Department for Education and its incumbents.

Structural causes

Reducing deliberation at the centre

Hennessy (Ross, 2011) has expressed the view that the present-day Civil Service is less willing to stand up to Ministers than it used to be. The Civil Service has traditionally performed a key function of providing Ministers with non-ideological expertise, a moderating influence and an intellectual challenge. By the 1990s, the Civil Service's role had, in some ways, evolved to become a crucial expert check on political power much needed by a system which had adopted the universal suffrage of a democracy, but retained the executive prerogatives of a monarchy.

As a junior official, I joined the DfE during the tail-end of this period. Civil servants then saw it as an important part of their professional role to act as a sounding board, a devil's advocate and, if not as expert themselves, at least to be able to produce the actual experts at the appropriate time – to provide the deliberative function which is so crucial to policy-making. I would argue that this role remained the core of DfE's activity until 1997.

When David Blunkett entered Sanctuary Buildings, the new administration quickly introduced two key changes which significantly reduced the quality of deliberation in policy-making within the DfE. The first was simply that Ministers made it clear they were no longer interested in the traditional 'pros and cons' advice officials would provide. They did not see the DfE's role as offering expertise and deliberation, but instead demanded that it solely focus on unquestioning 'delivery' of largely pre-cooked ideas. Those who still saw their role as helping to create better policy through questioning, challenging and deliberation soon discovered the hard way what the new approach meant.

One senior civil servant attended a meeting with Blunkett early in the new government. Blunkett wanted an announcement that struggling schools would be able to disapply the national curriculum in order to help them improve. The official pointed out some might argue that, if the national curriculum was hindering those schools' performance, then surely there was a case for disapplying it everywhere. Similarly, there may be criticisms of a policy which removed the entitlement of some children to a broad and balanced education. This was classic Civil Service advice: seeking to test policy against possible challenges, so as to either prepare for those challenges, or to shape better policy. Yet this was the new world. That civil servant was subsequently visited by an even more senior civil servant, told that the Minister found him 'obstructive', and instructed to find another berth in a different department as quickly as possible.

It didn't take many such examples before officials began to censor themselves. Policy submissions became uncritically enthusiastic about even the crassest idiocy. Obvious flaws were not just unaddressed in deliberations, but were often not even acknowledged. As a result, uncomfortable, complex, nuanced reality began to seep out of deliberation, to be replaced by the certainties of the journalistic editorial and ideological 'think-tank'.

The second major change was the arrival of the new breed of Special Advisors, or 'SPADs'. Special advisor roles had always existed, but with fairly clear delineation of roles. As a politician, the Minister was supported by SPADs, but as a Minister of the Crown she or he was supported by the professional Civil Service. That distinction vanished within days of the 1997 Election, with the arrival of a new breed of special advisors who saw themselves as being the key players in policy deliberation, rather than the political aides of the politician. In effect, SPADs became de facto junior Ministers. Policy advice which did not obtain SPAD approval wouldn't even reach Ministers. Some might argue that this was a change for the better, giving Ministers a firmly committed ally against the devious civil servants. However, SPADs necessarily tend to come from the same ideological space as Ministers, and also retain a powerful political interest in how the policy can be presented for party political gain. This goal is not always compatible with good policy-making. I recall one meeting with Conor Ryan, Blunkett's hugely influential SPAD, in which he listened to the deliberations of the civil servants trying to gain his approval for a policy to put to Ministers, and then asked, bluntly, "Yes, but how will it play in the *Daily Mail?*"

When the education profession looks with incredulity at an obviously flawed policy proposal emerging from DfE, we often assume that there are reasons why the flaws have been accepted. However, in many cases, it's simply that the process of deliberation which used to take place pre-announcement is now taking place post-announcement. Unchallenged policy – originating with detached ideologues, focused on winning tabloid headlines and unquestion-ingly 'delivered' by frightened officials without being exposed to expertise – is almost always bad policy.

Reducing deliberation on the ground

The second way in which the deliberative function in education has been undermined is the effective removal of local government from education man-agement, and its replacement with a national command-and-control structure whereby most secondary schools and many primary schools are effectively run directly by the DfE, often via sub-contracted private companies, or Multi-Academy Trusts (MATs). The century-old role of the LEA as the democrati-cally accountable, locally responsive intermediate tier in the education system has effectively been destroyed. This is often seen solely through the prism of service provision, but there is another, deliberative role, which has disappeared alongside that reduction in local accountability.

The DfE has long had LEAs in its sights. In the early nineties, many senior civil servants agreed with Ministers that LEAs were a weakness in the educa-tion system. This seemed to stem more from the classic central government superiority complex than any real evidence. While there were almost certainly some dysfunctional LEAs, it is also true that there were some excellent ones, and that there was never any evidence that the DfE in Whitehall could support 20,000 schools any better than LEAs could. Although there were occasional efforts to intervene in LEAs seen as particularly weak, the view which grudg-ingly persisted until as late as 2010 was that LEAs fulfilled a necessary role: if they didn't exist, we'd have to invent them. After all, by 2010, the DfE had considerable experience of trying to manage schools without LEA assistance, through policies such as GM schools and EAZs, and it was far from successful.

Nevertheless, since 2010, the DfE has been pursuing a policy of eradicating all but the most residual basic LEA presence from education. Ironically, the stance of 'if they didn't exist, we'd have to invent them' remains intact, and the need for an intermediate tier between DfE and schools is acknowledged. However, the tier which the DfE is now seeking to invent is not a publicly accountable LEA with the sort of historic and democratic legitimacy which allows it to challenge central government – rather, it is compliant private companies in the form of Multi-Academy Trusts, entirely dependent upon the DfE for funding, and controlled by businessmen who see their role as sub-contractors to central government, overseen by Regional School Commissioners who are effectively DfE employees.

No better example can be found of the net loss of deliberation in the system than May's announcement of the return of grammar schools. Increasingly powerless LEAs decried the policy – correctly – as a ridiculous, unevidenced throwback to darker days, and vowed to oppose it with all their diminished might. This was the sound of a voice which felt it had a mandate from, and a responsibility to, a constituency which was not the DfE. The large Multi-Academy Trusts, with which the DfE is replacing LEAs, were much more muted. A few mumbled that they would rather not have any grammars, but said they may be compelled to do so. None would go on the record to criticise or oppose the decision openly. They are a captive, compliant group, which dare not challenge policy for fear of losing their income stream. It bodes ill for the quality of future policy.

The deficit of accountability

Crewe and King (2014) note that in the British political system, Ministers like to talk about accountability, but rarely feel themselves accountable. Not all of this is the result of increasingly dishonourable Ministers refusing to shoulder responsibility for their Department. Much is about the ephemeral nature of Ministerial appointments. Often, blunders don't become apparent until the instigator has moved to a different post, and the Minister's successor doesn't feel bound to resign for her predecessor's mistakes. This is perhaps particularly true in education, where policies often have extremely long periods between implementation and impact. For example, Michael Gove began the process of changing history GCSEs in 2011, but the first cohort to complete those new GCSEs will sit their exams in Summer 2018, long after his departure from the DfE. Similarly, every story of a Free School's self-serving administration or corrupt practices begins with Michael Gove, yet it is his successor's successor who has to face the shocking headlines and the Parliamentary Committees.

This lack of long-term accountability means Ministers tend to be attracted to the short-term announcement of policy, rather than the long-term implementation of it. In some ways, *the announcement becomes the policy*. It also incentivises Ministers to look for policies which have short-term impacts. Free Schools and academisation fit this bill nicely, as Ministers can point to rising numbers on a relatively frequent basis – the fact that academisation has been shown to have almost no discernible impact on outcomes is neither here nor there. It was the ability to announce academisation which was the driver for Ministers, not the long-term impacts which they knew they would not be around to see. The advantage of opening a free school is that the Minister can smile on the photo with the new Head, safe in the knowledge that the first set of measurable outcomes are years in the future.

Behavioural causes

Ministerial hyper-activism

In *Why Is Britain Badly Governed? Policy Blunders 1980–2010*, Ivor Crewe (2014) wrote that ministerial hyper-activism is a direct result of the structural causes listed above. It manifests as over-confidence and it is empowered by a lack of accountability and the absence of effective checks and balances. In effect, Ministers are led to believe that any opposition to policy is either a result of self-interest or the fecklessness of civil servants in implementing it, and that any form of questioning is ostensibly obstructiveness. "Benign neglect – the option of doing nothing – is alien to the modern culture of Whitehall" (ibid.).

As Ministers have tried to gather greater direct control through abolishing other power centres, eliminating dissent and ensuring compliant quangos, schools have found themselves buffeted by initiatives. Desperate to respond to a system in which accountability flows downwards rather than upwards, they have bounced from one half-understood, poorly implemented policy to another as announcements spewed out of Sanctuary Buildings.

In education, this culture of hyper-activism is deeply harmful. In my decade at the chalkface: I had to teach three different GCSE syllabuses in three years; I had my subject in Key Stage 3 absorbed into 'Integrated Humanities' for two years, then liberated again; the National Curriculum for history changed; my school saw the number of students in Applied subjects rocket, then the Ebacc became king, leading to a crash in the number of applied students and the consequent re-allocation of staff and resources. Now multiply that sort of hyper-active meddling with all the other 'initiatives' which Governments have imposed in the last ten years, and one begins to see why the top of many Heads' wish-list is a period of no further change.

Cultural disconnect

Perhaps no observation of Crewe and King is more apparent in education policy than the problem of 'cultural disconnect'. They observe that policy-makers often struggle to understand that people have different attitudes, values and views. As a result, they design policy for the people they imagine exist, who tend to be rather similar to themselves and their immediate social and professional groups. Again, much of this problem can be traced to the removal of effective deliberation. The DfE used to be a conduit for the views of various expert groups – subject associations, SEN groups, teacher unions, academics, Heads etc. – and the much broader understanding of the various stakeholders in the education system would be thrown into the policy mix. The effective denial of access to these groups – or indeed their dismissal as a self-interested "blob" in the most egregious case of cultural disconnect (Garner, 2014) – has served to throw policy-making back onto a very small, homogenous group of people. It is, in effect, an echo chamber. The question is, which voices are echoing around in there?

Ministers, their SPADs and the think-tanks which feed and reflect their views, come from a remarkably narrow background. Disproportionately privately or grammar-school educated. Disproportionately male. Disproportionately white. Disproportionately middle-class. Disproportionately academically able. And, since 2010, disproportionately right-wing. Under New Labour, while much of that personal homogeneity existed, the political spectrum was fairly broad. Blunkett could on the one hand tolerate Chris Woodhead as HMCI, while also finding time for advice from Tim Brighouse. Since 2010, the political spectrum represented in DfE policy-making has shrivelled to a right-wing rump.

If one seeks evidence of the cultural disconnect prevalent in education policy-making circles, one need look no further than the ridiculous imbalance between policy targeted on higher attaining students and that targeted on lower attaining students. May's grammar school announcement has many fans in the right-wing education policy firmament, all of whom are relatively silent, or indeed dismissive, about the impact of such a policy on less able children. The Ebacc policy similarly demonstrates an inability to imagine different children with different abilities or inclinations. Where less academically able children are acknowledged, it is usually only in the context of a vacuous exhortation to them and their teachers to 'work harder', 'show grit' and 'close the gap'. Gove announced he wanted exams to be more difficult, and any questions as to how this would serve those already struggling with existing exams were dismissed as suffering from "the soft bigotry of low expectations" (Clare, 2012).

Operational disconnect

Crewe noted scathingly that fewer and fewer Ministers and their close policy advisors had experience outside politics, or closely associated professions like journalism (he tellingly named Michael Gove as a prime example). As a result, Ministers often take office without any real understanding of how their finely polished theories would be implemented in practice.

Ministers since 1997 have often made policy announcements which suggest they will find ways of leveraging private funding into state schools. One such policy under New Labour was specialist schools; Education Action Zones was another. Ministers confidently predicted a flood of private money into schools, and genuinely believed that it would be so, because they had, after all, repeatedly announced that it would. I recall the then head of the Specialist Schools team, complaining bitterly that Ministers would speak to audiences from the private sector about the initiative, and receive many pledges of money from businessmen keen to curry favour with the Government, yet my colleague's job was to follow up these contacts only to discover that, in nearly all cases, that cash would not be forthcoming. Instead, offers of 'in kind' assistance would be grudgingly offered, often meaning a few desultory lectures on management and leadership by executives of the private company, delivered to bemused teachers, charged at thousands of pounds per day.

I managed the Education Action Zone policy and discovered that many of the 'donations' required to gain influence in the Zones came in the form of obsolete IT equipment which had no value to the donor firm, or yet more 'leadership' training courses. The consequences were that private businessmen and companies were gaining significant power over local schools, without the quid pro quo of providing real additional resources. Yet Ministers were unable or unwilling to acknowledge that the reality of hard-nosed businessmen might differ from their imagined group of would-be philanthropists.

The exclusion of experts and deliverers from the policy formation process means Ministers can and do fall into traps which were predicted by those with greater understanding. A good example would be the Government-created crisis in teacher-training. Politicians and their entourage of SPADs and think-tankers on the New Right have long argued that university-led teacher train-ing departments are a dangerous hotbed of left-wing activism, 'trendy' teaching methods, and thus the root cause of educational failure. This bizarre belief is precisely the sort of article of faith which is dangerously reinforced when not exposed to alternative views during a thorough deliberation process. There is no clear record of the precise origins of the policy of slashing university-based initial teacher training and replacing it with schools-based training, preferably in schools controlled by ideologically sympathetic private chains. It emerged from the disconnected clique of right-wing think-tanks, SPADs and Ministers. Civil servants, teacher unions, academics and education experts knew that the policy would cause teacher shortages, and the latter groups protested loudly, but there is no longer any way in the policy-making process for such exper-tise to shape policy. Instead, the DFE slipped into its now-expected 'delivery' mode. Experts were dismissed as part of the self-interested 'blob'. The policy was pushed through. University ITT was slashed. Schools-based ITT didn't pick up the slack. A significant trainee teacher shortage ensued.

While Gove's dismissal of 'the Blob' and description of teachers who disa-greed with him as "bad teachers" may represent a particularly cloth-eared low point of operational disconnect, it is not new. John Bangs noted the phenom-enon already at play under New Labour. According to him, Minister of State, Stephen Byers wrote to Robin Alexander welcoming the cooperation of aca-demics, *but only to the extent to which they supported Government policies*. Perhaps more than any other field, education policy allows amateur politicians with no expertise to dismiss those with it out of hand, with ease, in pursuit of their own ideas.

Conclusion

Why do we have such consistent policy blunders in education? Leaving aside the narrow ideological echo chamber Ministers operate in, at one level it is as simple as this: Ministers tend to be very confident people. Very confident people are not always given to undue introspection. This unjustified over-confidence is particularly exacerbated when they believe that they have experience of the policy in question. And, unfortunately for education policy in particular, everyone once went to school.

Some of these flaws are easily rectified: greater *genuine* consultation with experts and practitioners; opening up policy-making to those outside the Ministerial echo chamber of ideological fellow-travellers; returning a degree of analysis and challenge to accompany the civil service's 'delivery' function; to suit the classicists, perhaps having a serving teacher standing behind the Secretary of State for Education during every public appearance, whispering "You are not a God" in his or her ear.

However, perhaps the most significant recommendation I would make is to cease and desist in the continual portrayal of the state school system as broken and in need of urgent substantial change. It isn't, and it doesn't. If more of the readily available expertise in the system was readmitted into the tiny bubble from which current policy emerges, then Ministers might begin to realise that. A period of 'benign neglect' would almost certainly be of greater value to schools, teachers and children, than the culturally disconnected, ideologically faith-based hyper-activism we have suffered for the last twenty years.

References

Clare, S. (2012), *Conservative conference: Michael Gove criticises teaching unions*, BBC News [online], available at http://www.bbc.co.uk/news/uk-politics-19885602 [accessed 21 May 2017].

Crewe, I. (2014), *Why is Britain badly governed? Policy blunders 1980–2010*, Political Studies Association [online], available at https://www.psa.ac.uk/insight-plus/why-britain-badly-governed-policy-blunders-1980-2010 [accessed 21 May 2017].

Crewe, I and King, A. (2014), *The blunders of our governments*. 1st ed. London: Oneworld Publications.

Garner, R. (2014), What is 'the Blob' and why is Michael Gove comparing his enemies to an unbeatable sci-fi mound of goo which once battled Steve McQueen?, *Independent* [online], available at http://www.independent.co.uk/news/education/education-news/what-is-the-blob-and-why-is-michael-gove-comparing-his-enemies-to-an-unbeatable-sci-fi-mound-of-goo-9115600.html [accessed 21 May 2017].

Ross, M. (2011), Interview: Peter Hennessy, in *Civil Service World* [online], available at https://www.civilserviceworld.com/profile-peter-hennessy [accessed 21 May 2017].

Chapter 28

Contrasting experiences of marginalisation and empowerment

Tony Gallagher

'There is little or no 'tolerance of failure' in top–down interventions, even though this is a necessary condition for the development of innovation.'

Northern Ireland's education system has its roots in the National School system established in Ireland in 1836 (Akenson, 1970). Since then, the general direction of policy has been to follow practice in England. The small size of the region allows for closer relationships between stakeholders in education and, traditionally, teachers have been held in high regard. This has not prevented the adoption of broadly neoliberal market-based approaches to education since the late 1980s. The local character of politics in Northern Ireland, allied with the dispersed nature of power in the system as a consequence of its divided and complex structure, has meant that the worst manifestations of neoliberal education strategies have been mitigated, to some degree. What is very evident, however, is that teachers' voices are weak in policy formation and teacher professionalism is mainly celebrated rhetorically. An alternative approach has emerged through an initiative designed for quite a different purpose: Shared Education, based on a conception of schools as an interdependent network, emerged as a new approach to promoting school improvement and social cohesion in the context of the peace process. This initiative has highlighted the importance of placing teachers' professional expertise at the centre of educational interventions and opens the possibility for new network-based solutions to old problems. This chapter will examine the implications of this work and begin with an outline of the development of the education system.

Education policy in Northern Ireland

Traditionally teachers' voices in NI have always been weak, in comparison with other parts of the UK. Schools in Northern Ireland are divided largely on denominational grounds, and this division was reflected for many years in the fact that there were many teacher trade unions, some of which represented teachers in particular sectors. This division among the unions is less important today, but the comparatively powerful role of the Churches remains strong, as does the level of political interest since the different school sectors represent important social institutions that overlap with communal interest.

Teacher training is provided in two universities and two university colleges: the two universities have always been secular institutions, but the two university colleges reflect the broader denominational divisions evident in schools and society. The problem is that Northern Ireland trains about twice as many teachers as it needs, and many students from the region undertake teacher training in the rest of the UK before returning to seek employment (Sahlberg Report, 2014). Efforts to rationalise this system have foundered on the rock of communal interest: attempts to merge the two university colleges (Chilver Report, 1980), or to merge them into one of the universities (Farren, 2012), were blocked by political and communal interests, and so we continue to train many more teachers than we need. Not only does this lead to a significant diversion of public resources, but it may weaken the bargaining power of the unions.

The broader theme of the absence of teacher voice can be illustrated by two examples. The first relates to an initiative which has been running for over a decade and has affected significant policy change in education, while the second is a government-led initiative.

The first initiative is termed Shared Education and resulted from a critical examination of the role of schools in promoting social cohesion during the years of political violence (Gallagher, 2004). Stepping around a much older debate on whether Northern Ireland should retain separate denominational schools as a recognition of identity, or move to a single system of religiously integrated schools, the Shared Education approach promoted collaborative networks of Protestant, Catholic and Integrated schools so that students moved between schools to take classes and teachers worked together to support collaborative processes: the genesis of the idea was in conceptualising schools as an interdependent network, rather than a system of largely autonomous schools, and seeking network solutions to promote positive interdependencies between schools. The impact of this initiative has been significant: following three major programmes of research and development between 2007–2010, 2010–2013 and 2012–2015, the Northern Ireland Assembly passed a Shared Education Law in 2016, and the main programme in support of this work is now run by the Education Authority (Gallagher, 2016).

For the present purposes, the most significant aspect of the Shared Education initiatives lies in the way we began working with schools in 2007. Schools invited to participate in the programme – the first wave had 12 partnerships comprising 65 schools – were not provided with a template for organising their collaborations. Rather, we invited teachers to co-create a model of effective collaboration, on the basis that they were best placed to identify local circumstances, challenges and opportunities. This also meant that each of the partnerships developed in different ways. This was enhanced further because the team supporting the programme consciously adopted an approach based on 'next practice', rather than 'best practice', on the basis that the challenge of collaboration in a divided society required a commitment to innovation, and that this, in turn, required a commitment to accept that not everything that was tried would be a success (Hannon, 2007).

To our surprise, this preparedness to tolerate failure turned out to be a novel experience for the teachers involved: top-down education interventions promoted by central authorities tended to be prescriptive in terms of the nature and timing of activities, and often adopted a singular character across the entire region. Most notably, there is little or no 'tolerance of failure' in top-down interventions, even though this is a necessary condition for the development of innovation. One of the most important lessons we gained from the Shared Education work, in other words, was the importance of teacher empowerment, by recognising and foregrounding not only their professional expertise, but also their local knowledge and understanding of their own and neighbouring schools, and the communities within which their schools were based.

Our second example concerns a Department of Education initiative on area planning. The roots of this go back to the Costello Report (2004), one of a series of reports addressing the issue of academic selection. *Inter alia*, the Costello Report highlighted the variable access to subjects for many students and recommended an 'entitlement framework' so that every student would have access to the same broad range of applied and theoretical subjects at GCSE and GCE. The Bain Report (2006) supported this idea and recommended that schools with enrolments below defined minimum thresholds should be reviewed, as part of a wider review of local area provision; that all education interests should be consulted in this area planning process; that community consultation should inform the process; and that options for collaboration between schools, and between schools and further education colleges, to provide the entitlement framework should be part of the process.

An area planning process was initiated in 2011, predicated on the claim that there were surplus places in schools (and therefore too much duplication and inadequate provision), but only the Department of Education, local authorities and the Council for Catholic Maintained Schools were directly involved, on the basis that they held managerial responsibility for schools. Other sectoral interests, the trade unions and communities were given opportunities to respond at different stages. A viability audit was published in 2012 and focused on the extent to which schools faced 'tension' due to enrolment, attainment or financial factors. The Education Committee in the Northern Ireland Assembly consulted on this and found widespread concern on key aspects of the methodology used in the audit. Later that same year a draft area plan was published for consultation and it provoked very mixed responses (NI Assembly Committee for Education, 2015).

The Education Committee of the Northern Ireland Assembly reviewed this process – I served as an academic adviser to the Committee on this work – and recognised a widespread perception that area planning was simply a cover for a school closure programme; that the method for calculating surplus places was inadequate; that the process used to project future needs was too linear and mechanical; that more engagement with local communities could have produced more innovative solutions; and that the consultation processes used by the Department generally ought to be reviewed.

A consideration of the outcomes of the process simply reinforced these criticisms. Thus, for example, analysis of the Viability Audit data suggested there was no correlation between enrolment size and attainment levels in schools. The planning process was supposed to consider options for shared education, or new forms of provision, but what happened in practice was that the ELBs and CCMS carried out parallel planning processes and sought intra-sectoral solutions before considering cross-sectoral or other solutions (Gallagher, 2015a). One consequence of this was that the Integrated schools were successful in winning a judicial review against the process since little had been done to implement the Department's legal responsibility to encourage Integrated education.

Since 2011/12, 76 schools have been closed, with some of these involved in mergers, but when the latest area planning proposals were issued in late 2016, they were more immune from criticism because they provided significantly less detail on the planning process. It is difficult to escape the perception that this process is bureaucratically driven, within very narrow parameters, and it has displayed limited interest in engaging with parents, pupils, teachers or communities to seek out creative or innovative options for educational provision.

A contrast can be seen with a deliberative polling process carried out in a small market town in NI in 2006 as part of the planning work for the Shared Education programme (Fishkin et al., 2007). In this exercise, a sample of parents were polled on their views on a series of specific options for future provision of schooling in their town; they were invited to participate in a deliberative process involving facilitated small-group discussions, with an opportunity to ask questions of leaders of the schools sectors, then were re-polled to see if their views on the options had changed. What this exercise demonstrated was that parents, by and large, were less wedded to specific sectoral systems, but rather were primarily interested that their children would get access to a good quality education, and they were open to change in the system if they felt this would help.

There is a further irony in the process. One of the key factors used to justify the need for area planning was the huge extent of surplus places in schools in Northern Ireland: the figure was claimed to be as high as 85,000 pupils overall, while the figure for post-primary schools was described as equivalent to twenty-two 600-pupil schools operating with no pupils at all. The claim was that surplus places were a waste of resources and that rationalisation would allow for the more effective use of resources. Yet, asked recently about the savings made, the NI Assembly Education Committee was told that no financial saving has been calculated as area planning was never about saving money – it was always about improving the quality of education.

Conclusions

Northern Ireland has operated as an autonomous region within the UK since 1922 and the education system has, for many years, reflected a conservative character, with attention more often focused on the high performance of grammar schools to the neglect of the inequities created by the selective system. In 1989 neoliberal reforms were introduced, and their predominant approach, based on markets, goals and accountability, continues to provide the framework for school improvement. The full impact of these measures has been mitigated somewhat by three factors: the dispersed nature of power in education, the bureaucratic tendency to retain power at the centre and the peculiar priorities associated with communal politics, but all of these marginalise teachers. All of these factors can be seen at play in the ongoing area planning process.

A contrast can be seen in the Shared Education initiative, the success of which was due in no small part to the role that teachers played in co-creating models for effective collaboration. Now that the Shared Education approach has been enshrined in legislation and mainstreamed under local authority control, it will be important that teacher empowerment, which was at the heart of the development of the model, continues to play a key role in its future. More generally, this experience highlights the importance for policy-makers of recognising and engaging with the professional expertise of teachers. Without it, it would seem, education will continue to suffer the iniquities of poor implementation.

References

Akenson, D. H. (1970) *The Irish education experiment: the national system of education in the nineteenth century*. London: Routledge and Kegan Paul.

Bain Report (2006) *Schools for the future: funding, strategy, sharing. Report of the Independent Strategic Review of Education*. Bangor: Department of Education.

Chilver Report (1980) *The future structure of teacher education in Northern Ireland. An interim report of the Higher Education Review Group*. Belfast: HMSO.

Costello Report (2004) *Report of the post primary working body*. Northern Ireland: Department of Education.

Farren, S. (2012) *Should we ignore our past? Reflections on teacher education in Ireland*. Belfast: General Teaching Council for Northern Ireland.

Fishkin, J., Gallagher, T., Luskin, R., McGrady, J., O'Flynn, I. and Russell, D. (2007) *A deliberative poll on education*. Newcastle/Belfast/Stanford: Newcastle University/Stanford University/Queens University Belfast.

Gallagher, T. (2004) *Education in divided societies*. London: Palgrave MacMillan.

Gallagher, T. (2015a) Review of the Viability Audit process: analysis of post-primary school data. In NI Assembly Committee for Education, *Position paper on area planning, together with committee papers relating to the position paper*. Belfast: Northern Ireland Assembly.

Gallagher, T. (2015b) Review of the area planning process (a). In NI Assembly Committee for Education, *Position paper on area planning, together with committee papers relating to the position paper*. Belfast: Northern Ireland Assembly.

Gallagher, T. (2016) Shared education in Northern Ireland: school collaboration in divided societies. *Oxford Review of Education*, 42(3), 362–375.

Gallagher, T. and Smith, A. (2001) The effects of selective education in Northern Ireland. *Education Review*, 15(1), 74–81.

Hannon, V. (2007) *'Next practice' in education: a disciplined approach to innovation*. London: Innovation Unit.

NI Assembly Committee for Education (2015) *Position paper on area planning, together with committee papers relating to the position paper*. Belfast: Northern Ireland Assembly.

Sahlberg Report (2014) *Aspiring to excellence: final report of the International Review Panel on the structure of initial teacher education in Northern Ireland*. Belfast: Department for Employment and Learning.

Chapter 29

A system with synergy

Bringing together all that is good in our system

Gareth Alcott

"The profession must examine how to harness professional identity and ensure collaboration is effective to avoid professional isolationism and protectionism."

There is no doubt that our current educational landscape is shifting. What was once a stifled system, held tightly in the grip of politicians and policy-makers, has demanded change. The knowledge, determination and passion of those within education are beginning to alter the face of the profession.

But what is the destination? Is it the elusive *school-led, self-improving system*? Few teachers would argue with this approach or the transformational changes proposed by those considering reform from an international perspective, like Hargreaves and Fullan (2012). Yet how many teachers have had the time or energy to consider how to achieve this, what they could do to support it, or what it might actually be like to work in such a system?

The SSAT (2015) *Vision 2040: Beyond Five-Year Policy Cycles* is a comprehensive and adventurous insight into a future school-led system, providing a compelling narrative by following an NQT's professional career. This particular career starts out in 2015 (in the "Decade of Deregulation") and finishes in 2040 (the "Decade of System Maturity"), when education is led by the professionals within it, research hubs provide evidence to inform practice and the Chartered College of Teaching offers support across the profession through its universities. This type of vision of education has long lingered before the profession like a promised land – but could continued commitment to system change, supported by further collaboration, provide improved synergy and greater teacher collective autonomy within education? In this chapter, I will consider whether the Teaching School network, along with grassroots organisations, holds the key to system maturity.

There is no shortage of lean, grassroots movements and educational charities in education, with growing numbers of supporters: for example, researchED has gone from four events in 2014 to 11 in 2017. Similarly, there is no shortage of connections in the Teaching Schools national network (in April 2013 there were 363 Teaching Schools, rising to 760 by February 2017), clearly showing that teachers and school leaders can create and sustain whole-system links.

Yet, at present the extent to which the two work effectively together is less clear. The challenge for those looking to a mature education system is how to maintain the passion of these movements and deploy it with the force of the Teaching Schools network – requiring both synergy and scalability.

Teaching Schools

In the 2010 White Paper *The Importance of Teaching* (DfE 2010), Michael Gove promised a national network of Teaching Schools and spoke of education being the "great progressive cause of our times" (p. 6). Around the same time, David Hargreaves put forward four think pieces[1] on a self-improving school system, outlining the importance of creating, leading and achieving system maturity. I would suggest that Hargreaves' work gave credence and credibility to Gove's vision of a national network; following the White Paper, the first cohort of Teaching Schools were designated in 2011. This period also saw the formation of the first Teaching Schools Alliances – clusters of Teaching Schools working in collaboration.

About the same time as the designation of the first 100 Teachings Schools, the Teaching School Council (TSC) was formed – a 'middle tier' set up to coordinate Teaching Schools and their Alliances. With ten Teaching School Council regions, the Council's primary purposes were, according to former TSC Chair Gary Holden, to "support coherence," and, according to TSC Vice-Chair Carolyn Robson, to provide a "networked way to transform education" through collaboration.

At their inception, Teaching Schools were given core areas of responsibilities, known as *The Big Six*:

1 School-led initial teacher training
2 Continuing Professional Development (CPD)
3 Supporting other schools
4 Identifying and developing leadership potential
5 Specialist Leaders in Education
6 Research & Development (R&D)

Teachers and school leaders were the driving force of these first Teaching Schools and their Alliances – most were allocated part-time Directorships whilst maintaining their role and responsibly with schools (a model which still exists today). Other teachers and school leaders supported these Directors: some designated as Specialist Leaders of Education (SLEs) or National/Local Leaders of Education (N/LLEs), working on School Improvement through school-to-school support. In many Teaching Schools, the CPD provision was designed, delivered and evaluated by teachers whose schools were paid so that these teachers could be released during directed time.

In 2013, the National College for Teaching and Leadership reviewed the work of Teaching Schools in the paper *First among Equals?* (Matthews and Berwick 2013), the titular question mark perhaps prompting consideration as to whether this approach to system leadership was effective or sustainable, although it was clear that there was a momentum building from professionals within schools who believed in a school-led approach. The paper stated that although innovation in schools was never lacking, "a framework for implementing and embedding successful practice" (Matthews and Berwick 2013, p. 3) now existed. Matthews and Berwick (2013, p. 4) also highlighted that the initial years of development provided "an excellent reminder of the power and promise of teaching schools and other partnerships, and of the immense potential of a school-led system."

The rise of the Teaching Schools was impressive. At their launch, the government set a target of designating 500 by the end of 2014. However, by January 2015, there were 598 Teaching Schools across 486 Alliances (Gu et al. 2015). So, Teaching Schools and their Alliances had succeeded in creating a national network as Gove had intended, but was the network delivering system-wide improvement?

The *Teaching School Evaluation Report* (Gu et al. 2015) looks at the "effectiveness and impact of Teaching Schools." One aspect of the report that is consistently clear is the successful development of a national network of professionals from schools leading the system:

> the analysis shows that almost all teaching school alliances had entered a new phase of development towards the end of the period of this study. In this phase, there are greater, more extensive, more focussed collaborations emerging between schools within a TSA. There are also increased strategic collaborations beyond the TSA – with local authorities, HEI partners and other school networks across and beyond the locality.
>
> (Gu et al. 2015, p. 188)

But perhaps the Gu report raises more questions than it answers. For the purpose of this chapter, it is certainly pertinent to consider if the Teaching School approach to system leadership really can deliver all it had set out to achieve; the impact on teacher identity and efficacy is unclear. Is there something absent from the Teaching Schools provision? Can lean grassroots movements fill this void to support system maturity?

Perhaps the 2017 rationalisation of *The Big Six* to four key themes was an attempt to become more focused in their work and address the absence of impact:

1 Professional Development and Leadership
2 ITT
3 School Improvement
4 Research and Impact

Since the 2015 Evaluation Report, there has been a continued commitment by the TSC to ensure Teaching Schools recruit more system leaders. The February

2017 Teaching Schools monthly report gives an indication of the size of the system capacity; 760 Teaching Schools across 595 Alliances, working with 1,231 NLEs, 8,500 SLEs and 497 newly designated National Leaders of Governance (NLGs).

Grassroots movement, organisation and charities

Concurrent with the growth of Teaching Schools and particularly in more recent years, I believe there has been demonstrable shift in confidence of grassroots leaders and other groups wishing to support improved professionalisation. Social media has afforded those in schools and classrooms improved access to those in positions of educational power and policy. I would suggest that the combination of these factors has in turn brought a sense of agency to many classroom teachers, providing them with greater professional identity and access to alternative routes to professional development, and as a result impacted on their self-efficacy.

Teachers like Ross McGill (*Teacher Toolkit*) and Tom Bennett are revolutionising how professionals engage with education, receiving acknowledgment both nationally and internationally with accolades including Finalists for Global Teacher Prize and among the "500 most influential people in Britain." Their efforts and the efforts of others are inspiring those within the profession, resulting in more and more education bloggers as well as school leaders and teachers publishing books on pedagogy, practice and leadership. Blogger Andrew Old recently compiled a list of all UK education blogs that totalled 3,741.[2]

Teachers with the drive and passion for system change have created organisations like the Chartered College of Teaching and the Teacher Development Trust. Think tanks led by Headteachers are beginning to challenge the political powers. The Headteachers' Roundtable's *Alternative Green Paper: Schools that Enable All to Thrive and Flourish* (2016, p. 3) states:

> Our goal is to provide a vehicle for people working in the profession to influence national education policymakers.

Twitter has also provided an ideal platform for teacher-led social movements like WomenEd and BAMEed to challenge and address the imbalance of gender and race within education. These examples of grassroots teacher-led change movements are equally essential to greater system maturity.

In response to the grassroots movements, Whitehall is recognising the need to involve more teachers and school leaders (albeit of their choosing) in the political decision-making process. This is evidenced by people such as Dame Alison Peacock and David Weston working with and leading DfE Expert Groups resulting in Government guidance, recommendations and policy for the profession. The recent announcement of more Research Schools, after the first five designations in 2016, could be perceived as a measure of the commitment of the Government to give schools the autonomy to deliver, in an evidence-informed way, in a school-led system.

But the most important outcome of these grassroots movements is the response from teachers, who are acknowledging this shift in power, finding their professional identity and supporting these agents of change. The energy and enthusiasm shown by the teachers for this approach to change is palpable to those who have experienced it. A clear example of this impact on teacher efficacy is the ubiquitous Teachmeet. After humble beginnings in Scotland in 2006 by Ewan McIntosh, Teachmeets are becoming a staple diet of informal CPD for those looking to learn from other classroom practitioners.

Perhaps one reason why Teachmeets and grassroots groups are having such a profound connection with teachers, and hence translating into drivers for increased professional identity, is their freedom from the establishment. Most run on a shoestring budget and are weekend/after-school events. This removes the needs for huge financial backing or, and perhaps more importantly, the need to ask for permission to attend – teachers are choosing to engage with their development in their own time and usually at their own expense. However, collaboration with Teaching Schools need not interfere with that. The sheer size of the Teaching Schools network gives grassroots organisations an ideal vehicle for promotion; the potential impact of engaging directly with more SLEs alone is an obvious win for all, and for education as a whole.

The grassroots voice

So, what of the profession's collective voice as the teachers find their agency? How effective are the grassroots leaders at delivering sustained change with a collective outcome? Hargreaves and Fullan's (2012, p. 150) description of system change may be apt:

> at the beginning it will be a broken front with a few brave souls from different quarters operating in semi-independent packs.

How are these grassroots leaders of change ensuring their efforts aren't pulling education in different directions and thereby adding more tensions to an already seemingly uncoordinated system? Applying Rosenberg's (2011) model of change to education, the profession must examine how to harness professional identity and ensure collaboration is effective to avoid professional isolationism and protectionism.

One example of effective collaboration within the system is the development of the DfE's Standards for Teachers' Professional Development – a Whitehall document that was warmly welcomed by most of the profession, as a result of work undertaken by a grassroots leader (David Weston, CEO of the TDT) to inform national policy.

So, could system change be more effective with greater synergy and collaboration? The work of Jelmer Evers and René Kneyber within the Dutch educational system may be proof enough. Since the release of *Flip the System*, "the [Dutch] system has [since] moved away from its ambition for high-stakes accountability and changed its perspective on the profession, as we're seeing a slow introduction of teachers into all levels of decision making" (Evers and Kneyber, 2016 p. xi).

For the profession, the potential benefits of a teacher-led, self-improving system, and the stakes of failing to develop one, are self-evident. The synergy of activist teachers/leaders within Teaching School Alliances may not be a panacea for the transformation of the education system in England, but it is, I contend, an achievable, high-impact and necessary next step in that journey.

Developing a system with synergy

In certain conditions, Hargreaves and Fullan (2012) argue political and professional forces can be pitted as adversaries. There is little doubt that the relationship between Government and the education system has, in recent years, been adversarial, but are Teaching Schools considered political? And are grassroots movements their adversaries?

Table 29.1 Grassroots movement views on collaboration with Teaching Schools and Alliances *(all views collected in February 2017)*

Teacher Development Trust	"We work with a few TSAs in different ways. TDT has very good relations with TSC although no formal links." David Weston (CEO)
researchED	"We have a more ad hoc approach but we're happy to work with networks when the circumstances arise. I have no issue working with establishment structures – it's often the best way to achieve change leverage – but at the same time it's crucial not to be beholden to them." Tom Bennett (Co-Founder)
#WomenEd	"Our events are indirectly supported by TS/TSAs. There are no formal links, it depends on whether members of the WomenEd community are in a TS/TSA. Many TS/TSAs have bid for Women Leading in Education Network but not all are formally collaborating with WomenEd." Hannah Wilson (Co-Founder)
Headteachers' Roundtable	From their Green Paper (2016, p. 35): • The "remit of Teaching Schools needs to be revisited." • The role of Teaching Schools should be retained with respect to the Initial Training of Teachers. • Teaching School Alliances should operate on a regional basis when training senior leaders, to benefit from economies of scale. • However, "the provision of professional development and research & development are not the sole province of Teaching School Alliances." • "Along with funding for SLEs and school-to-school support there should be a staged movement, in line with commitments given and contracts already in place, of monies from Teaching School Alliances to Partnership Trusts."

In recent conversations with a number of leading education activists, I have gathered their views on Teaching Schools and the status of their actual or potential links. Their responses, recorded in Table 29.1, seems to indicate that they are not averse to the idea of future integration.

Considering these responses and the current educational landscape, could this be what Mary Parker Follett refers to as both sides of polarity moving in the same direction? (Follett 1918). Considered a pioneer of organisational theory, and "a prophet ignored" (Briskin et al. 2009), her approach is insightful in reflecting on and exploring this educational dilemma. Her proposition is that giving rise to collective wisdom requires us to see the whole system. Briskin et al. describe her process as "the stance of deep listening, suspension of certainty, welcoming all that is arising and trust in transcendence" (2009, p. 90). She applied a simpler framework and motto: "Experiment. Record. Pool." (Follett 1918).

If we consider the evolution of Teaching Schools and the grassroots movements as separate *Experiments* and welcome what has arisen by their efforts (*Record*) as i) a labyrinth of links between schools and ii) passionate grassroots agents of change increasing teacher professional identity and efficacy, *Pooling* them together could have a profound impact on education (Figure 29.1). Using their combined momentum to shift the system towards maturity could be a catalyst for system change at a much quicker rate. It may indeed be a necessary step to flipping the system.

This representation does not work on the assumption that there are no passionate leaders in Teaching Schools, or that Teaching Schools do not have an impact on professional identity or efficacy. Nor does it assume that grassroots movements lack the networks and resources to promote themselves. Rather, in the spirit of "welcoming all that is arising," it encourages us to see the

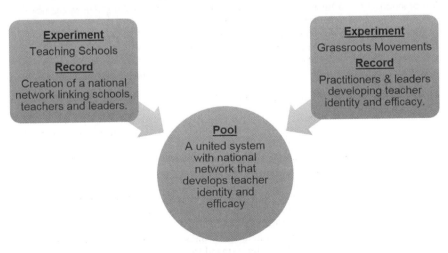

Figure 29.1 Combined pooling: a united system with synergy.

Table 29.2 Collaborative opportunities

Short term
- Mutual benefit – Teaching Schools and grassroots groups recognising that collaborating raises teacher awareness and the status of both their individual work within the teacher community.
- Connectivity – promote the Teaching School Finder app [4] so grassroots groups can find the nearest Teaching School to their event.
- System leaders – Teaching Schools to encourage more involvement of SLEs, NLEs and NLGs in grassroots movements/events.
- Marketing and promotion – Teaching Schools to actively seek out and promote local grassroot events like Teachmeets, #WomenEd, researchEd and #BAMEed. Actively engaging with the Chartered College of Teaching to promote its aims and help develop a system-wide membership.

Medium term
- An evidence-informed system – Research Schools and Teaching Schools commission research to find the most effective approach to use the Teaching School network locally and nationally.
- Making links – researchEd, Research Schools and the Chartered College of Teaching working to provide joint events with Teaching Schools promoting locally and nationally.
- Using existing capacity – More SLEs are used with the grassroots movements to support and develop their infrastructure.
- Hard to reach regional events – Teaching School Councils and grassroots groups to provide events in the new opportunity areas.
- Evaluation and impact – SLEs and the Teacher Development Trust develop a model for effective evaluation of Teaching Schools and their Alliances.

Long term
- Certified CPD – Teacher Development Trust and Teaching School Council to use the Standards for Teachers' Professional Development to create a quality mark for CPD to be used for Teaching Schools and their alliances.
- A collective approach – With its nationwide membership, the Chartered College of Teaching collaborate with Teaching Schools to provide a network and platform for grassroots organisations to impact across the system.

full potential of their collaboration. Away from theoretical models, to those who have experienced both, their combined force for change is undeniable. Table 29.2 outlines some practical suggestions for partnership, some of which may already be happening in ad hoc ways or be in stages of planning.

Educational systems around the world have demonstrated that with a meticulous action plan, patience and a collective will, systems can change. Hargreaves and Shirley (2012, p. 84) cite Lim, who refers to this process as "structured insurgency":

> It is not about driving change through people pushing them against their will, or making them deliver policies that others have determined.

It is about people working together with one collective vision.

Having a precise and structured approach such as this means all parties coming together, casting aside their differences, agreeing some common ground and finding a way to collaborate for future professionals and the pupils they serve. By far the most challenging question posed by this proposition of change is who can facilitate it. Teachers have to believe in it, Teaching Schools have to embrace and re-align themselves to it and grassroots leaders have to work within it without losing their pioneering drive or feeling beholden to it. One option could be the Chartered College of Teaching. With an ever-growing teacher membership, this independent professional body could be central in bringing together the grassroots organisations with the Teaching Schools network.

Whether through the Chartered College of Teaching, or by other means, it is clear that the benefits of greater collaboration are too great to pass up. They give us the chance to flip the system, to move towards system maturity and to truly realise a teacher-led approach that will give synergy to our profession in the future.

Notes

1 Hargreaves, D. H. (2010–2012), David H Hargreaves' thinkpieces on the self-improving school system, *National College for Teaching and Leadership*, available at https://www.gov.uk/government/collections/david-h-hargreaves-thinkpieces-on-the-self-improving-school-system
2 Old, A. (2017), List of UK Education Blogs Version 17, *The Echo Chamber*, available at https://educationechochamber.wordpress.com/2017/02/21/list-of-uk-education-blogs-version-17/

References

Briskin, A., Erickson, S., Callanan, T. and Ott, J. (2009), *The Power of Collective Wisdom: And the Trap of Collective Folly* (Berrett-Koehler Publishers).
Department of Education (2010), *The Importance of Teaching*, available at https://www.gov.uk/government/publications/the-importance-of-teaching-the-schools-white-paper-2010
Evers, J. and Kneyber, R. (2016), *Flip the System: Changing Education from the Ground Up* (Routledge).
Follett, M. P., *The New State* (1918), available at http://www.channelingreality.com/Education/Mary_Parker_Follett_New_State.pdf. Retrieved 07/09/2017.
Gu, Q., Rea, S., Smethe, L., Dunford, J., Varley, M. and Sammons, P. (2015), *Teaching Schools Evaluation: Final Report*. National College of Teaching and Leadership. Available at https://www.gov.uk/government/publications/teaching-schools-evaluation-final-research-report. Retrieved 07/09/2017.
Hargreaves, A. and Fullan, M. (2012), *Professional Capital* (Teachers College, Columbia University).
Hargreaves, A. and Shirley, D. (2012), *The Global Fourth Way: The Quest for Educational Excellence*. London: SAGE Publications.
Matthews, P. and Berwick, G. (2013), *Teaching Schools: First amongst Equals?* Available at https://www.gov.uk/government/publications/teaching-schools-first-among-equals. Retrieved 07/09/2017.

Rosenberg, T. (2011), *Join the Club* (Icon Books Ltd, London).

Secondary School Admission Test (2015), *Beyond a Five-Year Cycle*, available at https://webcontent.ssatuk.co.uk/wp-content/uploads/2015/04/A-vision-for-education-beyond-five-year-policy-cycles.pdf. Retrieved 07/09/2017.

The Headteachers' Roundtable: The Alternative Green Paper Schools – School that Enable All to Thrive and Flourish (2016), available at http://schoolsweek.co.uk/wp-content/uploads/2016/09/The-Alternative-Green-Paper.pdf. Retrieved 07/09/2017.

Chapter 30

Towards a teacher-focused system
Lessons from the Carter Review of ITE

Sam Twiselton

"Student teachers are often judged more on their ability to fit in than on the breadth and depth of their understanding."

Initial Teacher Education (ITE) has been a consistent subject of social and political debate in many countries in recent years. As many studies, including my own, have shown, teacher identity is formed early and is difficult to change once held. The formative years of Initial Teacher Education therefore represent a crucial period during which teachers need not only to develop beliefs and values that will help determine the actions they take in and beyond the classroom, but also develop the resilience and sense of agency to learn to navigate their way with integrity and professionalism through the minefield of those held by others. This can be particularly difficult where such beliefs conflict and where this lies with those who are in a position of power.

Introduction

> I call it a craft because it is something you learn in a work-based environment ... Everyone knows there are bright people who can't teach for toffee, and other people who may not have been the most gifted at university who have the emotional intelligence ... to really engage a classroom.
>
> Michael Gove – then Secretary of State
> for Education in England (*London Evening Standard*, 2010)

> Teachers and students thrive in the kind of settings that we describe as research-rich, and research-rich schools and colleges are those that are likely to have the greatest capacity for self-evaluation and self-improvement.
>
> John Furlong – Chair of the British Educational
> Research Association (2014)

These quotes capture some of the tensions in recent debates regarding how and where teachers are best prepared for their profession. In England, this has been particularly intense during the period since the Conservative and Liberal Democratic Coalition Government that came into power in 2010. This administration presided over unprecedented reforms to teacher education in the drive towards school-led Initial Teacher Training (ITT) in which schools have much more control and ownership. As a member of the expert panel that advised the recent Carter Review of ITT (Carter, 2015), I was able to witness at close quarters some of the impact of this policy drive and to consider potential strengths and weaknesses arising from this in relation to other models.

Background

It is commonly acknowledged that ITE plays a central role in the improvement of educational systems. However, what the best models for teacher education look like, where they should be delivered and who should lead them is much debated and has become a point of particular contention. As Ellis and McNicholl (2015, p. 7) state:

> Around the world, ITE continues to be in a state of almost continual reform, even crisis … In some countries, traditional programmes of professional preparation in which universities are in leading roles are positioned as ineffective, unresponsive and incapable of producing the human capital required for economies to be globally competitive. In these countries and others, 'alternative' programmes of professional preparation have arisen and have become favourites of reform movements and governments alike. … In these new forms of teacher education, the role of higher education is different and is differently positioned in the rhetoric. Higher education is more marginal in the reformist alternatives than in the traditional programmes.

Even within the United Kingdom, there is increasing divergence in policy discourse. Whereas all ITE in Scotland and Northern Ireland is led by higher education institutions (HEIs), and provision in Wales is primarily university-led, the range of approaches in England is noticeably much greater and more complex, with multiple providers and entry routes including university-led, school-centred, and employment-based programmes.

In contrast, in many other high performing education systems, such as Finland, Singapore and Scotland, there is a growing trend to offer ITE programmes at master's level in research universities. This mode of professional preparation requires student teachers to engage with research training and appropriate findings in order to conduct projects linked to their pedagogy or to aspects of their school-based experience. The intention is that this orientation to and experience of educational research provides a foundation for an enquiry-focused approach in continuing professional development. It aims to facilitate the emergence of teachers as reflective practitioners, and nurtures and reinforces the ideal of teachers as researchers of their own practice, committed to systematic self-study.

The BERA/RSA report *Research and the Teaching Profession: Building the Capacity for a Self-Improving Education System* (2014) particularly considers the role of research in four contrasting examples of education systems: Chile, the USA, Singapore and Finland, representing 'fair', 'good', 'great' and 'excellent' school performance as classified by McKinsey (2010). The comparative analysis claims that the education systems such as Singapore and Finland that consistently "come out on top" develop capacity from the bottom up, and rely heavily on methodologically rigorous research-based knowledge to inform their practice.

In these debates about systems and approaches, it could be argued that the needs and position of the developing teachers themselves can be somewhat lost. It is crucial to consider what conditions are most likely to empower, enthuse and equip student teachers in ways that will sustain them not just in ITE but throughout their careers. This is particularly important at a time when relatively high numbers of teachers are leaving the profession early in their careers and of increasing difficulty in teacher recruitment.

In the debates and comparisons that are made between models of ITE in some countries, the central ideological question – *should initial teacher education be led by universities or by schools?* – has become a dominant theme. A key question that is not often included in these discussions is the extent to which either approach puts teachers and student teachers at the centre of the process and most effectively meets their needs – not just as people developing knowledge and skills but also in the formation of professional identity and agency.

The review process

The Carter Review of ITT was commissioned by the then Secretary of State for Education in England, Michael Gove, in 2014 and reported in 2015, aiming to define effective ITT practice; assess the extent to which the system currently delivers effective ITT; and recommend where and how improvements could be made. The Review was not set up as a research project, but it did gather a wide range of evidence and views through a variety of activities, including 11 themed roundtable discussions with sector experts; 24 meetings and discussions with experts and stakeholders; 31 visits to ITT providers and schools involved in ITT, involving meetings with trainers, mentors, headteachers and student teachers; a call for evidence that received 148 responses from a range of individuals and institutions; a survey of student teacher and applicant opinions; and a review of the existing international evidence base.

Models of teacher development

Whatever the route student teachers followed, it was clear that the complexity of the process of becoming an effective teacher cannot be underestimated. The evidence we gathered suggests it is therefore very important that all programmes of ITE are underpinned by a clear understanding of how beginning teachers learn and how to support their growing knowledge and understanding at every step throughout this crucial period of their development. I believe there is a need for a much more widely understood and consistently articulated body of knowledge related to teacher education pedagogy as distinct from pupil pedagogy, e.g. Loughran (2005).

The experience of the Review illustrated the ways programmes deemed to be the most effective prioritised the student teacher and an understanding of their needs at any given point of their journey through ITE, and gave careful consideration as to how their learning experiences were structured. Models of learning to teach that privileged either 'theory' or 'practice' failed to take account of the necessity of integration between the two. Both globally and locally, systems that do not attend to this integration are failing to maximise student teacher development. What appeared to be needed most were models of 'clinical' practice, as articulated by Burn and Mutton (2014), where student teachers had access to the practical wisdom of experts and could engage in a process of inquiry, in an environment where they were able to trial techniques and strategies and evaluate the outcomes. Importantly, by making explicit the reasoning and underlying assumptions of experienced teachers, student teachers were encouraged to develop and extend their own decision-making capacities or professional judgments.

The quality of this approach was strengthened where schools saw themselves as centres of professional learning, where teachers collaborated in curriculum development, pupil assessment and school improvement. Where the principle of schools as self-evaluating institutions was taken seriously, the notion of the teacher as researcher was continuously reinforced. While there was certainly an important potential role for the university here, it was the school setting and the extent to which it was actively and explicitly demonstrating the above qualities that was the key determinant to the apparent effectiveness of the ITE programme. Schools with the commitment, vision and capacity to do this appeared to create extremely powerful contexts for student teacher learning.

Ongoing development beyond ITE

We found that however effective initial teacher education may be, it was crucial that structures were in place to ensure that newly qualified teachers were well supported during their induction year *and throughout their careers*. ITE programmes need to be structured in a way that takes careful account of the complex learning needs of student teachers in a staged and progressive way that leads seamlessly into a well-planned ongoing professional journey. Again, we found great potential in highly committed school partnerships to do this extremely effectively in a way that a university could not achieve on its own, at least in the English system. However, it was also clear that there was 'patchiness' in the extent to which this was guaranteed in all places. Too often NQTs and RQTs were not fully or systematically supported to continue to learn and reflect or to be fully engaged members of a self-sustaining community of learning.

Careful structuring of the student teacher journey and innovative use of time

One of the very clear conclusions I feel able to draw is that an ITE programme can cover all of the essential areas of ITE content, but, without effective delivery and careful structuring, programmes appeared less likely to produce outstanding teachers. In particular, our visits with ITE providers and schools revealed some excellent examples of innovative use of time over the programme to provide student teachers with a range of structured school experiences in contrasting settings. For example, some Teaching School Alliances had structured in time in Pupil Referral Units, Special Schools and schools in contrasting catchment areas with specialisms. This appeared to work well where the programme explicitly included careful preparation beforehand, a clear focus during and opportunity for reflection and transfer after placements. Where a superficial experience was deliberately avoided, student teachers showed a developing identity as agents of change with professional autonomy.

Teaching teachers to observe

Many student teachers and newly and recently qualified teachers reported that current practices of observation are often frustrating and not as impactful as they might be. We found that student teachers needed built-in opportunities to observe good and outstanding practice, to be helped to understand the importance of observation and to be taught how to observe effectively. Paired or partnership observation, it appeared, was used well to facilitate this, while some programmes made effective use of video to achieve this outcome. Indeed, the most useful observation experiences were conducted when student teachers were able to understand and analyse what they were seeing. If observation is confined to the early stages of ITE, learning is limited; student teachers are liable to miss or underestimate aspects of practice that they are later able to much more fully appreciate as significant.

Communities of practice

The most effective programmes we reviewed upheld the importance of communities of practice for student teachers, both in their school contexts and in wider subject-knowledge peer groups. This was particularly important in circumstances where student teachers were more likely to be isolated, where there were fewer student teachers in the school or centre, or where the partnership was small. There is a danger that student teachers can have a fragmented experience and become isolated from the structures and support needed to aid their development.

School- or university-led? Or should we say 'student teacher-focused'?

Across the English system, all the evidence emphasised the importance of genuine partnerships. This often included schools playing a leading role in many aspects of the provision. However, this did not always mean that schools themselves did all of these things on their own. We saw several examples of long-standing partnerships between universities and schools where responsibilities were allocated in a range of ways according to the strengths of both partners. The common feature with all of these effective partnerships was the deep commitment to the sharing of a common ethos and vision and recognition that both sides of the partnership had something to contribute that would have been weakened without this collaboration.

It appeared that partnerships where schools explicitly play a leading role were particularly effective, because the school setting itself is the greatest influence on student teacher learning. However, this can be both positive and detrimental. Findings from my own much earlier studies (Twiselton, 2003, 2004, 2006, 2007) clearly demonstrated the importance of context in learning and showed that de-contextualised experience can have limited value in helping student teachers to fully understand the complex processes involved in scaffolding children's learning. However, it also demonstrated that careful attention needs to be given to avoid a domination of the more superficial, easily observable features of classroom practice at the expense of deeper understanding of pupil learning that is less readily available without careful structuring and analysis. Both my study and the Review showed that it is not enough to place student teachers in school and expect the learning to happen without the right kind of support in place and without carefully constructed student teacher learning opportunities underpinning all aspects of the programme. It is very difficult to understand why and how a range of different types of knowledge are accessed, synchronised and utilised unless one is directly involved in the context surrounding it. It is also important to note that the relationship between contexts, learners and learning is not as straightforward as might be imagined.

The findings from Twiselton (2003) suggested that there is a tendency for school-based mentors to focus on management aspects of teaching in their support and assessment of student teachers. This focus on performance has the potential to lead both student teachers and mentors to focus on the more obvious, superficial aspects of teacher behaviour – the maintenance of order and becoming a confident figure of authority. This reinforces notions that limit the identity of the teacher to the management of learners rather than the management of learning.

Tensions in goals and outcomes

There is an inevitable disparity between the major aim of ITE – to develop the expertise of student teachers – and the major aim of schools – to develop the learning of children. This has the potential to lead to conflict when mediated through the different parties' perceptions of the nature of the expertise needed by student teachers and differing notions of what is involved in developing children's learning. Where pupil learning is the priority, there will be times when student teachers' learning cannot be maximised. When this is added to other school goals concerning accountability to a range of stakeholders, it is unsurprising that student teachers are often judged more on their ability to fit in than on the breadth and depth of their understanding.

These conflicts can leave student teachers with discordant roles to perform and with diverging goals, demands and expectations to meet. We found that the best school-based ITE programmes were those that could avoid or at least reduce this tension by securing a robust enough ITE infrastructure to allow some roles and efforts to be more explicitly dedicated to the needs of student teachers. It should be noted that this required a significant financial and professional commitment that should not be underestimated. It was clear that small-scale ITE is difficult for any partnership to sustain, whether school- or university-led.

The role of HEI and other partners

While I have argued that school-based learning is central to student teacher development, this does not mean that there is no place for learning away from school and for the potential importance of university expertise in supporting this learning. Student teachers need time and space to be able to distance themselves from the practicalities of the school setting, which can be overwhelming because of the immediacy of the demands. They need to be able to connect their learning with the subject beyond the curriculum, the world beyond the classroom and the broader knowledge base and research that underpins understanding. There is a case to be made for doing this in intense, focused episodes away from school, before using these ideas and/or pedagogies back in the school context. This needs to happen in a continuous, iterative process, so that connections can be constantly made, strengthened and reinforced in both places. There is still a very important potential role for universities in bringing their expertise to bear on this model.

Conclusion

The highly political and ideological way in which recent changes to ITE in England have been presented has polarised the debate to a point where it has become difficult to recognise both the strengths and weaknesses associated with different forms of ITE – both school- and university-led. It would be foolish to deny the enormous potential that exists in the new and emerging models we examined. Student teachers do need regular and ongoing access to practitioner expertise in a way that is carefully structured, critically deconstructed, analysed and evaluated for its impact on pupil learning and well-being. They also need to do this in a way that is situated in the literature, most up-to-date research and within an evidence-based, inquiry-driven framework. This leads to a conclusion that the best models of ITE do involve very deeply formed partnerships that thoughtfully balance experiences and expertise at every step. In my view, one of the most essential features is the deep integration of practitioner and research/inquiry expertise in a way that goes well beyond models that keep placement and 'input' learning as separate experiences that are not strongly and iteratively interrelated. The two polarised extremes of entirely school-led or entirely university-led ITE provision both present risks to the possibility of achieving this goal. Most importantly, programmes need to centre on the very complex learning journey involved in becoming an effective teacher and to do this in a way that gives student teachers agency and control over their learning.

References

BERA-RSA (2014). *The Role of Research in Teacher Education: Reviewing the Evidence.* London: BERA.

Burn, K. and Mutton, T. (2014). A Review of research-informed clinical practice in *Initial Teacher Education. Oxford Review of Education*, 41(2), 217–233.

Carter, A. C. (2015). Carter Review of Initial Teacher Training – Publications. *GOV.UK.* [online] Available at https://www.gov.uk/government/publications/carter-Review-of-initial-teacher-training [accessed 12 May 2015].

Ellis, V. and McNicholl, J. (2015). *Transforming Teacher Education: Reconfiguring the Academic Work.* London: Bloomsbury.

Laughran, J. (2005). *Developing a Pedagogy of Teacher Education: Understanding Teaching & Learning about Teaching.* Abingdon: Routledge.

London Evening Standard (2010). *Tories Prepare to Send Trainee Teachers Back to the Classroom*, 19/11/2010, available at https://www.questia.com/read/1G1-242466190/tories-prepare-to-send-trainee-teachers-back-to-the [accessed 22nd May 2017].

McKinsey (2010). *How the World's Most Improved School Systems Keep Getting Better.* McKinsey & Company Available at www.mckinsey.com.

Twiselton, S. (2003). Beyond the Curriculum: Learning to Teach Primary Literacy, in *Interactions in Language and Literacy in the Classroom*, Bearne, E. Dombey, H. and Grainger, T. (Eds.). Oxford: Oxford University Press.

Twiselton, S. (2004). The role of teacher identity in learning to teach primary literacy. *Educational Review*, 56(2), 157–164.

Twiselton, S (2006). The problem with English: the exploration and development of student teachers' English subject knowledge in primary classrooms. *Literacy*, 40(2), 88–96.

Twiselton, S (2007). Seeing the wood for the trees: learning to teach beyond the curriculum. How can student teachers be helped to see beyond the National Literacy Strategy? *Cambridge Journal of Education*, 37(4), 489–502.

Part V

The teachers' manifesto

Global agency

JL Dutaut and Lucy Rycroft-Smith

This book has had as its aim to look at the state of educational policy and teacher professionalism across the UK. In doing so, we have sought to gather evidence from England, Scotland, Wales and Northern Ireland, with limited success. While all four of the home nations find representation in the book, it is undeniable that the limited vantage point of classrooms in the South-East has made this a challenging aspect of the work. Nevertheless, we feel that useful comparatives have been made, and yet more can be drawn by its readers in each nation. Two points emerge for us from this endeavour. The first is that, while international comparisons are a powerful lever to shape our national policies, the possibilities for classroom teachers to engage with and critique them is highly limited. Second, for all the individualisation caused by the current working conditions of teachers, that there exists a broad range of opportunities to connect beyond our immediate circles.

Compare

Jelmer Evers opens this section on global agency with an overview of the international climate shaping our national educational weather patterns, and forecasts two alternative futures for the teaching profession. **Alma Harris** and **Michelle Jones** follow him with a worrying critique of the unintended outcomes of PISA's global comparison and rankings. They outline these outcomes as the erosion of public education, the devaluation of context and culture, the circumvention of the issue of poverty and the validation of top-down educational management, positioning teachers as recipients of change. One such recipient of change, **Natalie Scott**, describes her disillusionment with UK education, and how a stint teaching some of the world's most vulnerable children, in a place so poor no systems bothered to reach, re-connected her with her professionalism. Natalie's chapter is a testament to the power of comparison, and the importance of owning its method and its results.

Contrast

Testifying to the devaluation of context and culture, **Deborah Netolicky**, **Jon Andrews** and **Cameron Paterson** outline some of the ways in which

Australia, like the UK, has succumbed to policies that could just as well have been carbon-copied from others described in this book. Their call for a *Flip the System* of their own is echoed by **Per Kornhall**, who describes the ravages of a particularly unfettered experiment with New Public Management in Sweden, where a *Flip the System* title has recently been published. In stark contrast to this model of system management – one we hope to soon see wholly discredited – **Joe Hallgarten** and **Tom Beresford** offer Creative Public Leadership as a framework to imagine a teacher-led education system, one that is quicker to adapt, less likely to marginalise, and can make use of the global context of policy-making as a positive force for support, rather than as the lever of a competitive ideology ill-suited to public education.

Connect

We end this book with a personal favourite. In Sweden for a second visit, we hear from **Sara Hjelm**, who urges each of us to take ownership of our professional development, and to reach out beyond our contexts and constraints to collaborate in true networks. Hers are the book's last words and its last image because they illustrate perfectly why the system must be flipped, and how it will be flipped.

Demand global agency

The teachers' manifesto demands that teachers develop and be supported to develop the professionalism of all their colleagues. This must include:

- Teacher activism that promotes and develops professionalism in education locally, nationally and internationally;
- Qualifying and professional standards for teachers and system leaders that require demonstration of the promotion and development of professionalism in others;
- Working conditions for teachers and system leaders that make possible the continued attainment of such standards;
- Teacher involvement in the development and implementation of contextually and culturally specific measures of professional status with regards to:
    - Their access to, use and creation of professional knowledge;
    - Their access to, participation in and creation of professional networks;
    - Their access to, engagement with and creation of professional cultures;
    - Their activism for and impact upon education policy.
- Accountability measures for all stakeholders and policy-makers *at all levels* that require a commitment to, and the monitoring of performance in, upholding the professionalism of teachers with regard to their global agency as defined above.

Chapter 31

Systems matter

The future of the teaching profession

Jelmer Evers

"All over the world, teachers are leading change."

We live in interesting times. A cliché, maybe, but true nonetheless. Maybe this is true for every age, but the present feels more urgent than it did when we started on *The Alternative* in the Netherlands and even on *Flip the System* a few years later. It seems that history is back with a vengeance and the political, social and economic fault lines that are appearing nationally and internationally make the questions of what we educate for and how we build the systems to ensure a quality education all the more urgent. Starting to blog, being involved in national education policy and writing *Flip the System* made me realise how everything is connected, from the classroom to international education policy. Waking up to this created a sense of agency and urgency. I believe that, as a minimum, we need to be aware as teachers how global forces influence our classrooms. But the real solutions lie in being an active part in that global community.

One rewarding aspect of embarking on this journey was finding affirmation that in many cases teachers do have an influence. In my own case, the firm but positive message resonated with teachers, policy-makers, politicians, researchers and journalists. The fact that shortly after publishing *The Alternative* we were able to get the €5 million Teacher Innovation Fund – one of our conclusions – off the ground was a testament to that success. More importantly, I think it was an important step – one of many others, of course – in changing the narrative to put teachers at the core of educational policy and empower them to take responsibility themselves. Informal professional networks, both on and offline, have proliferated tremendously. Local meet-ups are springing up everywhere, and Facebook groups organised around subject and formative assessment are changing classroom practice as we speak. This in turn has led to a more politically active profession. A big grassroots movement called Primary Teachers in Action has activated most primary school teachers to call for a general strike – a move embraced by our traditional unions, though not led by them. This in turn could potentially kick-start union renewal and make teaching a more activist profession – in the most positive sense of the word – in the Netherlands.

Ideas spread quickly and globally nowadays. This book is a testament to that. Education policy has gone truly global, and these forces influence national policy and therefore our classrooms. Writing *Flip the System* made me aware of many policy actors that I didn't know about. Having interacted with them and having seen their influence in action the past couple of years, I can't stress enough how important it is that we teachers become involved. Most of the people I have met mean well and are extremely passionate about improving education, but without the countervailing voices of real teachers, they will continue to make mistakes.

International organisations play a very influential part, of course. They provide research, conferences and, most importantly, frameworks and benchmarks which national governments use to shape policy. Most prominently, the OECD has positioned itself as an international arbiter of 'what works' through their PISA and TALIS reports, which have expanded in scope substantially in recent years. Every PISA report makes national headlines and spurs governments into (unwarranted) action (Sellar et al. 2017). The United Nations, mostly through UNESCO, is also very influential. Most important was the adoption of the Sustainable Development Goals (SDGs). SDG4, on education, is one of the more detailed goals through the Incheon Declaration. This is the Education 2030 framework for action, which wants to "ensure inclusive and equitable quality education and promote lifelong learning opportunities for all" (UNESCO 2015). One of the ways in which these frameworks influence is though multi-stakeholder finance arrangements: the Global Partnership for Education (GPE), which since 2003 has allocated more than US$4.6 billion (GPE 2017), and the recently instituted International Commission on Financing Global Education Opportunity (Education Commission) seeks to mobilize US$20 billion for education in developing countries. How that money gets spent matters a lot. Will it be public or private? Public–private partnerships? What kind of accountability schemes and standards will they promote? These in turn will influence our own national policies. Besides UNESCO, the International Labour Organisation usually advocates for quality teaching. The closest thing we have to a global teacher standards was issued in 1966 (*and written by teachers!*) (ILO 2008). Not only are these standards quite good, but they set a precedent for advocating for our profession on a global platform.

We have seen the proliferation of Education Policy Networks, but these are increasingly dominated by private actors, think tanks, foundations, corporations, philanthropists and venture capitalists. Researchers have done a lot of network mapping in the past couple of years, and visualisations show a sprawling network where ideas travel fast and policy-makers are easily found (Ball 2012). Education providers like Ark and GEMS, and corporations like Pearson – through many subsidiaries – are at the centre of many of these networks, relentlessly advocating for Public–Private Partnerships (PPP) and neoliberal policies. Teach for America and its global spinoff Teach for All also figure prominently. Many of these organisations buy into the 'failing public education system' narrative contributing to the casualisation of teaching. Many of the 'leaders' that emanate from them become part of the education policy networks, strengthening this discourse.

If we want to flip the system, teachers need to shape the discourse and networks, of course, and to an extent that is already happening. Education's best kept secret to me is Education International, not only because they were instrumental in getting *Flip the System* published. EI is the global federation of teacher unions and professional associations. It represents around 32 million teachers worldwide and is the official teacher representative to many international organisations like UNESCO, OECD and the ILO. I first came across EI at the International Summit on the Teaching Profession (ISTP) in Amsterdam in 2013. The ISTP is a yearly joint initiative by EI and the OECD, where national delegations of ministers and teacher union leaders reflect together on PISA and TALIS findings and share best practices. EI leads the way on many issues. Without it, education would not even have been a Sustainable Development Goal. Through EI, *Flip the System* has been disseminated to many union leaders, researchers and policy-makers.

But that is not enough. For me the most profound discovery of the past two years is that I am not alone. Social media – Twitter in particular – was instrumental in this. Many teachers are now part of a global conversation and strengthened through many bottom-up networks. I have been privileged to meet teachers from many organisations which have had a profound impact, leading change for and by teachers: the Centre for Teacher Quality (CTQ) in the US, doing phenomenal work on teacher leadership; the HertsCam Network in England, running the first completely teacher-led master's programme; researchED, which has opened my eyes in so many ways and made my classroom practice more evidence-informed; and a powerful professional learning network set up by the Ugandan National Teachers Union (UNATU) and STIR, to name a few. All over the world, teachers are leading change.

We need to marry these bottom-up initiatives with more formal union organising. In many countries, teachers are under pressure with increasing workload, lower pay, increasing attrition rates and de-professionalisation. To counter this, an activist profession is needed, and this is where *Flip the System* plays a role. The international version strengthened the Dutch discourse and the fact that there are now more localised versions does so as well. A Swedish version has been published, an Australian version is in the works, we are looking at a Latin American version, and now there is this book. They all strengthen one another. But it is not only about publishing books; it is about organising around these ideas and acting upon them. Together these initiatives are all part of an emerging alternative education policy network. Part of the puzzle is connecting individual teachers with unions, grassroots movements and likeminded organisations to focus on both professional and industrial issues. The past year has been spent building alliances to create such a network. In the end, it is up to all of us as individuals. The recent global economic and political turmoil makes it even more urgent, and Hillel the Elder's saying more relevant than it been: "If I am not for myself, who is for me? But if I am only for myself, what am I? If not now, when?"

References

Ball, S. J., 2012. *Global Education Inc.: New Policy Networks and the Neo-liberal Imaginary.* London; New York: Routledge.

GPE, 2017. The Global Partnership for Education Factsheet, pp. 1–2.

ILO, 2008. *The ILO/UNESCO Recommendation concerning the Status of Teachers (1966) and The UNESCO Recommendation concerning the Status of Higher-Education Teaching Personnel (1997).* Paris: ILO/UNESCO.

Sellar, S., Thompson, G. and Rutkowski, D., 2017. *The Global Education Race: Taking the Measure of PISA and International Testing.* Canada: Brush Education Inc.

UNESCO, 2015. Education 2030. *World Education Forum 2015.*

Chapter 32

The unintended outcomes of PISA

Alma Harris and Michelle Jones

"Increasingly, teachers seem to be on the end of the food chain of reform and at the mercy of every policy whimsically borrowed from elsewhere."

The pathway to lasting educational improvement, at scale, is far from clear or straightforward. Almost twenty years ago, Louis (1998: 36) questioned whether systemic reform was indeed possible and argued "that educational change will, at least in the foreseeable future, continue to be characterised by disorder, discord, disconnection and turbulence". In the intervening years, this prophecy has certainly proved to be true, as schools and teachers, around the world, experience constant waves of intervention, experimentation and innovation (Hargreaves and Shirley, 2009; Harris and Jones, 2015; Shirley, 2017).

Fast-forward to the present day, and even though the educational landscape may have altered significantly, the goal of improving schools and school systems remains persistent and pervasive. At present, large-scale comparative assessments, such as PISA, define and determine the contours of international policy-making. While there have been numerous critiques of PISA and by association the Global Education Reform Movement (GERM) that has erupted from it (Sahlberg, 2015), PISA still remains a potent and ubiquitous policy influence.

While common sense would suggest that no single education system has all the answers, this has not deterred an international obsession, largely fuelled by PISA, with the high performing education systems. Alexander (2012: 4) notes that "it is hardly surprising that policy makers believe that the better performing systems have something to teach us", but also cautions that it is the translation of "what they discover into action that is the problem". Despite much concern about the wisdom of borrowing from the 'best systems', the motivation to raise PISA scores continues to be both attractive and seductive to policy-makers (Luke, 2011; Lingard et al., 2013).

While the unintended outcomes of PISA are the central focus of this chapter, it is first worth reflecting, initially, upon the more obvious positives and negatives of this dominant global benchmark. PISA was launched in 2000 and since then, a growing number of countries (both OECD and non-OECD) have taken part in this global beauty contest. One of the reasons for the huge popularity of PISA, particularly with policy-makers, is the key idea that improved educational performance leads to a better skilled workforce and ultimately to better economic prosperity. While there are those who fundamentally reject this human capital argument (Brown, Lauder and Ashton, 2010) competing in the knowledge society remains a potent rationale and chiefly explains the continued prominence of PISA (Schleicher, 2006, 2013).

There are, of course, some PISA plus points that should be acknowledged. On the positive side, the OECD's enormous data-gathering exercise has provided comparative evidence on a scale that previously did not exist. Its data sets have contributed to important empirically based country reports that have been valuable for those working in both policy and practice. On the negative side, however, it is exactly how PISA data is being interpreted, communicated and packaged that remains a cause for concern (Baird et al., 2011). Just like the side effects of a drug, the unintended consequences of PISA rarely make the headlines.

Unintended outcomes

To begin with, PISA has positioned discussions about contemporary educational reform and change at something of an impasse. On the one hand, there are those who advocate borrowing from the top performers (Tucker, 2011, 2012) and transporting what works across education systems. Conversely, there are those who promote contextualised, bottom up, teacher-led intervention where system reform is flipped and located within the profession (Evers and Kneyber, 2015). The Finnish educator, Pasi Sahlberg (2010), has argued that GERM, with its apparatus of standardisation, testing and accountability, has largely found validation and approval through PISA. In other words, that PISA has provided the approval and justification for certain policy measures and approaches but not others (Ravitch, 2013a and b).

Since Mourshed, Chijioke and Barber (2010: 16) produced the simple statement that "the quality of an education system cannot exceed the quality of its teachers", the teaching profession, in many countries, has been the focus for policy scrutiny, experimentation and innovation. This single phrase has given policy-makers, commentators and pundits almost carte blanche approval to focus on system failure or underperformance with the teaching profession. In the current debate about educational change and reform, teachers have become both the worst problem and the best solution. They are the worst problem because the available evidence from the best performing countries, such as Finland and Canada, suggest that teachers are key contributors to high performance. So, if the system is found wanting, then it is the profession that is to blame. Conversely, to improve the education system, teachers are the best solution, as they have the greatest effect on the quality of learning and teaching. Hence, for good or bad, teachers are centrally placed in the white-hot and constantly flickering spotlight of policy attention.

Eroding public education

In the wake of declining PISA scores, many countries, including the USA and England, have turned policy attention from public sector provision to private investment (Ravitcha, 2013). PISA has fuelled a powerful rhetoric that if public schools are failing the answer must lie in private provision. But what does the evidence show about private involvement in education, exactly? In the past decade, the United States has been at the forefront of market-driven reforms in education, including private–public partnerships (PPP). Evaluation data of the impact of PPPs, however, shows rather mixed results. There have been two studies of Charter Schools carried out by the Center for Research on Education Outcomes (CREDO). The first, in 2009, found no evidence that Charter schools were outperforming traditional state schools.[1] The second report, in 2013, once again showed that becoming a Charter School is no guarantee of improvement.[2]

Other research, which has indicated more positive outcomes for Charter Schools, underlines that relative gains remain quite modest.[3] Evidence about the Academy Programme[4] in England similarly raises questions about the benefits of private- and public-sector partnerships. In 2015, the NFER's Guide to the Evidence on Academies concluded that "there is no conclusive evidence of the impact of academy status on attainment in primary schools. There is some evidence that sponsored secondary academies have had a positive effect on pupil performance" (NFER, 2015: 1). In summary, the evidence is far from overwhelming for this particular brand of private–public partnership. Yet the Conservative Government elected in the UK in 2015 pledged to create and support hundreds of new academies, despite mixed reports of their impact and benefits.[5] While private–public partnerships are certainly not a new phenomenon, the scale of private sector intervention in education, particularly in developing countries, is dramatically increasing, providing the private sector with a unique and highly lucrative business opportunity. Evidence suggests that this private sector takeover is fast eroding and irreversibly replacing the public-sector provision it was intended to improve and assist (Ravitch, 2013a; Brown and Lauder, 2016).

Devaluing context and culture

The next unintended outcome of PISA concerns the relative dismissal and devaluation of contextual and cultural influences within considerations of education reform processes. While culture and context do not explain all the variance in education performance – both within and between countries – they account for a great deal more than current policy analyses would suggest (Chapman, 2011; Harris, Zhao and Jones, 2015). The current policy discourse about improving education performance tends to focus on single solutions or structural changes. Discussions about the 'high-performing countries' tend to erase any serious consideration of culture and context in favour of locating the best and most transferable solutions (Harris and Jones, 2016). Yet, evidence would suggest that approaches to school or system improvement need to be properly contextualised if they are to have any real chance of succeeding (Chapman et al., 2011; Harris and Jones, 2015). It matters greatly in which classroom, school, country and continent teachers and students reside. As a wealth of comparative evidence has shown, context matters and is of profound importance to the quality of teaching and learning.

Yet interpretations or attributions for system success or failure in PISA[6] rarely surface any cultural or contextual explanations. Instead, accounts of the high-performing systems tend to focus on social and human capital solutions (Jensen et al., 2012). While producing better teachers and leaders is certainly an important imperative for school- and system-level change, it is only part of the story. The latitude that teachers have over their professional judgment and expertise varies considerably from country to country. For example, in some of the high-performing systems such as Singapore and South Korea, teachers have relatively little scope to depart from the set curriculum and accepted teaching methods.

Side-stepping poverty

The next unintended outcome associated with PISA concerns the myopia regarding the pervasive and persistent influence of poverty on educational performance. While it is certainly not asserted that poverty is simply an excuse for under-performance, the stark reality is that the stubborn bond between disadvantage and under-achievement remains very difficult to break. The playing field is far from level for young people who come from broken homes or areas of significant disadvantage. Yet despite a recent focus on equity, as well as excellence, PISA continues to downplay the fact that in certain countries, cities, towns and villages, poverty is teachers' main obstacle to improving educational outcomes and performance. As noted earlier, certain groups of disadvantaged young people tend to be excluded from PISA samples, thus essentially removing some of the negative effects of poverty on achievement. In addition, those students who are absent on the day of the PISA test are disproportionately more likely to come from low-income backgrounds (Baird et al., 2011).

Without question, levels of poverty impact acutely upon educational performance and outcomes. A profound consequence of growing up in disadvantage is that attending school may simply not be an option. The available data on out-of-school children[7] shows that, daily, there are literally thousands of young people out of school. Proportionately, these figures are significantly higher in developing countries at the bottom of the PISA tables.

In the poorest families, it is more often the case that children work to provide extra income for their families or help look after younger siblings rather than attend school. Therefore, poverty determines participation in education and quite predictably this affects subsequent educational achievement and attainment. But despite huge gaps in wealth and dramatic income differentials between countries, the same standard PISA measure is used to judge educational performance.

Pasi Sahlberg[8] has repeatedly underlined that the success of the education system in Finland is premised upon a high degree of equity as well as excellence. He notes:

> Finland has followed the path of fairness and inclusion in building a more equitable school system. The country has invested fairly and more heavily in schools within disadvantaged communities and insisted the best way to provide equal educational opportunities for all is through public schools.[9]

The position in many other countries that sit toward the high end of the PISA league tables could not be more different. The inconvenient truth is that inequality is not only hard-wired into many education systems but also widely accepted, exploited and, in some cases, actively maintained. As Shirley (2017) notes, South Korea, which performs just below Shanghai in PISA, has scored "absolute rock bottom in an OECD survey assessing whether students feel good in school". It is also a country where income inequality is the worst among 22 countries in the Asia–Pacific region. The International Monetary Fund recently reported that in South Korea, the top 10 percent of the population receive 45 percent of the total income.[10]

Teachers as the recipients of change

The final unintended outcome of PISA is arguably the most harmful for the teaching profession. It concerns the way in which teachers have been re-positioned as the mere recipients of interventions or innovations rather than the main instigators of change. Various commentaries about the high-performing education systems have reinforced a view that teachers are critically important in securing better achievement and attainment levels for students. In reaching this conclusion, they are certainly right. But somehow this is translated into system under-performance equals poor or inadequate teaching (Tucker 2011; Rafee, 2011). While it is not contested that all teachers, even the best teachers, can get better, the exact means by which this is achieved has been a source of critique (Ravitch, 2013a; Shirley, 2017).

As highlighted earlier, the net result of the growth in GERM has been to locate teachers on the periphery of reform and to interpret their practice as a problem to be fixed. Increasingly, teachers seem to be on the end of the food chain of reform and at the mercy of every policy whimsically borrowed from elsewhere (Harris, Jones and Adams, 2016). The net result of responses to PISA, in many countries, has been to place more pressure, accountability and responsibility on the shoulders of school leaders and teachers without the concomitant support and resource (Ravitch, 2016; Whitty, 2016). Punitive performance-related pay schemes, teacher evaluation approaches and even key performance indicators have crept into many education systems across the globe.

It should come as no surprise therefore that in England, the USA and increasingly in many other countries, not only are there creeping teacher and headteacher shortages, but many of those new to the profession do not consider staying for the long haul (Edge, 2016). While the policy rhetoric underlines that teachers are our most important asset, in reality, they are increasingly treated as disposable and dispensable, as the mere receptacles for change rather than genuine participants in the change process. In *The Fourth Way*, Hargreaves and Shirley (2009) highlight the importance of teachers as drivers of educational change and reform. They underline the dangers of approaches to 'top-down change' that alienate teachers from the change process. In many countries and education systems, teachers continue to be marginalised and excluded from the process of policy-making and reform.

Future directions

The current global preoccupation with moving up the PISA league tables has undoubtedly diverted the attention of many policy-makers and politicians away from what matters most (Fullan, 2011). It has encouraged them to pay homage to quick-fix improvement strategies – approaches and interventions that they are told can lift educational performance quickly. The relentless desire for rapid improvement has meant that issues of poverty, inequality, contextual influences and teacher professionalism are often overshadowed or ignored as policy-makers seek a fast educational return. In short, the right things (i.e. the factors most likely to result in lasting educational improvement) are being replaced by the wrong thing (i.e. the most expedient, the borrowed or the seductive), all with the promise of quick-fix results.

Despite what has been written and even advocated by some, there are no silver bullets in educational reform. There are no certainties and no guarantees. The process of educational change, particularly at scale, is messy, complex and unpredictable. There are things we know about successful reform and inevitably a whole set of things that reside on the periphery of our understanding. But what we fundamentally know is that to improve any organisation or any education system there must be the internal capacity to deliver (Hatch, 2001).

This internal capacity is unlikely to be nurtured in education systems that are pushing teachers to do more, to be more accountable, work longer hours and deliver better results, but do so without trust, agency or any kind of dialogue. Evidence from England and the USA shows categorically that this devaluing of the profession is least likely to generate authentic long-term school or system improvement. The real answer resides elsewhere. It can be found in the power of teachers working collectively and collaboratively on real issues of learning and teaching that matter to them. The evidence is unequivocal:

when teachers learn, innovate and create together, the possibility of improving learner outcomes is significantly higher (Cordingley, 2016; Wiliam, 2016).

The answers to lasting school and system improvement are staring us squarely in the face. First, it is high time that policy-makers pushed the pause button on PISA with the clear acknowledgement that it is a measure, not *the* measure, of educational performance. Second, debates on educational performance, particularly of a comparative nature, need to be informed and enriched by serious consideration of contextual and cultural influences. We leave these factors out of the debate on educational change and transformation at our peril.

Third, and most importantly, teachers need to be repositioned as the active instigators and drivers of change rather than the passive recipients of more borrowed or unworkable solutions. Empowering those who have the greatest impact on learners to lead educational change and innovation is not only logical, but also essential in the current educational climate. As top-down change fails to deliver all it promised, teachers need to claim their place on the frontline of educational reform. Flipping the system will undoubtedly maximize professional capital and will ensure that the profession, collectively, builds capacity at the school and system level, so that all young people benefit.

Notes

1   Multiple Choice: Charter School performance in 16 States, Stanford University CREDO, 2009 http//:bit.ly/09Credo1 accessed December 22 2016.
2   National Charter School Study 2013, Stanford University CREDO http//:bit.ly/13Credoi accessed December 22 2016.
3   Impact Evaluation of Private Sector Involvement in Education 2012 CfBT, http://siteresources.worldbank.org/EDUCATION/Resources/PPP_impact_evaluation_report.pdf
4   The New School Rules, *Economist*, October 11 2014.
5   Henry Stewart 2014:www.localschoolsnetwork.org/2014/01/academy-chains-seriously-underperforming accessed December 15 2016.
6   http://nces.ed.gov/surveys/pisa/
7   http://data.worldbank.org/indicator/SE.PRM.UNER.FE
8   http://pasisahlberg.com/finnish-lessons/about-finnish-lessons/
9   http://pasisahlberg.com/wp-content/uploads/2013/01/Qualit_and_Equity_SA_2012.pdf
10   http://www.koreatimes.co.kr/www/news/biz/2016/03/488_200524.html

References

Alexander, R. (2012). *International evidence, national policy and classroom practice: Questions of judgment vision and trust*. Keynote address at the Third Van Leer International Conference on Education, Jerusalem (Vol. 24).

Baird, J., Isaacs, T., Johnson, S., Stobart, G., Yu, G., Sprague, T., and Daugherty, R. (2011). *Policy effects of PISA*. Report commissioned by Pearson UK, available at http://oucea.education. ox. ac. uk/wordpress/wpcontent/uploads/2011/10/Policy-Effects-of-PISA-OUCEA. pdf

Brown, P., Lauder, H., and Ashton, D. (2010). *The global auction: The broken promises of education, jobs, and incomes.* Oxford: Oxford University Press.

Brown, P., and Lauder, H. (2016). Higher education, Knowledge Capitalism, and the Global Auction for Jobs. In Gallacher, S. P., Parry, G., Scott, P., Gallacher, J., and Parry, G., eds. *New Landscapes and Languages in Higher Education*, 240. Oxford: Oxford University Press.

Chapman, C. P., Armstrong, P., Harris, A., Muijs, D. R., Reynolds, D., and Sammons, P. (2011). *School effectiveness and improvement research, policy and practice: Challenging the orthodoxy?* Abingdon: Routledge.

Cordingley, P. (2016). Knowledge and research use in local capacity building. *Educational Research and Innovation*, 139–157. Paris: OECD Publishing.

CREDO (2009). *Multiple choice: Charter school performance in 16 States.* Stanford University CREDO, available at http://:bit.ly/09Credo1 [accessed 22 December 2015].

CREDO (2013). *National charter school study.* Stanford University CREDO, available at http://:bit.ly/13Credoi [accessed 22 December 2015].

Edge, K., Descours, K., and Frayman, K. (2016). Generation X school leaders as agents of care: leader and teacher perspectives from Toronto, New York city and London. *Societies*, 6(2), 8.

Evers, J., and Kneyber, R. (Eds.) (2015). *Flip the system: Changing education from the ground up.* Abingdon: Routledge.

Fullan, M. (2011). *Choosing the wrong drivers for whole-system reform.* Seminar Series 204. Melbourne: Centre for Strategic Education.

Harris, A., and Jones, M. (2015). *Leading futures: Global perspectives on educational leadership.* Thousand Oaks: SAGE Press.

Harris, A., Jones, M., and Adams, D. (2016). Qualified to lead? A comparative, contextual and cultural view of educational policy borrowing. *Educational Research*, 58(2), 166–178.

Harris, A., Zhao, Y., and Jones, M. (2015). Why borrowing from the best sounds good but isn't. *Washington Post.* 11 September. Available at http://blogs.edweek.org/edweek/top_performers/2012/03/on_borrowing_best_practices_and_even_better_policies.html

Hatch, T. (2001). It takes capacity to build capacity. *Education Week*, 20(22), 44–47.

Hargreaves, A. P., and Shirley, D. L. (Eds.). (2009). *The fourth way: The inspiring future for educational change.* Thousand Oaks: Corwin Press.

Jensen, B., Hunter, A. Sonneman, J., and Burns, T. (2012). *Catching up: Learning from the best school systems in East Asia.* University of Melbourne, Grattan Institute.

Lingard, B., Martino, W., and Rezai-Rashti, G. (2013). Testing regimes, accountabilities and education policy: Commensurate global and national developments. *Journal of Education Policy*, 28(5), 539–556.

Luke, A. (2011). Generalizing across borders policy and the limits of educational science. *Educational Researcher*, 40(8), 367–377.

Louis-Seashore, K. (1998). 'A light feeling of chaos': Educational reform and policy in the United States. *Daedalus*, September 1998.

Mourshed, M., Chijioke, C., and Barber, M. (2010). *How the world's most improved school systems keep getting better.* New York: McKinsey and Company.

OECD (2014). *PISA 2012 Technical Report.* Available at https://www.oecd.org/pisa/pisaproducts/PISA%202012%20Technical%20Report_Chapter 204.pdf

Raffe, D. (2011). *'Policy Borrowing or Policy Learning' How (not) to improve education systems.* CES Briefing, No. 57, Centre for Educational Sociology, University of Edinburgh.

Ravitch (2013a). *The reign of error: The hoax of the privatization movement and the danger to America's public schools*. New York: Knopf.

Ravitch, D. (2013b). *We must out-educate and out-innovate other nations*. Available at http://billmoyers.com/groupthink/state-of-the-union-responses/we-must-out-educate-and-out-innovate-other-nations/

Ravitch, D. (2016). *The death and life of the great American school system: How testing and choice are undermining education*. New York: Basic Books.

Sahlberg, P. (2015). Britain should be wary of borrowing education ideas from abroad. Originally posted in the *Guardian*, 27 April. Available at http://pasisahlberg.com/britain-should-be-wary-of-borrowing-education-ideas-from-abroad/

Schleicher, A. (2006). The economics of knowledge: Why education is key for Europe's success.http://www.oecd.org/education/skills-beyond-school/36278531.pdf

Schleicher, A. (2013). Attacks on PISA Are Entirely Unjustified, *Times* Educational Supplement Scotland, 2 August. http://www.tes.co.uk/article.aspx?storycode=6345258

Shirley, D. (2017). *The new imperatives of educational change: Achievement with integrity*. Abingdon: Routledge.

Tucker, M. (2011). *Surpassing Shanghai: An agenda for American education built on the world's leading systems*. Cambridge: Harvard Education Press.

Tucker, M. (2012). On borrowing best practices and even better policies. *Education Week*, February 2016, available at http://blogs.edweek.org/edweek/top_performers/2012/03/on_borrowing_best_practices_and_even_better_policies.html

Wiliam, D. (2016). The secret of effective feedback. *Educational Leadership*, 73(7), 10–15.

Whitty, G. (2016). *Research and policy in education; Evidence, ideology and impact*. Bedford Way Papers. London: Institute of Education.

World Bank (2016). *The role and impact of public–private partnerships*. World Bank. Available at http://siteresources.worldbank.org/EDUCATION/Resources

Zhao, Y. (2015). Who's afraid of PISA: The fallacy of international assessments of system performance, in Harris, A., and Jones, M., *Leading Futures: Global Perspectives on Educational Leadership*. Sage Press.

Chapter 33

Teachers sans frontières

Natalie Scott

"Three parts, four parts, hooks, plenaries, mini plenaries. Restricted. Stepford teachers. Unhappy teachers."

Last November I quit teaching. Another statistic, another disillusioned teacher. I was frustrated by the constant hoop-jumping. I was torn to pieces by the thought that data was replacing children, that robots reading from generic PowerPoints were replacing teachers. I was devastated at stepping back but knew deep inside that I needed time out. I was worn out from working in a school which disempowered staff, took accountability to the extremes of fear and which banded the 'O' word around constantly. I was done.

It was at this point that I heard from a former colleague, an inspiring school leader who was in the process of setting up an educational aid charity. He had visited the illegal refugee camps of Northern France and had felt compelled to act, to change things for the children who called them home. These children – hundreds of them – had no access to education. They were a lost generation; bright, sweet, desperate to learn, but terribly lost in a bleak situation that not even our politicians know how to fix. Ultimately, they were just children and they were in these camps through no fault of their own. Like him, I had to find out more.

Grand Synthe camp in Dunkirk was about half an hour away from its more notorious older sibling in Calais, labelled by our media as 'The Jungle'. It had a different sort of resident, and a feel of its own. Whilst the Calais 'Jungle' grew rapidly into a sprawling grassroots city, Dunkirk was in its shadow, lesser known and, for the most part, somewhat under the radar of the press. The camp didn't boast the facilities, amenities or infrastructure that Calais did.

When I first stepped into its stinky mud, I was told there were somewhere in the region of 2000 refugees there, and I only counted 15 Port-a-loos on the whole site. Children were encouraged to use the small black plastic bags that back home we use for our pet dogs. I was appalled and stunned that this was the truth for some children, in modern-day Europe. I was also stunned by the bravery, resilience and smiles of the children who became my students, reigniting my spark for education over the following months.

So, a day in the life

Our catchment area was a squalid mess, with tents rather than the wooden huts or shipping containers of Calais. Between the tents were huge piles of rubbish and discarded clothes. There was a great deal of aid coming in, especially at weekends, but it quickly became a surplus; heaps of clothes would lie in the mud, many brand new, some still with tags. Lorries would come in and clear away these soiled, unwanted, kind donations like litter. Some tents had pairs and pairs and pairs of shoes and boots lined up neatly outside them, way more than I have ever owned.

Each day we would pick our way through the mud and stagnant brown puddles to our school tent, down a makeshift path made of wooden pallets covered in chicken wire to lessen our chance of slipping (not that effective, sadly), then over a makeshift bridge.

On arrival, we would unlock the classroom, a donated scout tent with half a sprayed alphabet on one side. We would get inside quickly to check what was still there and to prepare our learning environment. On one particular day, a plastic box had gone; it had only contained biscuits so was no significant loss, although it was a helpful makeshift table. A child's hat that sat in the corner had also gone, a particularly memorable tiger with long sides that would keep little ears warm on icy days. Sometimes we would arrive to find that our treasured teaching resources had gone, too. Books were a valuable commodity, and pencils and pens would vanish almost as quickly as they were donated.

Some of the children would amble alongside us as we squelched through the fetid camp in the morning. We'd greet their parents and they'd wave off their children proudly from their tents. It was like a walking bus. We'd stop on the way, pointing at cats and saying 'cat' together, and then 'chat', then at a chicken or two and do the same, smiling, pointing and shouting 'chicken' and 'poulet'. We were an international school and French was the local language that they needed and wanted to learn, too. Other children made their own way, or arrived with older siblings, getting dropped off at the tent door.

The lesson plan would vary each day, but I recall teaching the alphabet, then numbers, then body parts. There was no formal register but students told us their names. We'd say them back. Some children used to giggle at our poor pronunciation, whilst others simply repeated, patiently. They taught us, too. We'd often start by singing the alphabet. I don't have a good singing voice, but again the children would forgive me and their happy, enthusiastic, loud singing drowned out my tuneless attempts. We'd point at the sprayed alphabet and then move to a mini whiteboard for the final letters. We would do some written work, joining the dots on letters. Many of our students wrote their letters from right to left, bottom to top. They had learned Kurdish, or Arabic, as their first written language, so had to relearn a new European way. They were familiar with English to varying degrees, as many had learnt it from the age of 4 in Iraq. Differentiation happened. Learning was personalised; some students moved on to writing letters without dots or to a colleague who was using some tatty donated flash cards, looking at the pictures and the words and writing some of their own. They generously traded their words for ours, laughing in amusement at mispronunciations. Over the weeks words grew into sentences, spoken and then written, flowers in the mud.

It would get cold. Sat still for hours on end, focusing on written work, we'd start to shiver and opt to move into the playground (which was the same temperature as the tent) for some more active learning. We'd start off in a circle with 'heads, shoulders, knees and toes'. We got quite good at that bit, so would move onto 'and eyes and ears and mouth and nose'. I recall one little girl next to me, wrapped up like the Michelin man, with hands in pink gloves. She did the 'eyes' bit perfectly, but got stuck on the 'ears'. I pointed to my ear, pulling it out with my cold fingers and hoping she would remember the word. She didn't. Instead she beamed, a wide beacon of a grin spread across her flushed cheeks, and she proudly screamed 'EYES'. She was fluent in non-verbal communication and thought I wanted her to say it louder. We smiled and we started again. After a few attempts, she got it. Progress.

After lunch in their tents, the children would arrive back with us as and when, with no sanctions for poor attendance or being late. Often we'd get the little ones back for more; we'd look at some early reader books and point at images of dinosaurs or frogs, mouthing and practising the words: dog, then cat and mat. I recall one boy who loved helicopters and aeroplanes. I lost his attention each time one flew overhead. I remember spinning and twirling in the playground with him, being a rotor blade, then spreading our wings and soaring.

The winter sun would start to drop low in the sky by four in the afternoon and the mud would begin to harden once more. We'd stand waving goodbye, and the students would shout 'goodbye, my mamosta', 'thank you, teacher' as they made their ways back over the rickety bridge to their tents, with their carefully written letters of the alphabet folded neatly in their pockets. A couple would take reading books with them; we didn't sign them out. They were reliable students.

We would stand for a moment, feeling privileged and humble. We were simply teachers. Out there it didn't matter whether I was a traditionalist or progressive. Data was a simple headcount and feedback was predominantly verbal. As teachers, we held ourselves to account and taught because education was in our blood, because it can and did and will continue to change lives. What mattered in that school tent were the resilient determined children who reminded me how much I loved teaching, helped me to re-join a profession that had broken my heart a few months previously, who fixed me and made me smile. My students would go home and share their new words and songs with their families in cold tents each night. And then they would come back to school, with big brave smiles and boundless enthusiasm the following day, because they wanted to learn more.

Education really does change lives. We are in a time of educational and political shifting sands, where the system teaches our students to become trained dancers who simply recite steps, sequences and pre-determined routines, rather than equipping them with the skills to freestyle or the bravery to dance like nobody is looking. In the mud of the refugee camps, we remembered how to dance together, how to learn, how to teach.

Teachers, too, are increasingly paralysed by fear, as are senior leaders; pressure mounting, demonised by the media, marking for the wrong sets of eyes, teaching lessons in a dictated way. Three parts, four parts, hooks, plenaries, mini plenaries. Restricted. Stepford teachers. Unhappy teachers.

Data tells us that one in ten teachers leave the profession each year; that one in four who qualify are out after three; that more are running for the sunny promises of international schools than are training here in the UK each year.

But what if?

What if schools could lend the disillusioned to an educational aid charity? What if broken or bruised teachers could give some time to the education of a lost generation of refugee children and remember how simple it is to love the profession again? What if it could remind them that relationships between teachers and students do not need to be formulaic?

Humanity and kindness are far more effective tools for school improvement than data analysis and fear. And what if the truest measure of a great teacher as a giver of hope, a giver of words, a giver of a hand, is a thank you note from a small boy in a Spider-Man jacket who has never been to school before?

Chapter 34

Flipping the system

A perspective from down under

*Deborah M. Netolicky, Jon Andrews and
Cameron Paterson*

"**Teachers especially are habitually viewed as grunt workers at the bottom of the pecking order.**"

While we might conceptualise 'the system' in education as a giant, international web of intersecting relationships, a multi-tentacled octopus, it is often treated as a hierarchical pyramid. Teachers exist at the nadir of a system that saw schools emerge primarily as conservators, intended to safeguard and pass on the best of human knowledge. Schools have become highly bureaucratic institutions, and teachers are increasingly undervalued, constrained individuals. Teachers, including middle leaders, senior leaders, and principals, are largely voiceless in the public discourse on schooling. Teachers especially are habitually viewed as grunt workers at the bottom of the pecking order. In Australia, as in the UK, tacit knowledge – the wisdom of practice and of practitioners – is devalued. Mechanistic high stakes accountability, standardisation, and bureaucratisation are accepted as the means of controlling the unwieldy system. The soundbites of mass-consumed media, in Australia and around the Western world, intensify a narrative of an ailing system at odds with itself, thereby undermining the important work of teachers and schools.

At the apex of the system, with the most voice, power, and agency, are governments and policy-makers who make decisions in a manner largely disconnected from teachers. Those individuals or groups that wield influence on policy – yet who are physically removed from schools – dictate policy and "discount the expertise of teachers who are best placed to advise and share what works" (Harris 2015, p. 110). They create a sense of confusion and pessimism around the purpose of teachers' efforts. These few at the top construct narrow, publicly scrutinised measures of the success of schooling that impact on teacher agency, and from which students and their thinking are often obscured. This neoliberal apparatus has the regrettable effect of fuelling a culture of performativity and the fabrication of professional identities. As Ball (2003) explains, when stakes are high, visibility of work is demanded and a secure relationship between an intervention (as cause) and its outcome (the effect) requires accounting for. It is understandable that "a kind of values schizophrenia is experienced when commitment and experience within practice have to be sacrificed or compromised for impression and performance" (Ball 2003, p. 221). Teaching and leading schools become a dance of visible performance, a snakes and ladders game of avoiding punitive penalties while complying with the rules of the game. Rather than looking to one another, teachers and schools often look to experts who provide seductively simple answers to complex educational problems, or data that support their expectations of performance and the pursuit of evidence-based, 'scientific' teaching and school leadership (Eacott, 2017).

Professional action operates in the domain of the variable, not the eternal; it does not lead to pre-determined outcomes. Schools, school leaders, and teachers constantly navigate complexities, contexts, and uncertainties. As Wiliam (2016) stresses, the contexts in which teachers and school leaders work are so variable that research alone, de-contextualised, cannot tell them what to do. Neither, we would suggest, can those at the top of the current education system – government officials and policy-makers – prescribe effective top-down change. Context matters. Lived experience matters. Teachers' voices matter.

Sahlberg's (2011) theorisation of the Global Education Reform Movement (GERM) represents the international educational landscape as one in which policies, systems, and schools are infected by (among other things) a culture of accountability, performativity, and commodification. Negative drivers of education reform – such as merit-based, standardised, test-focused measures – develop a culture of fear and competition in education contexts (Fullan, 2011; Fullan & Quinn, 2016; Sahlberg, 2015). Cultures of fear and compliance are negative and unproductive drivers for individual and organisational development (Netolicky 2016a). High stakes testing, for instance, has been characterised as a villain, a virus, and a symptom of authoritarianism (Zhao, 2014). Shirley and MacDonald (2016) worry about the prevalence of 'alienated teaching' in which teachers capitulate, comply with, and perform to external conditions, while internally resisting. The notion of 'cruel optimism' (Moore & Clarke, 2016; Berlant, 2011) is relevant here: hopes and aspirations are not only likely to be unfulfilled, but can themselves have negative, constraining effects. That is: what the system desires actually hinders, complicates, and impedes it.

In Australia, the *Melbourne Declaration on Educational Goals for Young Australians* (Barr et al., 2008) outlines the push for data-driven accountability to inform education reform. PISA performance has become an end in itself in Australian education, evidenced by the national target of improving Australia's PISA ranking by 2025 (Sellar, Thompson & Rutkowski, 2017). The introduction of high stakes standardised national testing via the National Assessment Program – Literacy and Numeracy (NAPLAN) was intended to measure student achievement in order to drive education improvement. The complex web of policies and intergovernmental relations around national testing in Australia, and their largely negative effects, are explored in detail in Lingard, Thompson, and Sellar's (2016) book *National Testing in Schools: An Australian Assessment*. While in the UK SATs, GCSE, and A-Level dominate education debates, so in Australia NAPLAN, PISA, tertiary entrance ranks, and league tables drive public discourse, propelling competition between schools, systems, and teachers. Scores, numbers, and rankings are the gatekeepers to further study and work. The Australian government has been trialling and investigating further reforms, such as performance-based teacher pay. These initiatives continue the move towards the kind of standardised, de-humanised metrics described above, positioning Australia firmly as a cog in the global neoliberal education machine.

The articulation of perceived standards of professional action and engagement are enshrined in the Australian Professional Standards for Teachers, introduced in 2010. They are presented to the profession as an accepted set of reasonable, researched, and achievable principles; in practice, however, these standards are vague, imprecise, and open to varied interpretation, hardly the clear standards they claim to be. The assignment of career stage or competence labels, 360° evaluation, and outcomes-based evidence of effectiveness echo performativity. Furthermore, the use of standards for evaluative purposes comes hand-in-glove with goal setting and hollow, patronising development mantras commensurate with 'done-to' performance management and appraisal. This seems at odds with building professional agency such as that advocated for by Mockler (2015), who points out that it is a developmental focus, supplemented by high levels of teacher agency, which results in teachers' professional formation and renewal. Netolicky (2016b), too, found that it was deliberate, informed, contextual, agentic change from within schools that had transformational impacts on teachers, not external or evaluation-driven reform.

Flipping the educational system is about subverting stale and unproductive hierarchies. It is about teachers being trusted, agentic professionals with a voice in policy and practice. In their argument for democratising education reform, Evers and Kneyber (2016, p. 5) outline the need for "replacing top-down accountability with bottom-up support for teachers." So, flipping the system is less about handing over power wholesale to teachers as about supporting and empowering them to own and drive change. If teachers own reform, it becomes more sustainable and likely to result in deep, lasting change (Wiliam, 2016). Therefore, at system, state, district, and organisational level, the understanding and pursuit of developing agency is vital for Australian teachers – exactly as it is for British ones. Agency, as Biesta, Priestley, and Robinson (2015) point out, is not something we can have; it is something we do. To feel supported to explore practice, research, collaborate on new strategies, take risks, and be liberated from constraining standards and abstract ideas of quality, is a real priority. Teaching is unforgivingly complex (Cochran-Smith, 2003) and is impacted by so many variables. We should be excited to research practice, talk about practice, share practice, and drive change from a position of understanding that there are possibilities, not certainties.

To flip the system, we must start with the people in schools rather than mandating top-down accountability. As Shirley and MacDonald (2016) argue, "you can't be an outsider to the profession if you want to improve education." Instead of narrowing curriculum and fixating on educating for the known, David Perkins (2013) argues that "we need a vision of educating for the unknown, for the kinds of thinking and understanding that foster nimble adaptive insight in a complex world." However, students will only learn to take risks with their learning, co-create, network, play with ideas, and advocate for change if their teachers have the ability to do the same.

Too much education reform remains top-down, imposed on schools without drawing on or supporting the development of capacities within the system (Harris, 2015). We need to shift the narrative and reform from the bottom (our teachers) and the middle (those who lead within our schools). We need teacher and leader insider voices to be heard, rather than drowned out by outsider 'experts' or government rhetoric. In Australia and around the world, we need to galvanise and embolden our profession to be active agents in their own contexts and the wider education landscape, to not just flip the system but also to renew it.

References

Ball, S. J. (2003), The Teacher's Soul and the Terrors of Performativity. *Journal of Education Policy*, 18(2), 215–228.

Barr, A., Gillard, J., Firth, V., Scrymgour, M., Welford, R., Lomax-Smith, J., Bartlett, D., Pike, B. & Constable, E. (2008), *Melbourne Declaration on Educational Goals for Young Australians*, Ministerial Council on Education, Employment, Training and Youth Affairs, Carlton South, Australia.

Berlant, L. (2011), *Cruel Optimism*. Durham: Duke University Press.

Biesta, G., Priestley, M. & Robinson, S. (2015), The Role of Beliefs in Teacher Agency. *Teachers and Teaching*, 21(6), 624–640.

Cochran-Smith, M. (2003), The Unforgiving Complexity of Teaching. *Journal of Teacher Education*, 54(1), 3–5.

Eacott, S. (2017), School Leadership and the Cult of the Guru: The Neo-Taylorism of Hattie. *School Leadership & Management*.

Evers, J. & Kneyber, R. (2016), *Flip the System: Changing Education from the Ground Up*. Abingdon: Routledge.

Fullan, M. (2011), *Choosing the Wrong Drivers for Whole School Reform*. Seminar Series, 204.

Fullan, M. & Quinn, J. (2016), *Coherence: The Right Drivers in Action for Schools, Districts, and Systems*. Thousand Oaks: Corwin.

Harris, A. (2015), *Building the Collective Capacity for System Change: Professional Learning Communities in Wales*. In Helen J. Malone (Ed.), *Leading Educational Change: Global Issues, Challenges, and Lessons on Whole-System Reform*. Moorabin: Hawker Brownlow Education.

Lingard, B., Thompson, G. & Sellar, S. (2016), *National Testing in Schools: An Australian Assessment*. Abingdon: Routledge.

Mockler, N. (2015), From Surveillance to Formation? A Generative Approach to Teacher 'Performance and Development' in Australian Schools. *Australian Journal of Teacher Education*, 40(9), 7.

Moore, A. & Clarke, M. (2016), *'Cruel Optimism': Teacher Attachment to Professionalism in an Era of Performativity*. *Journal of Education Policy*, 1–12.

Netolicky, D. M. (2016a), Coaching for Professional Growth in One Australian School: 'Oil in Water'. *International Journal of Mentoring and Coaching in Education*, 5(2), 66–86.

Netolicky, D. M. (2016b), Rethinking Professional Learning for Teachers and School Leaders. *Journal of Professional Capital and Community*, 1(4), 270–285.

Perkins, D. (2013), *Presentation at the Project Zero Classroom Conference*, Harvard Graduate School of Education, July.

Sahlberg, P. (2011), *Finnish Lessons*. New York: Teachers College.

Sahlberg, P. (2015), *Fulfilling the Dream in Finland*. In H. J. Malone (Ed.), *Leading Educational Change: Global Issues, Challenges and Lessons on Whole-School Reform* (pp. 123–127). Moorabin: Hawker Brownlow.

Sellar, S., Thompson, G. & Rutkowski, D. (2017), *The Global Education Race: Taking the Measure of PISA and International Testing*. Alberta: Brush Education.

Shirley, D. & MacDonald, E. (2016), *The Mindful Teacher* (2nd ed.), New York: Teachers College.

Wiliam, D. (2016), *Leadership for Teacher Learning: Creating a Culture Where All Teachers Improve So That All Students Succeed*, Moorabin: Hawker Brownlow Education.

Zhao, Y. (2014), *Who's Afraid of the Big Bad Dragon?: Why China Has the Best (and Worst) Education System in the World*, San Francisco: Jossey-Bass.

Chapter 35

Flipping Sweden

Per Kornhall

"The neoliberal dream that competition and accountability would solve all our problems has crumbled before our eyes."

The image of a "Nordic model" consisting of rather similar, small, and orderly welfare states on and around the Arctic Circle is well established around the world. The image was probably valid from the end of World War II until the 1980s, but many things have changed since then that question the existence of such a unified model. The onset of New Public Management (NPM) and neoliberalism in the 1990s have left very different marks on the Scandinavian nations, creating big differences in how our welfare systems are constructed. Finland kept the "Nordic model", Denmark and Norway have seen some influence of NPM, but Sweden has gone all the way to what is probably the most neoliberal school system in the world.

If you don't treat teachers well

Figure 35.1, using data from the OECD's various surveys, shows the share of mathematics low performers (from PISA), plotted against the percentage of teachers who agree that teaching is valued in society (from TALIS). There are outliers, such as Mexico, Chile and Brazil, but most developed welfare states show a rather strong correlation between these two datasets. In the lower right corner of the graph are countries, like Finland and Singapore, with a very low share of mathematics low performers, and in these countries teachers view their occupation as valued in society. At the other end of the distribution is Sweden, with a very high proportion of low achievers in maths and teachers who do not perceive their profession as valued. The remaining Scandinavian countries, Norway and Denmark, are placed somewhat in the middle of the distribution. Interestingly enough, this also reflects differences in how much neoliberal policy has afflicted our respective school systems.

Finland and Singapore

I have had the pleasure of working with educators from both Singapore and Finland, and I've been struck by how highly they speak of the teaching

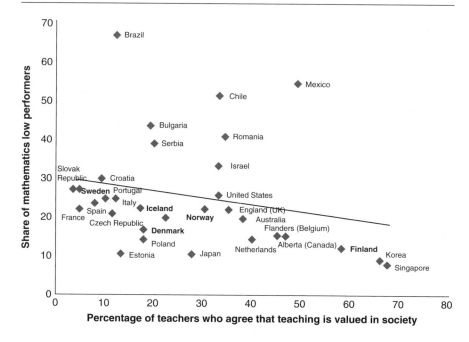

Figure 35.1 Relationship between lower secondary teachers' views on the value of their profession in society from TALIS 2013 and the country's share of low mathematics performers in PISA 2012.

profession. I once was part of an organising committee for an international research symposium on the teaching profession at the Royal Swedish Academy of Sciences. One of the highlights of the symposium was Professor Tan Oon Seng of Singapore ending his keynote on the importance of a strong teaching profession, in stark contrast to the highbrow event, by leading the audience in a singalong of his own version of ABBA's "I Have a Dream", which contained the line: "If you've seen the wonder of a teacher's role …"

As for Finland, when Finnish experts are asked why the country has done so well in PISA tests (which, incidentally, took them by surprise), their answer invariably includes references to trust in well-trained and highly motivated teachers. Finland's success has led to thousands of delegates from all over the world arriving at Helsinki airport in search for the keys to Finland's results, and the story has been well told by Pasi Sahlberg in *Finnish Lessons* (Sahlberg, 2015).

Sweden

Finland's school system was more or less modelled on the Swedish one. Finland basically created the same school system as its western neighbour, with a few years' lag. But all those delegates who travel to see Finland's success rarely stop over in Stockholm. Why? Sweden's results in international assessments and data from its national statistics have shown dramatic deterioration in nearly all aspects for the past two decades. Sweden has had the most negative development in PISA statistics among all participating countries, and the crisis has worsened with every successive round of assessment. In fact, the changes are so grave that the head of OECD's department of education, Andreas Schleicher, presenting a special report on Sweden's school system, emotionally announced he felt it had "lost its soul" (Dagens Arena, 2015).

Though Swedish results in the 2015 PISA and TIMSS assessments have shown some betterment, differences between schools are still rising dramatically. The National Agency for Education has written to the government stating that the situation is very grave, and that forceful measures need to be put in place to reinstitute equality in the system. What improvement there has been is most probably due to government interventions in the decentralised system through professional development initiatives and more focused national curricula.

We know that Sweden has a high share of low performers and one of the lowest perceived statuses of the teaching profession in TALIS. In fact, Sweden is the country where teachers regret most their choice of occupation (Skolverket, 2014). TALIS statistics also show that teachers in Sweden get very little of what they perceive as meaningful professional development and that their salaries are very low compared to other OECD countries. Nationally, the situation with regards to teacher recruitment is more and more often referred to as catastrophic by representative bodies and government officials alike. The Ministry of Education, in May 2016, calculated that in five years' time Sweden will lack more than 60,000 teachers (between a third and a quarter of the number now employed). One of the teaching unions has expressed it thus: certain subjects, like chemistry, physics, technology and modern languages, will be "eradicated" from Swedish schools in a couple of years if nothing happens (Skolvärlden, 2013). But why does Sweden's performance differ so wildly from Finland's, given both school systems' common history?

Devolution

In 1989, the Swedish social democratic minister of education, Göran Persson, wrote that the Swedish centrally governed school system had been very successful in results and, above all, in creating equity (Regeringen, 1989). But, he wrote, the time had come to move on. With those words, he started a transformation of the Swedish school system that continued through the 1990s, a trajectory Finland did not follow. It started with a radical decentralisation: 290 municipalities were more or less overnight given responsibility for all aspects of the school system, and the old national governing authority and its regional counterparts closed down. At the same time, the regulatory framework was dismantled and a NPM-inspired governing-by-objectives system was installed with new syllabi and national curricula. This initial decentralisation was brought about by a right-wing social democrat government and followed by one of the world's most neoliberal school reform agendas under a conservative government. They quickly – without deeper enquiry or risk assessment – opened the system to independent, for-profit schools and established a marketisation of the sector. Anybody, including foreign-based venture capitalists, suddenly had full access to the school system and its funding.

Sweden went from having one of the most centralised school systems to possibly – together with Chile – the most market-liberal school system in the world in less than a decade. This has included the construction of a voucher system giving parents choice. In most municipalities today, all schools are financed solely through vouchers, so that schools' budgets depend on the number of attending students *and on that only*. One of the effects has been a very strong school choice-induced segregation. Researchers talk about "white flight" (Trumberg, 2011) to refer to the phenomenon of better off, more educated parents using the voucher system to avoid their children mixing with those, for example, from a foreign background. Not only does this exacerbate social divisions, but it doubles down on them by creating large funding gaps that result in huge inequality in student outcomes.

Effects on teachers

One of the gravest effects of Sweden's neoliberal reforms is on teachers: their pay, conditions and professional status. In the frenzy of successive governments to install choice, accountability and competition, the teaching profession has experienced a number of changes that profoundly changed its heart. This list is not exhaustive:

- Becoming a teacher or a school leader was deregulated. Anybody could teach any subject, and anybody could become a principal without teaching experience or special training.
- Teaching hours were to be decided individually between the teacher and the principal (within a few national limits decided upon in union–employer agreements).
- A unique individual salary system was established (Nusche et al., 2011).
- Responsibility for schools was dispersed among 290 municipalities and countless independent school providers, weakening collective bargaining.
- The voucher system has led to de-professionalisation and grade inflation as grades are the chief means of competition among schools.
- Huge accountability is exercised through openly published standardised test results and through the Swedish School Inspectorate which, until very recently, was expressly forbidden to give anything but negative critique.

- A teacher education ideology and curricula based on rather extreme constructivist views dismantled pedagogical content knowledge in favour of general pedagogical knowledge and questioned the authority and skills of teachers.

(Ryve et al., 2016)

Where recent governments have tried to amend the situation, the underlying neoliberal model has not been questioned, resulting only in more pressure on teachers by means of the inspectorate and even more national testing.

The future?

The OECD 2015 taskforce delivered a report that urged Sweden to make comprehensive reforms, not least in order to reinstitute teaching as a respected profession (OECD, 2015). As a result, the government instituted a Swedish School Commission that in 2016 presented their first results. They write, among other things, that it is crucial to involve and strengthen the profession in the system. But how? To start with, consecutive governments have to commit to giving autonomy and responsibility back to a damaged profession. The neoliberal dream that competition and accountability would solve all our problems has crumbled before our eyes.

It is never easy – especially for policy-makers – to admit failure. One free school provider, Academedia, alone made €30 million (≈ €500 per pupil) in profit in 2015 (Dagens Arena, 2016) from its 500 "units". Its owners made an estimated €100 million in one day when the company floated on the Swedish stock exchange. Those huge profits mean the political discussion is awash with well-paid lobbyists and think-tanks working to keep the system as it is. Linda Darling-Hammond recently expressed to a minister of education that Sweden had "allowed the devil into the system" (Dalademokraten, 2016). Market mechanisms certainly risk corroding and corrupting the debate.

So, what would the Swedish lessons to the world be? Do not succumb to the lure of simple market logic in a complex and crucial establishment such as the school system. The road back is long when you have destroyed a functioning system. Lobbyists are working hard to push for more market mechanisms in England, and high-stakes accountability is already influencing the teaching profession negatively. More marketisation is the answer to a question nobody asked. Finland, with its comprehensive school system, least influenced by NPM and with no market forces at play, has better results than most nations, not only in Scandinavia but in the world. They have built on confidence in a well-defined national school system, with well-trained, trusted, autonomous teachers, and they handle education as a precious common good to be equally enjoyed by all children. Government can never abdicate its responsibility for the wholeness of the system. Market forces are blind, and the next generation of citizens deserve better than blind guides.

References

Dagens Arena (2015) *OECD: "Sveriges skolsystem har förlorat sin själ"*. [online] Available at: http://www.dagensarena.se/innehall/oecd-sveriges-skolsystem-har-forlorat-sin-sjal/. [Accessed 24 May 2017].

Dagens Arena (2016) *Lärarna rasar mot Academedias vinster*. [online] Available at: http://www.dagensarena.se/innehall/lararna-rasar-mot-academedias-vinster/. [Accessed 24 May 2017].

Dalademokraten (2016) *De skolor som finns till för att tjäna pengar kommer få stora problem om jag får som jag vill*. [online] Available at: http://www.dalademokraten.se/opinion/ledare/de-skolor-som-finns-till-for-att-tjana-pengar-kommer-fa-stora-problem-om-jag-far-som-jag-vill*. [Accessed 24 May 2017].

Nusche, Halász, Looney, Santiago & Shewbridge (2011) *OECD Reviews of Evaluation and Assessment in Education, Sweden*. Paris: OECD.

OECD (2015) *Improving Schools in Sweden: An OECD Perspective*. Paris: OECD.

Regeringen (1989) *Om kommunalt huvudmannaskap för lärare, skolledare, biträdande skolledare och syofunktionärer*. Regeringens proposition 1989/90:41.

Ryve, Hemmi & Kornhall (2016) *Skola på vetenskaplig grund*. Stockholm: Natur & Kultur.

Sahlberg, Pasi (2015) *Finnish Lessons 2.0. What Can the World Learn from Educational Change in Finland?* New York: Teachers College Press.

Skolvärlden (2013) Akut lärarbrist hotar flera ämnen. Skolvärlden. [online] Available at http://skolvarlden.se/artiklar/akut-lararbrist-hotar-flera-amnen. [Accessed 24 May 2017].

Skolverket (2014) *TALIS 2013 En studie av undervisnings- och lärmiljöer i årskurs 7–9*. Rapport 408. Stockholm: Skolverket.

Trumberg, A. (2011) Den delade skolan: segregationsprocesser i det svenska skolsystemet (Doctoral dissertation, Örebro universitet).

Chapter 36

Creating conditions for system-wide innovation

Humanising innovation in schools

Joe Hallgarten and Tom Beresford

"**While the mantras of reform have become ubiquitous across educa-tion systems the world over, the dominant models of change are not working.**"

Our report, *Creative Public Leadership* (Hallgarten et al., 2016), is a first, small step to a more global outlook in education systems innovation. Written for the 2016 World Innovation Summit for Education (WISE), we explored how school systems around the world could create the conditions for successful innovation that could in turn transform outcomes. This question arose from our shared belief that school systems that do not develop the innovative cultures, motivations and capacities of their leaders, educators and institutions are unlikely to see their efforts result in long-term, sustainable returns.

We have deliberately remained in a neutral space in the traditional versus progressive education debate. Some of the language adopted by those seeking radical changes to the 'desirable outcomes' of learning can be off-putting to those they need to convince. As one school principal told us: "Every time I hear the phrase '21st-century skills' I close my ears and reach for my periodic table, my handwriting ledger and even my Bible." The rhetoric of 'education revolution,' too, can close down the most important discussions, confining debates to the converted rather than the sceptical, and reassuring the confident rather than inspiring the constrained.

Our starting point is built on some key assumptions, all contestable. First, that the 'mandate the good, unleash greatness' mantra of school reform needs chal-lenging. The journey from poor to good cannot simply be mandated; and the journey from good to great cannot be 'unleashed' without creating the condi-tions in which the (implied) freedom can be exercised purposefully, with impact and in collaboration. Second, that it is wrong merely to await the tsunami of technological revolution in its many, and unpredictable, forms; we need to be proactive in seeking to reshape the architecture of public investment in learn-ing and encouraging the creation of ecosystems that are more open, inclusive and diverse. Third, that in this context, institutions such as 'the school' can and should sustain a crucial role. Finally, we need to find ways to emancipate the agency of learners, not just as consumers of technologies, but as makers, problem finders and solvers; entitled, invested players in their own right.

If, by sticking within their current tramlines, education systems were succeeding against the rigid criteria they tend to set themselves, then the (perceived) need for change would be minimal. The reality is more depressing. McKinsey's review of 30 years of education-reform efforts around the world concluded that there had been "lots of energy, little light." A trebling of spending in most OECD countries between 1970 and 2000 led to, at best, a stagnation in outcomes. In the global North, school improvement continues to struggle with multiple pressures: learner dissatisfaction, disengagement or stress, growing costs (often in contexts of reduced public investment) and frustrated educators.

The predicament of less established education systems is even more concerning. A recent study from the US-based Brookings Institution shows that without a fundamental rethinking of current approaches, it will take another 100 years for children in developing countries to reach the levels achieved in developed countries. And, as the Open Society Institute argues, "overall progress has actually resulted in a measure of greater inequity" (Williams, 2015). In the 1960s, Basil Bernstein famously wrote that education could not compensate for society. While this is of course much-contested, it is clear that education's 'compensatory' challenge grows as global wealth inequalities grow within and between countries.

Management failures

While the mantras of reform have become ubiquitous across education systems the world over, the dominant models of change are not working. For more than two decades, governments have pursued classic neoliberal reforms – the 'market constellation' of competition, choice and high-stakes accountability. Known as a new public management (NPM) approach, pioneered in the UK, this is described as 'steering, not rowing,' although the reality feels very different on the frontline. What is in essence a model of compliance has over time rubbed up against the natural desire of teachers to take responsibility for the learning of their students. In doing so, a significant source of educational wisdom has been systematically sidelined. Even those aspects of the NPM orthodoxy that have improved outcomes are having diminishing returns. Existing systems are enormously wasteful of human capital and continue to invest in failing programmes.

The logic of the current reform model has one central flaw: it is, at heart, doubtful of the value of teacher professionalism, seeing it as a mask for producer capture by vested professional interests. It has created a form of 'managerial professionalism,' driven by heavy scrutiny and linked to rankable performance measures. Despite the language of decentralisation and autonomy, the measurement systems entailed in these reforms put teachers at the bottom of an accountability chain that reaches only up, towards various offices of principals, school boards, local or national ministers and inspectors. While systems do recognise the importance of teacher quality, overall they are sceptical about trusting teachers to improve their own quality. This is the difference between management and stewardship; between rowing and steering; and the difference between holding to account and nurturing a sense of responsibility.

These dominant orthodoxies are being exported. The ability of developing countries to successfully adopt the features of more westernised schooling paradigms is used as a criterion to receive aid. Yet, as Lance Pritchett explains in his book *The Rebirth of Education* (2013, p. 90),

> Copying the educational fads from rich countries is not going to work: pedagogical and educational problems of developed countries are entirely different than those of advanced countries.

Moreover, the structures by which policy is made and handed down to schools in most jurisdictions disregard the fact that they are dealing with complex systems and tend towards simplistic solutions. The cognitive frames of policy-makers seem to be misaligned with the complexity of actually transforming learning.

Of course, education systems across the globe are full of innovations. In Lebanon, new temporary schools have been built to serve refugee camps that aim to connect with the other assets in the community. In the US, Big Picture Learning connects students with real-world, personalised learning by creating and maintaining innovative learning environments that ensure students spend at least two days a week working on personal projects or completing internships beyond the school gates. Beyond Tech, the Al Bairaq programme at Qatar University, trains and mentors secondary students in hands-on scientific activities to improve motivation in science and maths. In Nigeria and some Indian states, citizen-based assessment programmes are providing more reliable performance data and enabling high-quality community and parental engagement. Databases such as Edutopia, InnoveEdu and the WISE hub provide a myriad of education innovation exemplars.

System weaknesses

In spite of this volume of activity, we identified five weaknesses in the way that innovation appears to be emerging.

First, innovations seem to be *equity-light*. Generally, any interventions that do not explicitly aim for equity normally do the opposite; they increase achievement gaps. Too many education innovators see issues of equity as an afterthought, rather than central to their efforts.

Second, they are *teacher-light*. Despite countless examples of teacher-led innovation, it is not surprising that in the era of high-stakes prescription and measurement the overall role of teachers in innovation processes appears limited and devalued. According to the OECD's TALIS survey, three-quarters of teachers feel that they would receive no recognition for being more innovative. It is still rare to find the systematic involvement of teachers in education innovation. One important exception is British Columbia's 'network of inquiry'; another is the 'non-positional teacher leadership' programme, which ran across 15 countries, and is currently being trialled in Palestine and Egypt. Ontario and Singapore have also developed system-wide approaches to enabling teacher-led innovation.

Third, too many innovations are *evidence-light*, failing to develop a disciplined understanding of their impact. Evaluations are too success- and advocacy-focused, with little room for iterative learning. Hypotheses about change have not been 'good enough to be wrong,' so innovations have been doomed to appear successful. The more your pedagogies and practices break with existing conventions, the greater the need for a good understanding of the evidence base behind those conventions. While this is true across all innovations, those attempting to move beyond traditionally measured learning outcomes appear particularly prone to poor-quality relationships with evidence.

Fourth, the system is *replication-light*. The assumption that innovation-scaling is linear and procedural, rather than iterative and relational, is particularly unhelpful in education, where human relationships are a cornerstone of practice and play a fundamental role in determining outcomes. The concept of 'high-fidelity implementation' might be both undesirable and unrealistic in our classrooms. Unless practitioners are put at the centre of the innovation process, and invested in as innovators in their own right, the cultural shifts required in scaling new approaches that rely on relationships and ethos just as much as processes and functions will fail to materialise.

Finally, innovation is generally *transformation-light*. There are pockets of educational innovation that are beginning to rattle dominant discourses about conventional models, but the stubborn roots of the 200-year-old schooling paradigm remain. The structures that dictate the systems, processes and intended outcomes of the formal schooling system remain remarkably resilient. In the domain of organised tax-funded education, systems of schooling are for the most part in improvement mode: they take for granted the implicit parameters and metrics that maintain the current model of schooling. The incremental and piecemeal is overpowering the game-changing and revolutionary.

Towards collaborative innovation ecosystems

The most radical education innovators are doing so in guerrilla fashion, at the margins. The immense resources of states are still largely locked down into a model predicated on the values and assumptions of a previous age. Their work runs parallel with the systems run by states. Emerging economies have experienced the rapid emergence of a low-cost private school market. Omega in Ghana, APEC in the Philippines and Bridge International Academies across Africa are just a few examples in what is a sea of growing school chains, seeking to fill the void left by what they perceive as ineffective public school systems. Levels of innovative practice within these are often exaggerated (and innovation in public schools under-appreciated), but new school providers have the potential for positive disruption. Equally, in developed economies the philanthropics are increasingly investing in efforts to orient the system towards something more transformative, often against the grain of policy. The most recent high profile initiative comes in the form of EQ Schools, founded by the late Steve Jobs' wife, Laurene, that is looking to invest in a set of Super Schools, in an effort to shape the future of the US education landscape. In a similar, more targeted vein, Khan Academy founder Sal Khan recently opened the Khan Lab School, which aims to actively incubate, test and scale new research-based and innovative approaches to personalised learning.

The way in which public education leaders and institutions interact with these trends of change is fundamental to the ongoing challenge of equity within education systems. It is not about simply getting out of the way. Leaving transformation to market forces carries significant risks. We've known for some time now that the education landscape has been experiencing some game-changing shifts:

> the penetration of digital technologies; the opportunities for other providers to by-pass schools altogether; the closer interest by employers and business in the outcomes of schooling; the interest and expertise in learning of a range of other institutions (e.g. in the creative sector) all entail that we should be thinking of 'learning eco-systems' – interdependent combinations of different species of providers and organisations playing different roles with learners in differing relationships to them over time and in varying mixes.
>
> (Hannon, 2013, p. 2)

While the role of government/state remains crucial, we need to draw on resources from both within and beyond traditional public institutions to create the enabling conditions and cultures for innovation. The task for jurisdictions should be to enable these learning ecosystems to become ecosystems of innovation; mobilising and stewarding a diverse range of players (including schools and practitioners) conditioned by the values of equity and democracy. While plenty of agencies within government have the title 'innovation' somewhere in their remit, they rarely venture beyond incremental improvement. With a few exceptions, for instance the NYC iZone, and the Creative Partnerships programme in England, there is a lack of curation of these efforts; this diminishes their collective potential and contributes to widening gaps in opportunity and achievement.

Humanising innovation in schools

School systems should create intentional platforms for innovation that are long-term focused, equity-centred and teacher-powered. In doing this, leaders need to reinforce that profound learning, great teaching and, indeed, transformative change, are ultimately predicated on the power of human relationships. We therefore need to aspire towards a humanising innovation, defined by Chappell et al. (2012, p. 3) as "an active process of change guided by compassion and reference to shared value," and teachers must be front and centre.

Leading educationalists are beginning to think about what these platforms can and should look like, and what they must focus on. Jal Mehta at Harvard School of Education proposes a 'human-centered system design' approach that begins with the needs of teachers and students, while appreciating that new ideas are never divorced from the system in which they are realised. It is a marriage of bottom-up design with the idea that working at scale requires the development of good systems.

In conducting a set of interviews, he and his colleague, Renee Reinhart, identified a fundamental breakdown in trust between teachers and system leaders across the US education landscape. Amongst teachers they found "absolute puzzlement and/or outright hostility about the ideas and even motives of those further up the chain" (Mehta, 2016), with state and district officials acutely aware of this perspective, yet making little progress in overcoming this 'buy-in' deficit.

> 'buy-in' assumes that people 'on the top' have the wisdom and the problem is that people 'on the bottom' won't do what they want. A better world would recognize [...] that our best chance is collaboration that privileges the perspectives of those closest to teaching and learning.
>
> (ibid.)

To the same end, our Creative Public Leadership approach is based on a conviction about the potential for education as humanity's best hope; one that can both assemble and communicate a compelling case for change, and mobilise and enable school leaders and teachers, parents and students. We need leaders who understand that this is not a quest to converge on a single solution, who have the political savvy to create the legitimacy for radical change, and draw on international networks as a source of imaginative ideas rather than prefabricated policies.

To test our thinking, we set out nine first steps to reorient the role public system leaders might play:

1 Build the case for change.
2 Desist from waves of centrally driven short-term 'reforms'.
3 Develop outward as well as upward accountability, to learners and localities.

4   Create and protect genuine space for local curriculum designs.
5   Prioritise innovations that transform approaches to assessing students.
6   Place intentional, rigorous focus on the development of teachers' innovation capabilities, throughout their careers.
7   Redirect some proportion of a jurisdiction's education spending to an explicit incubator program, tasked with radically innovating on behalf of the system as a whole.
8   Build systems of collaborative peer learning to support the adaptive scaling of innovation.
9   Put system entrepreneurship at the heart of system leadership.

Each of the steps above is designed with the teacher at their heart. Education systems must reconnect with the significant source of wisdom that teachers offer, if they are to create the conditions for system-wide innovation. They must re-orientate the role of teacher as one of innovator and change-maker, working in partnership with local and national system leaders.

This will be a long journey – one that requires persistence and a willingness to fail forward. Our next steps are to talk to a small number of education system leaders around the world who might want to adapt our 'half-formed' ideas for their context. We will then look to turn our community of education change-makers into a global community, willing and able to develop, interrogate and share practices and campaign for change.

References

Chappell, K., Craft, A. R., Rolfe, L., and Jobbins, V. (2012). Humanizing Creativity: Valuing Our Journeys of Becoming. *International Journal of Education & the Arts*, 13(8). [online] Available at http://www.ijea.org/v13n8/. [Accessed 5 June 2017].

Hallgarten, J., Hannon, V., and Beresford, T. (2016). *Creative Public Leadership – How School System Leaders Can Create the Conditions for System-wide Innovation*. RSA Innovation Unit. [online] Available at https://www.thersa.org/globalassets/pdfs/reports/creative-public-leadership.pdf. [Accessed 22 May 2017].

Hannon, V. (2013). *ILE Strand 3: Innovation, Systems and System Leadership*, OECD/CERI. [online] Available at https://www.oecd.org/edu/ceri/Hannon%20paper_ILE%20strand%203.pdf. [Accessed 22 May 2017].

Mehta, J. (2016). The Case for Human-Centered Systems Design. *Education Week*. [online] Available at http://blogs.edweek.org/edweek/learning_deeply/2016/01/the_case_for_human-centered_systems_design.html,m. [Accessed 22 May 2017].

Pritchett, L. (2013). *The Rebirth of Education: Schooling Ain't Learning*. Brookings Institution Press.

Williams, D. (2015). Global Education Goals Shouldn't Just Be a Numbers Game. *Open Society Foundation*. May 20. [online] Available at https://www.opensocietyfoundations.org/voices/global-education-goals-shouldn-t-just-be-numbers-game. [Accessed 22nd June 2017].

Chapter 37

Someone to discuss with ...

Sara Hjelm

"No one needs to be an island."

There are networks and then there are *true* networks. The first kind is often imposed from above, to promote or to guard the interests of one group against another in specific issues. If you're lucky useful things get done, but just as often they don't. The second kind can be private or professional, and all have in common that members give and receive freely. They have a purpose, and communication flows both ways. This story is about that kind of network.

I am a keen reader. I always was. And I have a genuine interest in organisational theory and change processes. During two gap years when I studied archaeology, these were far more interesting to me than the excavation of artefacts and the snapshots of moments passed they provided. By comparison, theoretic applications in education are next to irresistible in their complexity. This is why I was more than thrilled when I was offered a new assignment in November 2011; our Managing Director asked for implementation of at least some of the impressive things he'd seen on a visit to Ottawa. From a group of four, the task of researching fell to me – to figure out what had happened in Ontario, what current educational research had to say, what lessons could be learned, and to make recommendations about what to do and how to do it.

I wasn't completely ignorant to begin with. I had read Hattie, the impact of the McKinsey reports was hard to avoid, and long before the 2012 PISA report was published, people in high places had already begun to panic about what the results might reveal.

In March 2012, the fundamentals for our organisation's new Program for Quality Development – primarily statements for a desirable mutual culture and guidelines for peer assessment – were presented to principals and leaders. In May of the same year, Michael Fullan, who happened to pass through Sweden, offered that very group a day of professional development.

In the first two years that I worked with the Program, I learned more than I thought possible in such a short time. I became an expert internet surfer, read hundreds of reports and articles, scrutinised the Ontario reforms down to school budget level, bought as many books as the budget would allow, and looked through an endless number of video clips and slideshows. Very soon we launched an intranet site for the Program for Quality Development, and I set out to fill it with information and resources, all the time trying to find the small portions accessible enough to share, with all or with different target groups. I even dabbled in translations of my own in an effort to increase accessibility.

An assignment can be highly interesting and engaging, but it can also be lonely. Eventually, you reach a point when you really need someone to discuss with. If there's nobody around with the same role, no peer to collaborate with, it gets increasingly difficult to deal with the slow pace of change. I reached that point sometime in early 2014 and I got lucky. By recommendation from Dylan Wiliam, or perhaps his wife, Siobhan Leahy, I found Eva Hartell. Through our mutual interest in trying to introduce formative assessment, we started to talk on the phone, sharing material and discussing the thesis she was writing at the time.

Then in October Eva sent me the link to a video of Dylan Wiliam, and there was researchED. On the website was a newly advertised event, the 2014 Research Leads Christmas Conference, a special event for the likes of me. I persuaded my boss that I simply had to go, and after many emails about my missing researchED invoice, followed this:

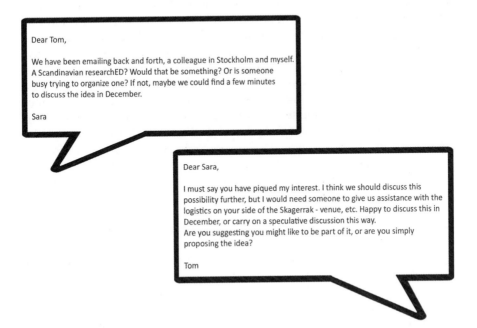

Dear Tom,

We have been emailing back and forth, a colleague in Stockholm and myself. A Scandinavian researchED? Would that be something? Or is someone busy trying to organize one? If not, maybe we could find a few minutes to discuss the idea in December.

Sara

Dear Sara,

I must say you have piqued my interest. I think we should discuss this possibility further, but I would need someone to give us assistance with the logistics on your side of the Skagerrak - venue, etc. Happy to discuss this in December, or carry on a speculative discussion this way.
Are you suggesting you might like to be part of it, or are you simply proposing the idea?

Tom

Figure 37.1 Reaching out: an email exchange between Sara Hjelm and Tom Bennett.

I have to credit Eva. It was her idea, thrown out as we rued together that she would not be able to attend the Christmas conference. *Why don't we arrange something like this here?*

To this day, I can still feel the disappointment of the evening of December 12th, when air traffic computers in Swanwick completely broke down. While a traditional Swedish Saint Lucia and her procession of handmaidens walked back and forth singing among surprised foreign travellers at the airport, Eva and I talked over the phone and put together a list of questions about researchED – conditions, strategies, responsibilities, and how the Sydney conference (at that point the only overseas researchED to be confirmed) had been planned. Before all flights to London were finally cancelled and I took a taxi home, the list of questions was long and diverse.

Someone noted that researchED *is Twitter*, which is probably true in a way. Sometime between Christmas and New Year's Eve, I, who had *sworn* to stay off social media, finally gave in and registered a Twitter account for the sole purpose of interaction with Tom Bennett. Of all the communication that followed across the North Sea, to plan and prepare that first researchED Scandinavia in Gothenburg, most was done via Twitter. Venue and catering for the conference in Gothenburg had already been granted when I finally made it to my first researchED conference in Cambridge and met Tom in person, and then, that very rainy summer of 2015, Eva and I set out to put together a high quality Scandinavian part of the speakers list.

In 2015, very few in the four Nordic nations had heard of researchED. Even fewer knew who Tom Bennett was. Fewer still used Twitter. All I remember of that summer holiday is constant rain and an endless stream of emails, presenting the concept of researchED and asking for assistance to spread the word, perhaps contribute or give tip-offs of who might be interested – all preceded by as much internet surfing as I was capable of to find out whom to contact. It was a very different process than the mere search for new research and interesting discussions and papers. This time I had a reason to communicate as well. One thing was obvious then and still is: channels for communication differ a lot, not only between countries, but also between academic communities and the education sector, and within those subgroups. But there was also the experience of being met with generosity and enthusiasm. There were so many positive people out there, very willing to contribute, to help and to connect, even those who couldn't come to Gothenburg themselves.

In the end, my gain is so much greater than I could have imagined at the start. The lesson I learned is that such true networks are instrumental to our professional lives. Where they exist, they should be celebrated. Where they don't, they ought to be created and nurtured.

To all in the education sector who see ICT only as resources for the classroom or for administrative use, to researchers who see it primarily as a digital toolkit for writing and processing data, I'd like to send the message that there is quite another dimension out there. No one needs to be an island.

To everyone serious about education as an evidence-based profession for the maximum benefit of all: *Reach out and take part!* Participate in the live, ongoing multitude of voices – sharing, informing, communicating, collaborating. Do it with an open mind and you will not only get help when you ask for it, but also learn to be a better judge of what you encounter and make better decisions.

And there will always be someone to discuss with ...

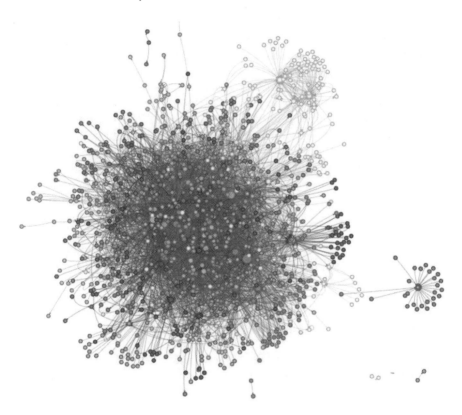

Figure 37.2 Network connections of Twitter users of #rED16 or @ResearchED1, 10/09/2016

List of contributors

Gareth Alcott Teacher, Assistant Head Teacher and Director of Oxfordshire Teaching Schools Alliance

Jon Andrews Executive Director of Teaching and Learning

Sheila Ball Programme Leader for HertsCam Network and Teacher at Meridian School, Royston

Tom Bennett Founder of researchED, Independent Behaviour Advisor to Department for Education

Tom Beresford Senior Associate and Project Lead, Innovation Unit

Zeba Clarke Deputy Head Academic

Julian Critchley Ex-Department for Education, Ex-Head of History

JL Dutaut Teacher of Politics, Media and Drama

Jelmer Evers Teacher of History at UniC, the Netherlands, writer and co-founder of TEN Global

Gary Farrell Principal of Our Lady's & St Mochua's PS Derrynoose Co Armagh

Jonathan Firth Psychology Teacher, author and researcher

Peter Ford Head of Studies Digital and iBusiness, Blackburn College

David Frost Trustee of the HertsCam Network

Tony Gallagher Professor of Education, School of Social Sciences, Education and Social Work, Queen's University Belfast

Simon Gibbs Reader in Educational Psychology

George Gilchrist Recently retired Primary Headteacher of two Scottish schools. SCEL Fellow

Ross Hall Education Director, Ashoka

Joe Hallgarten Senior Associate and Project Lead, Innovation Unit

Andy Hargreaves Brennan Chair in Education, Lynch School of Education, Boston College

Alma Harris Professor of Educational Leadership and Policy, University of Bath

Sara Hjelm Quality Development Manager, Göteborgs Stad Utbildning

Michelle Jones Assistant Professor, Department of Education, University of Bath

Debra Kidd Teacher and teacher trainer

René Kneyber Teacher of Mathematics, writer and Crown member of the Dutch Education Council

Simon Knight Director, Whole School SEND

Per Kornhall Consultant and researcher at the Mälardalen University, Sweden

Sarah Lightfoot Programme Leader for HertsCam Network and Early Years Education Consultant

Robert Loe Executive Director and CRO (FRSA, DFOCT)

Ross Morrison McGill Deputy Headteacher and Director of Teacher Toolkit Ltd.

Darren Macey Framework Writer, Cambridge Mathematics

Deborah M. Netolicky Honorary Research Associate, Murdoch University; Dean of Research and Pedagogy, Wesley College Perth

Cameron Paterson Mentor of Learning and Teaching, Shore School

Jeremy Pattle Recently retired teacher

Alison Peacock Chief Executive, Chartered College of Teaching

Lucy Rycroft-Smith Freelance writer and researcher

Natalie Scott Teacher, SLE, Blogger and Trustee of the Chartered College of Teaching

Julie Smith Director of Teaching and Learning at Wyedean School and doctoral student at UWE Bristol

Rae Snape Headteacher of The Spinney Primary School, Cambridge. National Leader of Education and Headteacher of The Kite Teaching School Alliance, Cambridge

Howard Stevenson Professor of Educational Leadership and Policy Studies

d'Reen Struthers Lecturer in Education, SFHEA at UCL–IoE

Sam Twiselton Director of Sheffield Institute of Education, Sheffield Hallam University

Jackie Ward Behaviour and SEND Consultant

Steve Watson Lecturer in Education, Faculty of Education, University of Cambridge

David Weston Chief Executive, Teacher Development Trust.
Chair, Department for Education (England) Teachers' Professional Development Expert Group

David Williams KS4 Coordinator for English

Phil Wood Associate Professor in Education, School of Education, University of Leicester

Index